THE TO-DO
LIST ✓
AND OTHER
*DEBACLES

EBURY
PRESS

This edition published in 2021 by Ebury Press, an imprint of Ebury Publishing
First published by Ebury Press in 2019

1

20 Vauxhall Bridge Road
London SW1V 2SA

Ebury Press is part of the Penguin Random House group of companies whose
addresses can be found at global.penguinrandomhouse.com

Penguin
Random House
UK

www.penguin.co.uk

A CIP catalogue record for this book is available from the British Library

ISBN 9781529103434

Printed and bound in Italy by Grafica Veneta S.p.A.

The authorised representative in the EEA is Penguin Random House Ireland,
Morrison Chambers, 32 Nassau Street, Dublin D02 YH68.

Penguin Random House is committed to a sustainable future
for our business, our readers and our planet. This book is made
from Forest Stewardship Council® certified paper.

MIX
Paper from
responsible sources
FSC® C018179

AMY JONES

THE TO-DO LIST ✓

AND OTHER

✳DEBACLES

To everyone who feels lost, alone, or like they're not good enough.

It's okay to feel lost. I promise you, you're not alone. And more than anything else, please know that you are enough.

TO-DO

- ☐ *Put washing on*
- ☐ *Brunch with girls*
- ☐ *Pick up meds*
- ☐ *Monthly reflections*
- ☐ *Hang washing up*
- ☐ *Pay energy bills...*
- ☐ *...or at least open them*
- ☐ *...or at least check out prices for other energy providers*
- ☐ *...or at least look at other providers*

- ☐ Yoga? To calm down after all the energy stuff?
- ☐ Do online shop
- ☐ Make sure to get decaff tea on online shop
- ☐ Do some mindful baking
- ☐ Clean kitchen to calm down from the stress of mindful baking
- ☐ Write mental health newsletter on coping better (ahahahahahaha!)

ONE

If I had to pick an ideal time to write a To-Do List, I thought, as I sat cross-legged on my bed in my pants and a bra bought three years earlier when I was a few pay rises poorer and several stone lighter, *this would not be it*. Twenty minutes before I'd been in a hot shower and ten minutes ago, frantically blow-drying my hair, so now my face was sore, pink and shiny from all the heat. I was covered in a thin sheen of sweat, thanks to the heat of the blow-dryer and the stress of getting ready, and my shocking mop of badly dried, frizzy hair was sticking to the back of my neck. Yet, there I was, tapping away on the Notes app on my phone. This was the cage I had built for myself, so I might as well make the most of it.

See, I live according to lists. I keep lists of books I've read, books I want to read, films I want to watch, recipes I want to make, presents I've given and presents received, potential future baby and pet names, restaurants to try, clothes I want, annual goals, and probably a few other ones I've forgotten. I should start a list, really, so that I can remember them all. The lists I cherish most are my 'To-Do Lists' – little lifebuoys that keep me afloat. I used to imagine I'd forgotten vital things and that I wouldn't be able to remember I'd forgotten them until it was too late and the world was falling apart around my shoulders. I would panic about the things I was supposed to do on Monday and hadn't had time for: how on earth was I going to remember to do them on Tuesday with all of Tuesday's tasks to think about? I'd get ideas for one task or project midway through another and completely forget about it until I was just about to fall asleep, when it'd burst out in front of me and I'd come out in a cold sweat with the stress of having forgotten it in the first place. There's so much going on in my head that one brain is not enough to keep track of it all.

To-Do Lists made all of this nonsense better. Now, I can make neat lists of everything I have to do, from washing my hair to finishing a report on time, and even if my stupid, broken brain forgets something, my Notes app will keep it safe for me. If it's on my list, I don't have to worry about it – I'm already halfway there. And, y'know, there's that little *rush* you get when you tap the checkbox and the item disappears. A tiny little rush, a little sparkle in my chest, and I can do it whenever I want with no consequences. Some people do drugs, I add things to a To-Do List just so I can tick them off. And who's having more fun, *really*? If Frank had told all those kids about To-Do Lists, the war on drugs wouldn't be necessary.

Which brings us back to me, on my bed, in my pants. I was panicking about having to leave the house, which is why it was necessary for me to make a list *now*. I needed to feel grounded, in control, and I needed a quick win to boost me out the door. As I scanned the room wildly for something to add to the list, I spotted yesterday's jeans crumpled inside-out in a corner. Yesterday's red knickers were still wrapped around the bum, like something Superman might wear on dress-down Friday. I wrinkled my nose at myself: *That's one thing I could do, then: put the washing on.*

What else, what else …? I mentally scanned the day: brunch with girls. Now, that could go on. I needed to pick up my medication. And that reminded me, I should do all that self-care stuff I'd been meaning to do – yoga, mindful baking, planning ahead. And I should hang the washing up once it's finished in the machine. What else? I checked yesterday's list and felt an ice cube slide unpleasantly down my throat and melt in my chest: energy bills. I really needed to sort out the energy bills …

Don't judge, but at that point I hadn't paid my energy bills in two years. I thought about this every time I opened my email and saw a line of unopened emails, all with the placid subject line 'Your latest energy bill is now ready'. They were all so *bastarding* polite! That only made it worse. It's like my mum's face popped out of the screen, sighed, and said, 'I'm not angry at you, I'm just disappointed I've managed to raise such a dysfunctional human being. What a waste of a perfectly good vagina *you* turned out to be!'

Just to reassure you that I'm not a dysfunctional human, about to ask you to donate to my Kickstarter, I'm up to date on every other bill: council tax, water, TV licence, even the house insurance. I'm responsible enough to pay extra for comprehensive contents insurance, but not to make sure I can keep the heating on. While there's every chance soon I won't be able to turn my TV on in order to watch it, at least I know I'm covered if someone tries to nick it.

In my defence this situation arose when I moved into my new flat just over two years ago. I trusted those stupid meerkats and tried to find a cheaper deal online, but ended up fighting online with my supplier for three months about a contract that I (a) didn't sign up for, (b) didn't want, and (c) they wouldn't let me out of. There's only so many three-hour crying fits down a phone to some scared-sounding bloke called Nelson you can have before you give up and accept your fate, you know? There was food to eat and *Gilmore Girls* to watch; life is too short to fight off *all* the shit coming your way. This was the shit I was going to let slide.

It didn't help that all this happened around the same time my sanity took an alarming nosedive. This happens fairly regularly as I'm a bit mad, but this was a *particularly* bad bout and it left me terrified of all energy companies. Too scared to complain, too scared to switch, way too scared just to deal with it. So I had done nothing. For two years. Thankfully, they didn't seem to have noticed.

I finished my list feeling if not better, at least slightly more in control. Rummaging through the washing basket, I found an outfit worn earlier in the week so I didn't have to deal with trying to dress myself or contemplate how I looked when I was already feeling shaky. I put it on, sprayed myself with perfume to cover up any BO (*classsssy lady, Jones!*) and threw an armful of remaining dirty clothes into the washing machine. After wetting my hands in the sink, I smoothed down the mad hair, twisting the rest of it into a couple of buns either side of my head. I threw my make-up bag and a book in my bag and ran for the door. Then I sprinted for the bus, thus undoing all my good work, and once in my seat, applied make-up while trying not to cry about what I'm going to do about energy bills for the 20 minutes it took to reach my stop and Dévoré, the best brunch place in London – or, at least, the only place a convenient distance from all of us where we don't have to queue to get in and which serves a flat white deemed acceptable by Penny.

Speaking of Penny, she was sitting in the window and so was the first thing I saw as I approached. Her hair, a thick, artfully mussed dirty blonde curtain, was tucked behind her ears and shining where the sun hit it. Self-consciously, I reached up and pulled my hair from its buns, loosening it with my fingers and hoping it didn't look too awful. As I entered, I noticed the two women in their early twenties at the back of the cafe were doing an awful job of pretending not to check social media to verify if this really *was* Penny Williams, and I smiled. She'd gotten a lot more notorious since her book came out and I'm only 30 per cent jealous of her, 35 per cent tops. *Really.* Mostly, I'm proud. But yes, okay: very, very, *very* fucking jealous, too.

When I pushed the door open, she stood up immediately. 'Amy!' she cried, pushing her chair back to pull me into a hug. I hugged her hard and breathed in the smell of her; it's crying over GCSEs and screaming with laughter over terrible dates and her staying over at my flat on the nights Garry was working when we first moved to London and the nights spent in the spare room of the house she has with her husband all wrapped up in one breath. How can one person make you feel so safe and so self-loathing at the same time? Because that's what Penny does for me. She held me at arm's length for a second and her beautiful, perfect face beamed into mine. There's not an ounce of cynicism or self-doubt in her. She's everything I love in the world, and everything I hate myself for not being. We broke away before I started weeping and I turned instinctively to the right, where I knew Janae would be waiting with a wide, easy grin and a new set of electric blue box-braids.

'Aaaaaammmmmmy!' she said, grabbing me. We hugged tightly and rocked from side to side with joy, just as we've always done. I've known Janae since I first came to London and she feels like my sister, despite us being as physically and mentally different as humanly possible. When we let go, Frankie was there waiting for me. Frankie is far more reserved than Penny and Janae, but they say still waters run deep for a reason. We hugged silently, briefly, fiercely. She's seen some shit from me, and I've heard some shit from her. We've gone past the point of needing to loudly proclaim our love: we know. We *just know.*

As I sat down and smiled into the faces of the three people aside from my husband who know and love me best in the world, I felt myself relax. I didn't have to worry about the energy bills right now. They're a problem, yes, but I didn't need to solve it just yet. After all, I could have a *few* hours without thinking about what I'm terrified of, couldn't I?

Turns out, no, I couldn't. Within five minutes my best friends managed to get me to tell them what was wrong and they were all giving me advice. It's the only problem with spending time with people who've known you for years: they know you well enough to recognise and immediately call you on your bullshit.

'Everyone has something like this, don't they?' said Penny (garden-variety mad like me, though more anxious than depressed, and with a fun streak of hypochondria that means more student doctors have stuck their fingers in her arse than sexual partners have). 'Like, mice. I'm terrified so I just don't deal with them – I make Ollie do it.'

'At least Ollie *does* it,' Janae (not mad at all, now, but had a fairly serious self-harming problem as a teen because the contraceptive pill is a horrible bastard that does terrible things to a girl's brain) said, nudging a chunk of poached egg around her plate. 'Garry doesn't even know about the bills, does he?'

'He knows,' I said, my chest slowly filling with cold, wriggling eels as I thought about just how crap the situation was. 'But he's about as inclined to do anything about it as I am. I think his is laziness, though, whereas I'm just scared.'

'Do you want me to do it?' Frankie offered (she teeters *just* on the okay side of disordered eating. Currently not eating sugar, dairy or gluten because a wellness influencer told her not to, so her breakfast was avocado and poached egg and a fuckload of bacon, which she was carefully stripping the fat off), eyebrows furrowed in concern. 'I'll do it, I can pretend to be you.'

'It's fine, it's fine,' I said, smiling brightly. One of the eels was wriggling upwards and I really needed them to shut up before it got in my throat and I wouldn't be able to breathe (add to list: find way to calm the wriggling eels, they've caused more public panic attacks than anything else). 'I'll do it eventually. It's just a ... it's a thing, it's a weird thing, but it's fine, it's *fine*. We all have weird things ...'

'We do all have things,' Janae pronounced solemnly. 'You avoid energy bills because they make you feel sick and scared, I avoid ironing for the same reason.'

'That's because you're a lazy bitch, not because you've a fear of it,' Frankie deadpanned. Under the table, Penny squeezed my hand.

'It's okay, you know,' she said quietly. 'This isn't that bad.'

'Thanks, but it is,' I replied. 'I should be better than this. I should be more ... *together* than this.'

'Who the fuck says you "should" be anything?' interjected Janae, stabbing the final bit of egg with a flourish.

'The law? Society in general, expecting me to pay for a service I've used fairly extensively for two years?'

'Eh,' she said, waving her hand vaguely in front of her face. 'You do what makes you happy, fuck society!'

'But this is very much *not* making me happy, that's the problem. I keep remembering it and feeling terrible about myself.'

'Just go home and do it, you'll be fine.'

'You *will*, you'll be fine.'

'*Totally* fine.'

I agreed and nodded, and smiled at them determinedly, all the while thinking, *Fuck off fuck off fuck off fuck off fuck off fuck off ... Just fucking fuck off, you fucking fucks*. It wasn't *that* easy, it just wasn't. They're right that I do things I'm scared of all the time, but I'm scared of ordering a coffee in Pret, for God's sake. If I didn't do things I was scared of, I wouldn't *do* anything. And a lot of the things they think are scary – being on camera, talking about things that make me vulnerable, standing up in front of big groups of people – I don't find scary at all. But dealing with this teensy piece of life admin? Hell, no! I can't. I just *can't*.

I went quiet for the rest of brunch. While they had the usual argument over who should pay what I said nothing, smiling vaguely whenever they looked my way and clarifying any facts that needed it. I handed over my card and paid whatever they said I should, and then we left the restaurant and went our separate ways. Penny had a judo class, Frankie was going over to the house of a man she was almost certainly going to have sex with, Janae was off to a pop-up exhibition of vintage canned food with her girlfriend. I put on some on-ear headphones, but didn't play anything through them. It muted the world around me, like I was underwater or listening to my neighbours argue through a wall. The outside world was there, but I didn't have to engage.

By some miracle, I managed to get a seat on the Tube. I was on there for three stops before I realised that I was pressing my thighs together and clenching my shoulders, tightening my whole body as if about to be attacked. So, I took a deep breath in, willing my shoulders to drop and my fists to unclench. With every breath, I loosened up a little more. I kept going until the rush of oxygen made my head spin and I had to press my cool palms onto my hot, sticky forehead to stop myself from feeling like I was floating away. It was a sensation I knew well, the kind of feeling that precedes a panic attack. I was jittery enough already, and everyone knows the single worst place to have a panic attack is while sat alone on the Tube.

Usually, when I start panicking, I can calm down, provided I have fresh air and someone I know next to me and talking me down. My success rate miles underground, surrounded by judgemental strangers who don't want to be near you in case whatever you have is contagious, is not high. The man opposite scowled because, I imagine, I was breathing so loudly. I resisted the urge to scream: 'I don't *want* to be like this. Have some *fucking* compassion, won't you?'

When I finally emerged from the Tube, blinking at the winter sun, I managed to dart onto a bus before it pulled away. I got my To-Do List up on my phone and ticked off the first two items, feeling a little rush of achievement as I did so. Before I left that morning I'd duly put my washing on and brunch with the girls was had. Success! Even better, I'd managed to get through the whole thing without crying or being embarrassing – a real achievement.

I imagine a lot of people, my friends included, would be horrified if they learnt that I put social engagements on my To-Do List as if they were chores, akin to mopping the kitchen floor or filling in my tax return, but I'm a bit fragile and really bad at dealing with uncertainty. I need to know everything going on in my life. I hate the feeling that someone knows something that affects me that I don't know, or is keeping a secret – which is frustrating when a lot of people, my parents included, keep things from me because of the aforementioned fragility.

But I *need* to know things. And I need to *know* them, not just suspect or believe them. If I don't know, I will imagine, and the things my anxious brain imagines are far worse than anything that could ever exist. That's why the lists are perfect: they reassure me that I haven't forgotten anything, they remind me what I need to do in the moment, and they help me plan what's coming up. They help keep me on track and, frankly, I need all the help I can get.

The bus pulled up to my stop, near the chemist, and I hopped off, yelling, 'Thanks, Drive' to the driver in the way my parents taught me to, which makes my husband pretend he doesn't know who I am. The old man who hangs round my neighbourhood shouting unintelligibly was there, outside Sports Direct, angrily waving his hat at passers-by. I smiled ruefully at him, then put my head down and scurried past. There but for the grace of God, a lifetime of privilege and a prescription for Citalopram, go I …

The familiar waves of guilt swam over me as I stood in the queue, clutching the piece of green paper in my hand. What did I have to be depressed about? What exactly was so horrible about my upbringing? I had parents who adored me, teachers who encouraged me and enough money to buy food, clothes and all the Jacqueline Wilson books I could carry, so what left me unable to function without chemical help and repeated bouts of therapy? What right did *I* have to feel the way I do? What reason did I have to hate myself and my life? How *dare* I fantasise about walking out in front of traffic when people who have so much less keep on going and are perfectly happy about it? Of course, I know that's not the way things work. Still, by the time I got to the front of the queue I was shaking with the effort of keeping my emotions concealed.

'Next, please,' the assistant said. I stepped forward, thrusting my prescription into her hands. She scanned it quickly, then glanced up at me and paused. A slow, sick blush started to prickle at my neck.

'It'll be about ten minutes, is that okay?' she said, keeping eye contact.

'Sure, I'll just … um … hang around.'

She turned away to do whatever magic they do with filing and organising prescriptions. Head down, I sloped off, desperate to be somewhere less embarrassing but still near enough that I could hear when they called my name. I ended up lurking between the 'Weight-Management' and 'Family Planning' aisles. The sexiest aisle, no? Considering I'm in a place which also sells constipation medicine and orthotic insoles, that's quite an accolade.

Do other people get The Stare, I wondered, as I watched them step up to the counter and hand in their scripts. *Did I even get The Stare?* It was getting to the point where I didn't even know what was real and what my brain had cooked up to torture me with. The burning, sick feeling I got certainly *felt* real, but just because things feel real to me doesn't mean they're necessarily real out in the world. Maybe I imagined it. Maybe that's just her face. But, no. Other people were coming up now and handing their scripts in. They weren't getting The Stare, or at least not to the same degree. It must be real, mustn't it? Partially real, at least.

I kept watching as others handed in their scripts. None of them looked particularly sick, so they couldn't *all* be getting antibiotics for generic illnesses. That one looked like the type to shag around; maybe he had an STI, a nasty one that makes your balls swell like melons. Why wasn't the assistant giving *him* The Stare? Previously, I've gone to get heavy-duty meds for a bad bout of thrush (the extra-thick kind that could be used to make enough to bread to feed the 5,000) and I'm sure the assistant was perfectly fine with me then. If my yeasty foof didn't merit The Stare, why does my Citalopram?

Everyone thinks I'm mad, I thought sadly. Sadly … Sad … It's such a small word that doesn't quite fit my meaning, this feeling that's so enormous and confusing, but it's the only one I had. My entire body felt *sad*. I was steeped in it, saturated. Every pore and my brain and my heart and my soul were full of sadness, every inch of me dripping with it, heavy with it – it was suffocating.

Once, Caitlin Moran described Elizabeth Taylor as being so beautiful she looked 'heavy, like wet roses'. She meant it to show how luscious Taylor was, but it's also exactly how I feel sad. What would the depression version of that quote even be? Heavy, like a flannel sat under a dripping shower for days, which smells a bit weird? Heavy, like the sediment at the bottom of a pint of milk that's gone off, the stuff that schloops into the sink and explodes when you pour it away? I am heavy, like the thousand tiny straws that break the camel's back, like the bags of wet sand thrown in front of leaks in dark basements and forgotten about until they fall apart. I am heavy. And I am *sad*.

Standing in the Weight-Management aisle, I thought back to how my trips to the chemist had started. My friend Laxmi had come to stay for a few days in between her hospital placements. This was about 18 months after I first moved to London, and I was cheerily texting her to announce that I'd be able to spend the whole time with her, even though it was midweek, because my job was so flexible. It wasn't true. My job wasn't flexible at all, really, but I worked from home and I was so ignored and alone that I didn't think my boss would've noticed if I'd gone on holiday to Australia for three weeks and come back ten shades darker, with a new tattoo and a nose piercing to boot.

Of course, I was wrong. Two hours after Laxmi arrived, I was given a huge task and had to spend the day tied to my laptop while she watched daytime TV on my shitty rental sofa. With one eye on *Bargain Hunt*, she asked how things were going, how my life was, how I enjoyed living in London. I was so focused on getting my research done in time that I didn't quite lie to her properly ('Oh, he's great! I mean, he's the coolest man I've ever met, which obviously makes me feel like a slug in comparison. But it's really good! I've got business cards!'). As the day went on, I became more frantic and she grew quieter and quieter, until eventually, she stopped talking entirely and watched me carefully as I flapped around.

That evening, I cooked for me, her and Garry in my tiny kitchen.

'I totally fucked up and ended up having to work most of the day,' I announced brightly (*too* brightly), sitting down to hastily thrown-together pasta and meatballs.

'It was fine,' Laxmi said, taking a big spoonful of sauce. 'We still got to talk, and that's the main thing.'

'Yeah, sure, sure ...' I said, rolling my eyes mock-cheerfully at Garry. 'I'm sure you *wanted* to come all the way down to London just so you could talk to *me* rather than going out and about and seeing things.' Garry was silently helping himself to pasta and looking down steadfastly at his plate. I was convinced my oldest friend and the love of my life hated me for being such a pathetic mess – I couldn't even have a friend to stay without getting it wrong somehow, for God's sake. *Why would anyone want to hang around with me?*

Thankfully, Laxmi was good enough to stick around anyway. She watched quietly the next morning as I typed up a presentation and sent it to my boss, nodding at my increasingly hysterical jokes and bringing me tea as the hours before she had to go home slipped away. We ended up having a couple of free hours together, so rather than doing anything remotely exciting, we went for a walk and ended up in M&S. There, as I was frantically weighing up whether I wanted the £30 nightie reduced to £7 because the strap had been ripped off, Laxmi gently suggested I go to the doctor and get some help for my mental health. I burst into tears, nightie in one hand, a bag of Percy Pigs in the other, and she put her arms round me and hugged me while mildly alarmed mothers tried to hurry along their staring children.

Four years, two courses of therapy, a year on Sertraline, two years of pretending I was okay again and eight months of Citalopram later, and there I was: describing myself like a waterlogged flannel because a pharmacist gave me a dodgy look. Aren't brains great?

The pharmacist called my name and I jumped. Collecting my medication was nowhere near as stressful – the pharmacist barely looked at me for longer than customer service dictated, let alone sized me up like I was about to take an overdose right in front of him – and I felt slightly cheerier.

Yeah, look at me go! I'm just as repulsive as the guy with the STI, no more, no less! Look at me go!

I got home, put the little bag of pills on the shelf, settled into my yellow armchair, waited for the cat to settle herself in between the crook of my legs, then opened up my Notes app.

Pick up meds: tick!

I scanned the rest of my list, and frowned. There was quite a lot of energy stuff on there to tackle. And I *did* tell the girls at brunch I would do something about the situation. Opening my inbox, I eyed the unread emails nervously. I also knew that in the drawer I could see out of the corner of my eye there was a pile of letters I could have looked at. Even if I didn't actually pay the bills today, or find out what I owed, maybe I could go on to other sites and see what I could pay there?

I could do it, it would be so easy.

But then, I can do that any time. To be really productive – and that's the *whole point* of a To-Do List – I should do all the stuff that just needs to be *started* and then left to do its thing first, and do the energy stuff while I'm waiting for the first stuff to finish. By doing the energy stuff first, I'm *wasting* time. I'm actually being worse than I would be by just ignoring the energy stuff altogether. Right? *Right!* I instantly felt better so I stood up, earning myself an annoyed little chirrup from the dislodged cat, and marched towards the kitchen: I should start by hanging up the now-clean washing.

Four hours later, I settled back down in the chair with a notebook and a stack of pens. The washing was hung, another lot had gone on. *I am a domestic goddess*, I thought proudly. I'd made some brownies, cleaned the kitchen while they baked, photographed them in case I wanted to put them on my blog (add to list: Blog brownies) and ate three of them with a big cup of tea while wiggling my toes under the duvet for the cat to pounce on. I'd written my mental health newsletter, done the online shop. By anyone's standards, it had been a productive day.

I consulted the list: only a few things left for today. I needed to do my monthly reflections – a task set for me by a former therapist, and which I still tried to do – and the energy bill stuff. And considering my energy bill stuff was being sabotaged by my mental health stuff, I reasoned that I should really do my reflections first. Opening my notebook carefully, I wrote the date on a fresh page in my neatest handwriting, and in a different colour underneath wrote out the first question of the set my therapist gave me at the start of our sessions together.

What have you been doing this month to improve your physical well-being and relationship with your body?

I've kept up my swimming, but mainly because I'm obsessed with the teeny-tiny arm muscles it's giving me. It's like my upper arms have baked potatoes growing under the skin now and I love it, although thinking about it, that's a weird thing to enjoy. I stopped putting lotion on my body after showers because I felt too bad about the way my stomach and thighs felt under my hands. But I'm sleeping a lot – last weekend, I slept for 24 hours out of 48. Is that good? I don't know.

I'm cooking a bit more, and feeding myself good things more, so that's good. I just need to get to a point where I can cook myself something that's both healthy and as delicious as a Domino's Pepperoni Passion and Sainsbury's White Chocolate cookies, then I'll be laughing.

What have you been doing this month to improve your intellectual health?

Not beating myself up for not yet having read any of George Eliot's books and not really enjoying any of Jane Austen's novels apart from *P&P*, mainly. Although I've also stopped arguing with people on the Internet and muted anyone on Twitter who talks about Piers Morgan more than once a day, apart from the days he's done something Exceptionally Stupid rather than just Generally Stupid. Still having that problem where I come home from work with every intention of doing something to improve myself, but end up lying on the floor and staring blankly at a wall for two hours, but I'm starting to think maybe lying on a floor and staring at a wall is a thing I enjoy doing and I shouldn't beat myself up for it.

What have you been doing this month to improve your spiritual health?

My lack of belief in God, the healing power of crystals or moon-charged jade eggs you put up your vagina continues to make this a difficult one, to be honest. But I've been looking at trees a bit. Last week, I saw a fox and it made me quite happy. Especially when it saw me looking and jumped three feet in the air in shock.

What have you been doing this month to improve your social health?

Talking to people. Also, *not* talking to people. There's a particular joy found in cancelling plans the afternoon before you're supposed to do them – even better if they cancel the plans rather than you – and I'm taking as much pleasure as I can from it. And even if I'm not talking to people I'm listening to them, scrolling endlessly through social media, flicking through Twitter to Instagram to Facebook to Tumblr to Snapchat and back again, and even though I don't often have something to say back, at least I'm interacting in some way and that counts.

Overall, how do you feel you are coping?

. . .?

How *was* I coping? I hated that question. In a way, I was coping when I was spending every waking moment in my pyjamas, crying daily and eating nothing but entire boxes of cereal. I was coping when I was perfectly happy, meeting new people and making them into solid friends, and having fun experiences and absolutely bossing my job. I was coping when I spent my entire 45-minute walk to and from work each day wondering if I should throw myself into the road or the nearest canal. No matter what stage of mad I was in, I was still doing the work I needed to do, paying my bills (apart from the fucking energy bills, I KNOW), saying the things I needed to say to the people I needed to say them to. I was, technically, coping. But two of those 'copings' weren't right, really. I know they weren't. So, which 'coping' am I doing now? What does the word even mean?

The front door slammed. I lifted up my head and the cat streaked past to stand in the doorway and meow at the person coming through the living-room door. He looked tired, his curly black hair fluffy at the front where he'd been running his fingers through it all day. Shrugging his backpack off, he bent down to fuss the cat, then stood up and pushed his glasses back onto his nose. He smiled at me across the room, stretching sleepily; his

Ghostbusters t-shirt rode up and the hint of fuzzy brown hair I saw on his soft belly made me feel a rush of love. I smiled.

'Hello, sweetie,' he said, bending down again to fuss the cat as she wound her way around his legs. 'You okay?'

'I'm good, you okay?'

'Tired.'

He scooped Flick up and cuddled her; she stayed there for a few seconds, then clawed her way over his shoulder and down his back. As her claws dug into his shoulder, he winced.

'You busy? Want to snuggle up and watch some *Peep Show* before I cook tea?'

I looked down at my notebook, then back up to him. 'Sure!' I said brightly, snapping it closed and standing up to hug him. My forehead rested perfectly in the space between his collarbone and his shoulder, and Flick rubbed herself happily against both of our legs. It doesn't matter that I haven't done the energy, I'll do it tomorrow. And I'm not going to bother answering that last question. Because I'm coping, I am. *Look at me go!* I'm baking brownies, writing newsletters, making lists … I'm doing fine, I really am.

I'm *fine*.

TO-DO

- ✓ Put washing on
- ✓ Brunch with girls
- ✓ Pick up meds
- ✓ Monthly reflections
- ✓ Hang washing up
- ☐ Pay energy bills... £
- ☐ ...or at least open them!
- ☐ ...or at least check out prices for other energy providers
- ☐ ...or at least look at other providers
- ☐ (Yoga?) To calm down after all the energy stuff?

✓ Do online shop

✓ Make sure to get decaff tea on
online shop

✓ Do some mindful baking

✓ Clean kitchen to calm down from
the stress of mindful baking

✓ Write mental health newsletter on
coping better (ahahahahahaha!)

☐ Find a way to calm down the
wriggling eels

☐ Blog brownies

All this, and
I didn't cry once.
Coping? Mate,
I am FLYING

TO-DO

- ☐ Get up at 6.45am
- ☐ Go to the swimming baths
- ☐ Ten lengths of breaststroke
- ☐ Ten lengths of backstroke
- ☐ Ten lengths of front crawl
- ☐ Wash hair
- ☐ Get ready
- ☐ Make-up on
- ☐ Healthy breakfast
- ☐ Healthy lunch
- ☐ Walk at lunchtime

TWO

There are multiple alarm pre-sets on my phone, but only one has a name attached to it so when I roll over to turn it off, I get a little note from past-me. It's the one for 6.45am, and the message is: 'Get up, go swimming. You'll feel better'.

When it went off this morning, I groaned. It's so tempting to roll over and go back to sleep for another 90 minutes, but I know that if I don't get up, I'll have future-me chastising me for being a lazy git, so I get up and drag my exhausted arse out the door.

One of the first things you learn about mental health, probably even before you realise depression is going to curl up in *your* brain and rot there for a while, is that exercise helps. Every fucker and the dog they go jogging with is keen to tell you that you can fight depression and anxiety with a brisk walk three times a week, or by playing tennis with friends, or doing anything that gets those magical endorphins whooshing round your body and crushing the brain spiders like they're a giant rolled-up newspaper made of sweat and smugness.

What these leggings-wearing wankers don't tell you is that when you're feeling crap, exercise is the hardest thing in the world. Lying on my bed, staring silently at the ceiling for three hours, even though I was *rationally aware* that if I got up and went for a walk I'd probably feel a bit better, not an atom in my body had the motivation to do anything other than stay exactly where I was. There were several days when I was so anxious that I couldn't leave the house, weeks at a time when I didn't have the motivation to shower. How on earth was I going to get up the energy to run? The only exercise I was getting was beating myself up, and although I was certainly putting enough effort in to get nice and sweaty, the only water leaking from me was coming from my eyes and dripping down my face, forming puddles on the duvet below.

I spent many years silently hating all those people who extolled the virtues of exercise in managing their mental health. 'I just feel so much better after doing a quick 5k in the morning!' they'd trill, and I'd smile and nod and give them the finger the second their back was turned. You don't *know*, I'd think. Even though you used to know, you've forgotten. You filled your head full of kilometre splits and running shoes and terrible, terrible running playlists, and it's pushed out the memories of how *fucking awful* it is to be depressed and be told that the secret to feeling better is to *exercise*. Occasionally, I would take myself out for a run because I knew it was good for me, but I was so bad at it, and it made me feel so bad about *myself* that I could never keep it up for more than four or five days. I tried it because it was cheap and easy, and I used to dream about being the kind of person who could elegantly and effortlessly do a 5k three times a week before work. When I ran, I didn't feel elegant or effortless, I felt dumpy and plodding. My running speed was often beaten by others going for a brisk stroll, and the longer I ran, the heavier I felt. And as much as people say no one pays attention when you're running, I know that's not true: people noticed me, they made fun of me. A man once saw me coming across the park at the end of a run, Week Three of Couch-to-5k jog that I was incredibly proud of myself for managing, and started lumbering up and down while pointing at me to make his wife laugh.

What's worse was that I knew he had reason to laugh. The first time I started running I was still living at home, and after a few jogs Mum came with me. She was better at it than me. I was 18, ostensibly at the peak of my physical life, and a 53-year-old woman was better at running than me. After that I gave up fairly quickly; she went on to do longer runs and charity runs and made it a part of her daily life. I was happy for her – I *am* happy for her – but it still makes me feel sick with shame.

And it's not just Mum. I once went for a jog with Penny, and when we went our separate ways to go home, I took the first opportunity to throw up in a bush. Once, when Garry came for a run with me, I noticed he was bobbing up and down quite a lot.

'Hey, I read in *Running Like a Girl* that you should push yourself *forward* rather than bobbing up and down. It saves energy!' I told him brightly. There was a pause.

'I'm going up and down because it's the only way I can run slowly enough for you,' he said kindly.

'Oh,' I replied. Mentally, I had stopped and screamed in his face, opening my mouth wide enough to swallow him whole like a snake. But I didn't say anything other than 'Oh'. We ran on, and when I got home, I locked myself in the shower and cried. We never went running again, and I stopped going altogether shortly afterwards. Running made me feel terrible, and I was doing that to myself well enough on my own.

The fact, therefore, that I'd become one of those people who exercises for their brain rather than their body surprised no one more than me. Towards the end of my last lot of therapy, I went for a swim one Saturday – I had to psyche myself up for four hours beforehand and ended up trapped in a changing cubicle for 15 minutes before I was brave enough to get in the pool – and followed it up with a few swims before work that week. Then I got a membership to the pool. Then I bought a new swimming costume and a swimming cap. And now I'm going three or four times a week, before work and after work and on my own and with friends and in different pools around London, and if I *don't* go, I can feel it in my chest and my stomach and behind my eyes. It feels fuzzy and jittery and uncomfortable, and the only thing that can blast it is 30 lengths of very slow swimming.

I try really, really hard not to become one of those arseholes who forgets how difficult it is to just stay alive when you're tits-deep in depression, so I'm not going to lecture you on how great I feel after a swim; how the secret was finding an exercise *I* enjoyed rather than one everyone else told me I should do (running can still die a fiery death for all I care) and how you should all sign up to your local leisure centre. I don't think swimming makes me feel great, necessarily, it just stops me from feeling shit, and just because it works for me, doesn't mean it'll work for you. Maybe painting makes you feel not-shit. Or rap music. Even yoga. Or masturbating in the toilets at work twice a day. Who knows? But my thing is swimming, and it's why I have that little nagging message on my phone. No matter how crap I feel getting up to go, I know I'll always feel a bit better afterwards.

And my God, do I feel crap when I get up to go. Sat on the train, I could feel the eyes of all the suburban commuters on me. I didn't have make-up on, obviously, and my greasy, unbrushed hair was pulled back in a bun. My swimming bag was a stained tote with 'Harry Potter Book Club' on the front. I was wearing my costume underneath my clothes so, because I could buy a two-bed flat in Zone 3 for the price of one cossie with decent tit support, my enormous boobs were resting near my belly button. One thing was clear: my fellow travellers hated me. Usually I'd meet their disapproving looks with a glare, but my face was still puffy from sleep so I stared blearily at them until they felt uncomfortable instead.

One-nil to the baggy-eyed bag lady, motherfuckers!

The swimming pool is on my way to work, and close to home. I leave the house at 6.55am and I'm in the changing room by 7.20am. I think I like this pool so much because it's a bit crap: it's cheap and cheerful, and in the morning frequented mainly by people in their sixties who go because it's free and they've been awake for two hours so they might as well do *something* – although yes, there are still a few people Instagramming themselves crushing a workout before drinking a green smoothie and going to a glamorous City job while probably/hopefully secretly hating their lives. But hey, nowhere's perfect!

As I stuffed my bag and clothes into a locker, I smiled at Laura (cheery 50-something who goes to the gym for half an hour before doing a half-hour swim *every damn morning*), who in turn was chatting to Maud (being taught to swim by Laura). I pointedly ignored the two gym bunnies behind me slowly drying every inch of themselves while completely naked, tiny nipples pointing to the ceiling and perfect strips of pubes adorning neat and tidy crotches.

I *say* I was ignoring them, but I obviously wasn't. Otherwise I wouldn't be able to comment. I was *totally* checking them out! Just as I was checking out Laura and Maud, just as I was checking out the big beefy woman on the other side of the room whose bottom was covered in dimples, just as I was checking out the naked 70-year-old showering woman as I walked from the changing room to the pool, just as I was checking out the bodies of the women on the poolside, who hoisted themselves in and out of the water while I was swimming.

It's not in a pervy way – well, it's not *always* in a pervy way. It's just that I can't help myself. I can't walk down a street without checking out the body of every single woman who walks past and comparing it to mine. On the Tube, I'm ranking everyone's body to see where I fit. At work, I stare at thighs, collarbones, arms, stomachs, seeing who has a smaller bum than me or who has nicer boobs, or whose stomach is flatter than mine (spoiler alert: *everyone. Always. Absolutely everyone*). Friends, family members, strangers, colleagues, people who serve me in cafes and restaurants ... no one is safe. The only difference is the people in a changing room are usually a lot more naked than the ones on the street.

This isn't the healthiest thing to do, I know, but I can't help it. I need some point of reference to understand my own body, I can't do it on its own merit. In the past six years I'd lost, regained, part lost and fully regained five stone. I'd ranged from a size 10–12 to 20–22. The jeans I'd pulled on that morning were a size 20, and according to my last, furtive weigh-in I was 16 and a half stone. To me, it's fascinating in exactly the same way as those videos of spots being popped. And it's a good thing I didn't start swimming to lose weight, because I haven't lost a pound since I started.

I may be fascinated by my growing body, but that doesn't mean I'm not also ashamed of it. I wish I wasn't, I knew I shouldn't be, but it's *hard* to not feel like I was wrong when that's the message society was giving me. As I neared the pool, I scuttled to the steps and got in as quickly as possible, sucking my breath in as the cold water hit my warm body. Submerged to the neck, I pushed away and stood at the head of the pool for a second, breathing in the familiar smell of chlorine and damp, letting the water seep into and soothe every single inch of me.

I like being in the water. According to the fancy scales I bought (and hate), I am roughly 50 per cent fat, so there's a lot of me to float when I'm in the pool. My breasts lift away from my body and bob around happily. My tummy doesn't hang over my crotch but floats slightly, so it becomes rounded and pleasing rather than saggy and shameful. My thighs go from big and meaty to smooth, pale and soft. The cold water both covers and comforts; the heavy, burning shame I carry round with me is washed away. When I'm in a pool, I feel unencumbered. I feel light, I am free.

I took a deep breath and pushed off from the wall, heading into my first ten lengths of breaststroke, my least favourite. I can't do the frog-legs thing without somehow kicking a flood of water up my vagina. My breaststroke, therefore, involves doggy-paddle legs. It's slow and steady, a perfect warm-up, and something I would be far too embarrassed to do if I was anywhere other than with the 7am crowd, all too sleepy or non-judgemental to care.

When I go swimming, I usually stay in the Slow Lane. I *should* be in the Moderate Lane: the sign at the head of the lanes says the Moderate Lane is for swimmers who do lengths in 30–60 seconds, and my average speed is about 40 seconds. However, what *actually* happens is that in the Fast Lane, you get the people who think they're in training for the Olympics, who thrash up and down doing overly dramatic strokes while wearing goggles and fucking *flippers* and causing waves that make the swimmers nearest bob up and down like seagulls on the tide. Those who should be in the Fast Lane, therefore, go in the Moderate Lane and tut at anyone doing their lengths less quickly, pushing all us Moderates into the Slow Lane and getting in the way of those who swim at the speed of a space hopper rolling up a hill.

And then, there's *her*. My nemesis. I don't know anything about her apart from the fact that she has a pink swim cap, gets in the pool earlier than 7.20am, and I would happily kick her in the face if the opportunity arose. It never does, though; she shoots up and down, weaving in and out of paddling pensioners, rarely stopping for breath and never looking anyone in the eye. I couldn't get my feet near her when I tried – I mean, even if I tried, obviously. *If …*

She makes me furious. I can never properly relax until she's out of the pool. As I reached the foot of the pool to complete my first length, she was there, ready to come back the other way. Her eyes were already focused on the wall behind me, arms ploughing through the water like it's air. I had to swerve to the left to avoid her – difficult when you're in water and only going 25 metres a minute – but she didn't acknowledge me. She just shot off, cutting her own line through the water, quickly overtaking a man in the Moderate Lane. *Dickheads, the pair of them!*

It doesn't feel like she's purposefully shoving it in our faces that she's so much faster, and I often wonder if she truly *believes* that she belongs in the Slow Lane. I can't decide if this is her being an inconsiderate dolt, or if she's undermining herself. Either way, I can't hate her for smugness so I hate her for her sheer inconvenience instead and for her tiny, perfect frame. I bet she shops in the petite section. I *long* to be like her – little, but powerful. I spent the next five lengths fantasising about tapping her on the shoulder and saying, 'Oi, you're too fast for this lane, why not move over?', but obviously, I never would.

After ten lengths, I flipped over onto my back and started doing backstroke, my favourite. Big and meaty as they are, my legs kick me backwards and I can feel the water tickling my cheeks as it rushes past. When I swim, I feel faster and more graceful than I ever do on my feet. Whenever I think about what my Patronus might be – I have a Harry Potter swimming bag, of course I think about it – I always think it'd be a seal. Cumbersome on land, but get them in the sea and they're strong, powerful and beautiful. I'm not a good enough swimmer to believe water is my natural habitat, but it gives me hope that one day, I'll find an environment where I feel like I fit.

I was pulled from this soothing train of thought by a spray of water hitting me right in the face and going up my nose. I coughed, doubling up and treading water. An old man whose name I don't know was doing backstroke the other way up the pool, and because his right arm wouldn't go back properly, he was flailing it around somewhere over his shoulder, sending a spray of water across anyone who happened to be within a three-metre radius. He heard me choking and popped his head up.

'Shorr, m'dahhhrr,' he said, in what I think was an Irish accent hiding behind the inability to pronounce his words properly.

'Don't worry about it, lovely,' I said, just as my nemesis flew past on the inside, making me jump. *Fucker! Absolute fucker!* Furious, I lay back and tried to catch her up, hips up (just as Laura taught me to do. The burst of speed it gave surprised me so much that I didn't keep myself straight and shot straight into the wall), arms thrashing. I wasn't even two-thirds of the way there before I spotted her gliding past me on the other side – I hope her fancy swimming costume gives her thrush.

I prefer swimming in the morning because after work, the pool is full of my nemeses. In the evening there are swimming lessons, and this is fine because everyone has to learn and I'm not selfish enough to get annoyed by the existence of children, but the knock-on effect they have is infuriating.

While the majority who come to exercise in the morning are bleary-eyed and happy to gently do their 30 minutes with only a few people coming to Work Out, in the evening, the balance shifts. The pool is full of wankers with waterproof smart watches, Speedos and goggles, doing elaborate stretches at the end of the lanes. These people have the utmost competitive respect for *each other* and so give each other space, but absolutely none for general swimmers so when they do these stupid stretches, they go in the Slow Lane, where they stretch for *fucking ages*, getting in the way of everyone else. I don't ask for much in life, but I really don't want to have to contort my body to avoid touching some-bloke-wearing-nothing-but-a-lime-green-swim-cap's naked body when I do my ten lengths of pseudo-breaststroke.

And then, because there's no general swimming lane when there are swimming lessons going on, the Slow Lane is *filled* with idiots. Did you know that *adult human beings who have money and homes to go to* will visit a shitty leisure centre swimming pool *for a date* in the year of our Lord 2017? *Did* you? Because they do! They hang around in the water and chat to each other and generally get in the way. Why? Do they know they're allowed to have sex? That they don't have to make excuses to see each other semi-naked? If you're ever debating taking a date to a swimming pool for a Monday evening, don't! If you're going to actually swim it's a shitty date because you can't really talk, and if you plan to hang about in the water then you're an idiot, and no one wants to have sex with an idiot.

Somewhere between my tenth and twentieth length, the sky started to lighten. The pool has a big mottled glass section on the roof. Lying on my back as I worked my way up and down, I watched it turn from black to purple to lilac to grey. After finishing my ten lengths of backstroke, I flipped over, taking a deep breath and pushing myself underwater. I stayed in a glide for as long as I could before breaking the surface and taking an enormous breath, feeling my body swell and shudder with it, before reaching my arms out and over and pulling myself through the water. I timed my breathing with my arm movements, putting my head underwater in between breaths. Breathe-one-two-three-four-five, BREATHE-one-two-three-four-five, over and over until I reached the end. I clung to the wall and gasped before doing the whole thing again. And again; again and again, until my limbs were heavy and it felt like I was moving through custard; until my lungs stung like I was about to sneeze with every breath, until I had to stop to let myself return to normal.

It's that feeling, that horrible, heavy feeling, that has always stopped me from exercise. Or rather, the hot shame I feel in every atom of my being whenever I try and get my big, lumbering body to move. You can only make your body good at exercise by practising it, but I could never get past the painful, inescapable humiliation of how *bad* my body was at anything other than eating a lot of KitKats to get to that point. Maybe that's why I like swimming. No one can see how much you're struggling or how tired you are. Maybe that's why I like swimming at 7am with pensioners – because I'm just as slow as they are, so I don't have to feel bad about myself around them. Maybe that's why I resent being pushed out of the Moderate Lane – the one time I've ever done exercise and not been the slowest, and I resent not being able to prove it.

And maybe, if I'm entirely honest, it's why I hate my nemesis so much. It's not that I hate her for getting in the way, but I hate how she forces me to confront the truth: even though I've been swimming three or four times a week for months, I'm still slow and awkward. I can hide it with a blanket of water and by removing people I could possibly compare myself negatively to, but she reveals the truth: my body is still useless, and I am still ashamed of it.

Cheery thought, isn't it? Anyway, although I hate it when I'm exhausted, I still push myself once or twice every swim session. It feels nice, making my body hurt a little. Like I'm showing it who's boss: 'I don't *care* if you ache, serves you right for being so unfit!' And when I'm timing my breaths and making my legs and my arms and my lungs move in tandem, I feel like a machine rather than a human. Who can have emotional feelings, positive or negative, about machines? No one, unless you're one of those blokes who buys a robot wife because they can't be doing with real women. Or someone with a Kate Spade watch, because I would VERY QUICKLY get very emotionally attached to one of those.

By the time my ten lengths of crawl were over, I was done. My hands clasped the wall of the shallow end and I pulled myself to it, panting so hard I accidentally inhaled water and made myself cough. I glanced up at the clock: a few minutes left before I'd been in for 30 minutes. I pushed off to paddle a couple more lengths and bring my distance up to a round 800m (my Fitbit likes round numbers). My heart rate slowed, my breathing evened out. If the last ten lengths were punishing my body, this felt like forgiving it. Or actually, like hugging it better while it cries; it was filled with remorse, so now I could be gentle with it and make it feel better.

As I came back up to the top of the pool, a few women were walking from the changing room towards it. One was tall and very slim, her legs lean and long, her black swimming costume showing off a neatly nipped-in waist and defined collarbones. Is she too thin? I wondered. Maybe she's got a problem. Maybe she's really strict on calories and she over-exercises, that's why she looks so slim. Almost immediately, I felt guilty. I can't start diagnosing strangers with disordered eating, especially when I feel bad about how good her body is.

Just behind her was a woman who looked like Beyoncé's little sister. She had a narrow torso and waist, but her hips and thighs were wide and rounded. As she walked towards the pool her thighs jiggled; when she turned to drop her bag on the side I saw that her bum stuck out and her tummy was the perfect level of cute roundness. Now, as well as sick with shame I was sick with longing. *Time to get out.* As I pulled myself up the ladder, I felt a moment of satisfaction as the cold, stinging air took the edge off my emotions. I couldn't stop staring at the two women as they sat on the edge of the pool and slid in. One trim body, one round body, both utterly beautiful.

God, how I wish I was utterly beautiful.

Steadily but speedily, I walked back to the changing room, stomach sucked in and hands on my waist at the back to try and cover up my back fat. I grabbed my Harry Potter bag from the hook on the wall and headed for the shower cubicle, steadfastly ignoring the two fat naked 50-year-olds chatting away happily in the communal showers. I closed the door behind me, and closed my eyes.

How do they get so confident? How can I get that confident? Does it just come from not caring? I turned on the shower and peeled my costume off my exhausted body. The warm water felt nice on my skin, easing the knots from gently aching shoulders and hips. I squirted shampoo in my palm and massaged it into my hair; the gentle groan of my arms as I lifted them above my head felt like the 'Oooof' you involuntarily make when you sit in a low chair. Could I do it, let my pendulous boobs and rounded hips and saggy belly free, with a roomful of strangers there? A room full of strangers who categorically don't care about me, let alone the details of my body and how more and more, it's resembling a melting ice cream.

No, absolutely not! Not in a million years.

Because strangers *do* care how you look naked. We all check each other out when we're getting dressed. Those glimpses when I'm getting in the pool are nothing; when I've nothing to do but dry myself, I can spend a lot of time staring at other women's bodies, and staring at them staring at me, and staring at them staring at other women and ... you get the picture.

We all look. How could we not? Other women's bodies are *fascinating*.

I re-emerged in the changing room, towel wrapped tightly around me, and tried not to obviously look at the plethora of nakedness surrounding me. Until I came swimming, I didn't know just how *different* boobs can be. I knew there were the boobs you see in film and TV and porn, then there were mine – ones that point downwards and kind of sideways and start so low on my body, I can put my palms flat on my chest without feeling any tit – but I assumed the media tits were right and mine were wrong. Whenever I saw tits that were different, in those body positive campaigns occasionally re-blogged onto my Tumblr dashboard, I assumed these were the tits of older ladies who'd had babies or whatnot. Flat boobs, saggy boobs, misshapen boobs, pointy nipples … I thought that was the result of breastfeeding, and bullied myself for having the body of a woman who'd had a kid without being able to brag that I'd made a whole human with my vagina.

But no, I was wrong! Some of the elderly ladies I swim with have a perfect handful, tiny pink nipples pointing north at all times. Some have boobs like used Pret bags, flat and weirdly square and wrinkly. Then again, some of the young ladies have these too. And some have big ones that hang like mine, some have boobs which rest to the side, others hang perfectly in front of them like twin soldiers in a row. Some are pointy, others perfectly round. Some look so full to bursting, others so empty, they can basically be folded in half. *And the nipples!* Some have big nipples, others have little ones. Some stick out at all times, like tiny torpedos. Others point *inwards*. Then they come in all sorts of colours. Pinks, browns, purples, reds … even shades of deep purple on some of the black ladies. I never knew how many types of boobs there were. I wish I had – it would have saved a lot of agonising in my youth.

Other parts of women's bodies I like looking at: what they're doing with their bushes (Brazilians are still *very* much in, no matter what women's magazines try to tell you), whether they shave their pits (elder ones yes, younger ones no. I would've thought it'd be the other way round), their tummies (the amount of women who have little rounded bellies when they're not tucked into control pants or tight trousers is astonishing), their thighs (more women than you'd believe have thigh gaps, but not usually the thinnest) and whether or not they wear matching bras and knickers (overwhelmingly YES, even if they've clearly just bought a plain black bra and a bunch of black knickers to go with it. Is everyone wearing matching knickers and bras except me? Note to self: check that out). And their faces … I'm always fascinated by faces, whether they're furtively shoving still-damp bodies in clothes underneath their towels like me, or naked and proud like Frankie, who occasionally comes swimming with me and therefore has a body I know almost as well as my husband's.

As if she knew I was thinking about her, my phone buzzed with a WhatsApp from Frankie. I read it, my face cracked into a smile, and I sat on the bench to reply.

FRANKIE: Do you find it more uncomfortable when people walk around naked in the changing rooms or talk about all their business to friends?

AMY: All their business

AMY: Purely because everyone here is walking around naked. There are five distinct fannies at face height within five metres of me RIGHT NOW. I'd have to get comfortable with it or I'd never come here again

AMY: Also, they all have such sculpted pubes I feel like I should admire them, not be made uncomfortable by them

AMY: You?

FRANKIE: The business. NO ONE CARES

FRANKIE: Also, right?!

AMY: No one cares

AMY: Not even a bit

FRANKIE: I only do my pubes if I have a date

FRANKIE: While we're on the subject …

FRANKIE: How are yours doing?

AMY: They were completely untamed but they kept escaping my bathers so when I went swimming with you last week, I ran Garry's beard trimmer over them

FRANKIE: Hahahahaha! I love you

AMY: I'm getting quite relaxed on the body hair front, tbh.

AMY: Until the weekend I had v hairy legs and armpits and just didn't care

FRANKIE: Good for you!

FRANKIE: Kind of freeing, eh? I love not caring about what my body looks like in the changing room, now

FRANKIE: Although it took a couple of weeks before I stopped scurrying into the gym toilets to get dressed

FRANKIE: Now I'm all hey gals, here are my tits and clunge, won't be long till they're covered

AMY: Not a good enough reason to use the word clunge

FRANKIE: Like I need a reason

By the time we'd stopped texting I'd gotten dry(ish), put my clothes back on and was standing in front of the mirror with my make-up bag. Most days I happily turn up to work without anything on my face, but secretly, it's because I go so many days without showering that the shadows of yesterday's make-up still make me look vaguely human and so I don't need to apply more. Fresh from a swim, my face is red and blotchy and without mascara I look like my dad, so I take five minutes to smear things on my face so I can feel vaguely like myself again. I pull my wet hair into a bobble, and set off for work.

The Tube was busy, but I've learnt to cope with it: I bought a pair of comfy, squashy on-ear headphones last year so when commuting, I can snap them on, press play on the latest episode of the podcast Penny makes with her colleague, Rosie, and forget the rest of the world exists. Them chatting about the new episode of *The Good Place* and the feminist implications of Janet saw me all the way to Old Street and the cafe near my office. There, as I do every time I buy breakfast, I became trapped in front of the fridge.

Croissant or fruit? Croissant or fruit? Or their granola pots? No, not the granola, there's loads of calories in one of those for what they are. So, croissant or fruit? I know I should have fruit – a pot of mango and lime is barely 100 calories and I can nibble on it all morning. But I also know that I don't want the mango and lime. I want the croissant; I want the buttery pastry and the chocolate and the feeling of something warm and satisfying in my stomach, which is growling at me after the swim. But the mango and lime won't undo all the calories I just burnt. I should get the mango and lime. I should. *I should* ...

So, I reached forward and grabbed the pot of mango. I stood in the queue, pleased with myself and my decision. Healthy breakfast, healthy lunch. I'll do it ... a whole healthy day.

The woman behind the counter waved me forward. She glanced at the pot in my hand and started tapping at the screen in front of her.

'Anything else?' she asked disinterestedly.

'A chocolate croissant, please,' I said before I could help myself. 'And a hot chocolate.' Hurriedly added before she stepped away.

Fucking hell!

As I sat at my desk, I ate the croissant in six large bites. I sipped at the hot chocolate slowly as I went through emails and wrote my To-Do List for the day. The mango and lime sat on my desk, untouched, until the cleaner threw it away long after I went home that night. Later, curled up on the sofa with

Garry and the chilli I made for dinner, I suddenly remembered something. I reached for my phone, opened up my Queens group chat, and typed out a message.

> AMY: Hey, do you guys wear matching knickers and bras?
> JANAE: Lol, no, who has time?
> PENNY: Maybe about half the time? I buy loads of M&S knickers to go with the matching bra, but if I buy an expensive bra, I'll only buy one or two matching pairs of knickers
> FRANKIE: Not really

I felt cheered. Then I noticed that Janae was typing another message.

> JANAE: Why?
> AMY: Just loads of women at the pool have matching sets and I was surprised
> JANAE: Oh, I wear matching sets if someone else is going to be seeing them
> PENNY: I always wear my matching ones when I'm going to judo
> FRANKIE: Me too. And when I think I'm going to be having sex
> PENNY: Oh yes, that's when I get the expensive ones out

The conversation descended into innuendos and fire emojis, so I locked my phone and turned my attention back to the TV. Matching knickers … Right, let's add that to the list.

TO-DO

- ✓ Get up at 6.45am
- ✓ Go to the swimming baths
- ✓ Ten lengths of breaststroke
- ✓ Ten lengths of backstroke
- ✓ Ten lengths of front crawl
- ✓ Wash hair
- ✓ Get ready
- ✓ Make-up on
- ☐ Healthy breakfast (well-fucking done Jones!)
- ☐ Healthy lunch
- ☐ Walk at lunchtime
- ☐ Buy matching sets of bras and pants

Is everyone wearing matching bras and pants except me? ✓

NOTES

Trying to convince myself that spending my lunch eating a katsu curry while reading BuzzFeed was emotionally nourishing and so it doesn't matter that it wasn't _physically_ good for me

TO-DO

- ☐ Team meeting
- ☐ Finish the YouTube scripts
- ☐ Chase on schools' copy
- ☐ Try to figure out why Adam hates me
- ☐ Take a lunch break

THREE

As the lift doors opened I took a deep breath and walked out onto my floor. My job isn't that bad, really – Garry often quips that I've had 'another hard day down the glittermine' – but I don't think I'm overreacting to say my soul seeps out of every pore for every single second I'm here. No matter how content I feel after a morning swim or a long weekend, it only takes 30 minutes of being in the office before I feel complete and utter despair at having to do this for another 40 years.

My boss, Adam, was at his desk across the table from me and in no way acknowledged my presence when I arrived. I'd be offended, but I'm long past that. If he quit, our little sub-team (the youth-facing part of a mental health charity) would fall into total chaos, and maybe he feels absolutely no need to waste a single second of his day on such things as initiating pleasantries with subordinates.

'Good morning!' I said with as much chirpiness as I could muster.

'Morning,' he muttered back – the bare minimum without being actively rude.

'Alright, pet?' said Claire, smiling cheerily from directly across the desk. Like me, Claire is a senior content producer at Youth Steady and although she can be relied upon after a few gins to get weepy about Adam's behaviour, she's not so obsessed as me. 'Good weekend?'

'Fine, thanks. You?'

'Yeah, good. Took Edie down to Brighton to paddle in the sea for the first time.'

'How'd she like that?'

'She screamed the whole time, poor love, but liked the ice cream for afters.'

I half-listened to Claire prattle on about her adorable toddler while I loaded up my computer. Steady is a charity, and not even a sexy charity which has people clamouring to run marathons for us, so our equipment is *incredibly* old. If you took the case off my computer tower, I'm sure you'd find a tiny old man sat on a penny-farthing, shrugging and saying, 'Eh, what do you want me to do about it?' in a voice that's 90 per cent tobacco ash. The whole reason Claire and I arrive 20 minutes earlier than we have to is so that our computers can be up and running by 9am. I'm not sure why Adam arrives so early. To be honest, I'm not sure he ever leaves.

I opened up my emails. There was one from Adam marked with a little red exclamation point. My stomach lurched.

I'm happy with this but as it's advertising the service we need to get Marketing & Elias to sign off too ASAP

He liked what I wrote last week! I'd feel relief, but I'm already so tense that at this point I'd need an orgasm and a family bar of Dairy Milk to unclench. Instead, I exhale the breath I didn't know I was holding, open a new email, attach the school leaflet copy to it, and begin to type.

Hello! So, this is the copy we're proposing for the new school leaflet. It's got an introduction to the service and the website, and then an extract from our page on self-esteem, as that's the theme that comms really wants to push this year.

We need your sign-off on this before it can be sent to the printer. Can you cast your eye over it and let me know if there are any problems, please?

Any questions, just ask.

> *Thanks!*
> *Take care,*
> *Amy*

I sent it to Elias (head of youth activities) and my favourite person in Marketing, Joe. Struck by a sudden fear that I'd started the email with 'Dear fuckheads' or something along those lines, I checked my sent-folder. I hadn't, thankfully. Almost immediately, I got a reply.

> *Hi there. Thanks for your email. I'm out of the office this week. If you need anything urgently, please contact Rosie Lucas.*
>
> > *Thanks,*
> > *Joe*

Fucksticks! I don't know Rosie Lucas, I don't have a relationship with her. I don't know if she's a quick replier, when her meetings are, if I can call her a lazy git without her reporting me to HR. I have no fucking idea how to proceed, which means I have no fucking idea how this week is going to go. Why are the tiny, admin-based things always so much more stressful and so much harder to deal with than the big ones? I can do a presentation to a hundred donors about exactly how we used their money no problem, but the idea of getting sign-off from someone I didn't know was bringing me out in a cold sweat. Swallowing my nerves, I click on the link to Rosie's email in Joe's out-of-office and start to type.

> *Hi Rosie. I'm Amy, and I'm senior content producer in the youth arm of the Editorial Content team. I tried to email Joe Hart and his OOO directed me towards you …*

I copied and pasted the email sent to Joe into the email, hit send and let out my breath. Without realising it, I had curled my toes into tiny feet fists in my shoes. I needed to get this done, or Adam would hate me even more than he did already. I glanced at him miserably: he was still absorbed in his phone. I wouldn't mind that he hated me so much apart from the fact that I quite liked him. Most people here are killing time until they can retire, but not him. He's hungry. He wants to keep doing things bigger and better, to win awards and impress people, and give talks and all that work stuff we're supposed to aspire to #girlboss #goals #leanin. And I don't know why he hates me. Everyone else seems to get on with me. My constant need for validation and desire to please mean that I work hard, I work fast, and I work long. Also, I'm not so far into my self-loathing that I can't see the objective truth: I'm clever, I'm capable, and I'm good at my job – no matter how I feel most Friday afternoons.

Our office was filling up. The main Editorial team arrived in groups of two or three, talking about taking bike rides down to the coast or the incredible hangovers they had this weekend. I glanced over longingly at their head of team, Rowena, who has a mane of golden gingery hair and is simultaneously incredibly friendly and so calmly powerful you get the impression she'd make your eyeballs into earrings if you disappointed her.

When Youth Steady's junior content producers, Fee and Nish, arrived together, they were discussing the latest episode of *Agents of S.H.I.E.L.D.* with an intensity most people reserve for political debate. Nish was wearing a t-shirt that I knew for a fact had moth holes in the armpits, and Fee looked ... well. Like Fee. They had once joked to me that, as a non-binary babe, their goal was that people would look at them and feel nothing but confusion about what their gender was. Their amazing dress sense meant they achieved that goal every day of their lives.

Adam cleared his throat, typing something with such ferocity it was like he was trying to punch through the keyboard.

'Team meeting at two, yes?' he said tersely, eyes not moving from the screen. We muttered in agreement, turning to our screens in silence.

The morning passed in a blur. I was half-editing scripts for the new videos we were about to produce for the *Steady: On Now* YouTube channel, half-obsessing over why Adam hated me, and half-WhatsApping Penny about whether or not I should be applying for jobs. I realise that's too many halves for one person, but I don't think you appreciate how quickly I was working. By the time lunch came around, I was nauseous with the stress of it all and had to focus on keeping my hands steady.

AMY: I think I'm going to be sick
PENNY: Then go and be sick, darling
AMY: I don't want to be sick
PENNY: If you're going to be sick, you might as well just go and be sick. In private, not all over your desk
PENNY: But also, your job shouldn't be making you want to be sick
AMY: I know
AMY: I need to leave
PENNY: You do. Your job is an utter shitshow.
PENNY: Just remember, they're cunts, my love, and they don't deserve you
AMY: Okay. Yes. Cunts. The lot of them, cunts
PENNY: Exactly. A veritable *bouquet* of cunts. Time to find you a non-cunty workplace. What have you applied for?

I was typing out a reply to Penny, telling her about the job at an indie art charity which would have required me to travel to Zone 6 and paid slightly less than I was on now, when I sensed someone coming up behind me. Quickly, I closed the WhatsApp Web window and when Adam appeared at my chair, I spun round to face him.

'Any luck with the school copy yet?' he asked.

'Uh, no,' I said, spinning slightly back towards the computer so I could open my email and gesture vaguely at the screen. 'Joe

is off, so I've emailed someone called Rosie Lucas about it …?'
I trailed off, hoping he might go, 'Oh, Rosie Lucas! I know her,
I'll just go and have a word,' but nada. I'm usually quite good
at reading body language, but Adam's shoulders stayed set, his
eyes didn't flicker, his mouth didn't move. MI6 agents give away
more.

'But no response yet, from her or from Elias. I'll wait until
after the meeting, and then I'll … chase?' I phrased it as a
question rather than a statement and cursed myself – according
to the people who write long articles for the *Observer* about how
the pay gap is all down to the way women communicate, that's
exactly the *wrong* thing to do. Then again, I could probably
write a statement on a giant plate, smash it over Adam's head
and he'd give it only a passing amount of interest.

'Sure,' he said. 'Do you want to take us through the new
scripts in the meeting?'

It's not really a question.

'I can do.'

'Great.'

He walked off without another word. I turned back to my
desk, digging my nails into my palm. *Shit. Okay, two hours to go.
I need to actually get some work done.*

I work better on a deadline so I snapped my headphones
on, blasted film scores, said goodbye to dreams of sitting outside
in the sun to eat my lunch, and got it done. By the time 2pm
rolled around, I had five copies of a passable script on OCD
printed out. I would have felt proud of myself if I wasn't too
busy feeling sick.

My little team schlepped to the meeting room, Fee wiping
crisp crumbs from around their mouth and Nish with his usual
array of pens and pencils he uses to take precise, incredibly
detailed notes. Adam sat furthest from the door, tapping
furiously on his phone; he didn't look up when we came in.
Claire, Fee and Nish were having an enthusiastic conversation
about *RuPaul's Drag Race*, which I am the only person in the

world not to have seen, so I sat quietly until Adam looked up and the conversation faltered.

'Right,' he said, putting his phone face-down on the table. 'Fee, stats for this week?'

They flipped open their notebook, which had a glittery unicorn on the front. 'Twenty-four thousand uniques, 33 per cent new users. Up on last week, but our time on page has suffered because of it. Most popular section is the self-harm section. I've done a bit of digging and there's been a *Hollyoaks* storyline on it this week, so that'll be why, and search has been the biggest driver of traffic this week.'

'Have you told the social team?' Adam asked.

Fee met his gaze unflinchingly.

'No, do you want me to?' they asked.

'Well, yes. If they know that *Hollyoaks* is driving traffic, they can reference it in their posts and catch anyone who knows *Hollyoaks* but doesn't know *us*,' he replied. He kept his voice and tone neutral, but I *swore* there was a glimmer of irritation there. Fee didn't seem to notice – or if they did, they didn't care.

'Cool, can do,' they said brightly, making a note in green ink. Adam was still staring unblinkingly. Something twinged heavily in my gut. *Oh, God, this is excruciating! How are they not panicking? Why are they so unbothered?*

'Claire,' he said. She jumped next to me. 'What's the progress with the new site structure?'

Claire took us through the new information architecture planned for the website, then Nish went through the research he'd been doing on the new therapeutic games. I was half-listening, half-daydreaming about going to work as a primary teacher in a small seaside town when Nish suddenly put his notebook back on the table, picked up a pen and looked at me expectantly. I glanced round. Everyone was looking at me.

'Amy,' said Adam. 'Take us through the work you're doing on YouTube.'

'Sure,' I said, somehow making my voice sound a lot steadier than I felt. I passed round the printouts of my script, cleared my throat, and started to talk.

'So, we've decided to go for three topics initially – OCD, social anxiety and self-harm,' I began. 'We've gone for –' I interrupted myself with a cough. 'We've gone for these first because we know from the message boards and feedback that OCD is one of the most misunderstood conditions, social anxiety is becoming more and more searched for as … as celebrities talk about it and the issue gains awareness, and self-harm is consistently a big issue. So … I … yeah, I decided that these are the first three to look at, and the OCD script is what you've got here …'

I looked around the room. Claire was smiling encouragingly. Fee was reading the script and nodding. Nish was scribbling in his notebook, colour coding and drawing little symbols that make no sense to anyone apart from him. Adam was looking at me blankly.

'What are you trying to do here?'

'Right! Right, so, our first videos are going to be very Mental Health 101 …'

Even though I'd spent all morning on the script, it was only a three-minute video and so it didn't take me long to talk it through. My heart was buzzing, my chest filled with butterflies, and I pressed my fingertips into the desk to try and hide the fact that my hands were shaking. Even so, I felt a weird swell of pride as I re-read the script out loud and explained my choices. *I'm good at this, this is a good script! This will make a good video!* By the time I'd finished, even though I was still incredibly nervous, I was also strangely hopeful. Nish, Fee and Claire were looking at me with interest, agreement – maybe even respect? *Huh! Maybe I did okay?* But then Adam cleared his throat, and my swollen chest deflated to a balloon that's been forgotten about and hidden under the sofa for two days.

Oh, God! Clearly, it's terrible and I did everything wrong and ...

'When do you think you're going to have the other scripts ready?' he asked.

So that was it. No comment on whether it was good or bad, no praise, no suggestions, no indication he's paid any attention to the ten minutes I spent explaining a piece of work I'd poured my heart into for the past two hours, nothing. Just a question of logistics.

'Hopefully, by the end of tomorrow, if I can keep ...'

'Fine. Have you heard back from Elias and Rosie yet?'

'N ... no.'

'Don't forget to chase them. We need to get that signed off as soon as possible.' He locked his phone, shoved it in his pocket and stood up. 'Thanks, everyone.' Except when he said 'Thanks', the subtext was very much 'Fuck off'.

Not making eye contact with anyone, I walked steadily back to my desk. I dumped my notebook and printout on the keyboard, turned and headed straight out of the building and into the cafe across the road, where I bought a large mocha and a salted caramel brownie and brought them back to my desk. I worked my way steadily through both items, even when full, even when the sugar overwhelmed me. I kept going, *especially* when sugar overwhelmed me; it overwhelmed my fear and my sadness and my shame at being *me*. By the time I'd finished, I felt more physically than emotionally sick, and that's what I put all my focus on. I threw the wrapper and the cup in the bin, returned to my desk, put my headphones on and hid behind the computer screen until it was time to go home, sit quietly while Garry watched TV, and regain the strength to do it all again tomorrow.

TO-DO

- ✓ Team meeting
- ✓ Finish the YouTube scripts ▷
- ✓ Chase on schools' copy
- → Try to figure out <u>why</u> Adam <u>hates</u> me — move to tomorrow
- → ~~Take a lunch break~~ — try tomorrow
- ☐ Find two other jobs to apply for

TUESDAY, 7 MARCH
TO-DO

- ☐ Schools' copy sign-off
- ☐ Try to figure out why Adam hates me
- ☐ Take a lunch break
- ☐ Find two other jobs to apply for
- ☐ Organise school's copy meeting

FOUR

You can learn a lot about someone from the way they pee. There are so many different ways *to* pee – there are the people who sit down and tinkle away cheerily, the ones who do a number of nervous squirts, terrified at the sounds being made by their own bladder, people who force it out like the toilet bowl has wronged them personally, those who fart away unconcernedly – and often, you can find out a lot about a person's true nature from listening to them in the toilet.

I don't think I need to explain that I am a nervous squirter. I live in absolute envy of the people, like Claire, who happily parp away as they wee, chatting about this and that while their body releases some of its most pungent odours and liquids. I live in fear of those who force it out – I thought Fee was harmless and a bit dopey until the first time we happened to be in a toilet together and they weed with such force, I clung to the sides of the bowl in shock. Never fully trust a person who pees with that level of power: they've got some stuff going on that you don't want to get in the way of.

If only I could find myself in a toilet with Rosie Lucas, I mused, as I spent my twelfth consecutive minute hiding in the far-left stall of the fourth-floor women's toilet. I'd know how to handle the fact that she still hadn't replied to my email despite it being 2pm the following day. I knew she was in – I could see her 'Online' icon on our internal messaging service – so why wasn't she replying? What should I do about it?

Was she a nervous squirter like me? Could I talk to her, one nervous squirter to another, and reason it out? Or was she a cheery parper, motivated but not intimidated by a stern follow-up email? Or was she a forcer, and I should really stand back and let Adam deal with it? I didn't know, and the stress had once again driven me to my favourite cubicle to hide out and play Bubble Witch 2 until I'd stopped crying.

After a further 18 minutes, listening to several more people come and pee (two nervous squirters, one tinkle, and one person who I don't think knew I was there and did a massive poo, which required two flushes), I felt brave enough to leave. When I got back to my computer, I had five emails: all from Rosie and Elias. I gripped the mouse so hard, my knuckles went white, then opened the first one from the mysterious Rosie.

> *With Joe out of the office, I'm not across this. Can we meet face to face to discuss?*

I let my breath out. *Okay, organise a face-to-face meeting. I can do this.* I opened the second email, from Elias, noting it was sent at the exact same time.

> *Thanks for this, Amy. Before I sign off, I'd like a meeting to discuss this. This afternoon?*

The next email was also from Elias, replying to Rosie's email.

> *Great minds think alike! I'll get a meeting in at 4pm, in the ground-floor meeting room.*

The next email was from Rosie, replying to Elias's first email.

> *Our emails must have crossed. Can't do this afternoon, though. Tomorrow?*

And the final email was also from Rosie, replying to Elias's second email.

> *Can't do this afternoon … Tomorrow?*

I took a deep breath, counted to four, and blew it out. Adam gave me a glance of irritation; I resisted the urge to kick him under the table.

Shall I do a Doodle so we can find a suitable time for all of us?

I replied less than five minutes after Rosie's last email, but didn't get a reply for the rest of the day. At 4pm, Adam suddenly stopped still and stared over his computer at me. He didn't say anything until I nervously looked back at him.

'Amy,' he said slowly, like he was speaking to an idiot, 'do you have sign-off on that school leaflet copy yet?'

'No. They want to have a meeting, but –'

'Have you organised it yet?'

'No, I'm trying to, but they're not replying and –'

'Right,' he said icily, cutting me off. 'Just get it in as soon as possible.'

'No problem!' I said cheerily. 'I'll email them again now.' I opened a new email, typed 'I hate myself I hate my life I hate my boss I hate everything oh God what is the point of me and my life just kill me now please' over and over until the counter said I'd hit 250 words, and sent it to my personal account. I smiled reassuringly at Adam, who'd been watching me the entire time. He didn't return the smile.

When the fundraising team came round with a cake sale trolley, I used all the cash in my purse to buy myself a cornflake cake, a faintly curry-smelling brownie, and a slice of banana bread. I made a cup of tea and slowly ate my way through everything while cursing myself for (a) not contributing something to the bake sale, and (b) not having spent more money. When I got back to my desk I was so full of cake, I collapsed in my chair and clicked between the same three tabs until it was time to go home. I spent the evening rewatching *Gilmore Girls*, eating my way through a box of Mornflake Chocolate Squares, and looking into retraining as a primary school teacher. I don't think it's financially viable, though. *Fucksticks!*

TUESDAY, 7 MARCH
TO-DO

→ *Schools' copy sign-off* ⟶
— progress made, move to tomorrow

→ *Try to figure out <u>why</u> Adam hates me*

→ *Take a lunch break* — nope

→ *Find two other jobs to apply for* ⟶ progress made, move to tomorrow

→ *Organise school's copy meeting* — progress made, move to tomorrow

WEDNESDAY, 8 MARCH
TO-DO

- ☐ Schools' copy sign-off
  . . . .
- ☐ Try to figure out why Adam hates me
  . . . .
- ☐ Take a lunch break
  . . . .
- ☐ Find two other jobs to apply for
  . . . .
- ☐ Organise school's copy meeting
  . . . .

FIVE

Around lunchtime, I get an email from Elias, replying to the last email Rosie had sent yesterday rather than my follow-up.

Can do 3pm today?

As I'm typing a reply, something comes in from Rosie.

Sorry, meeting external agency then. 10am tomorrow?

And then as I'm typing a reply to *that*, another email comes through from Elias.

Can't do that. When can you do? I can do tomorrow afternoon.

There's silence for a few hours. Then, at 4pm, an email comes in: it's from Rosie.

Sorry, misread your email! I thought you said 3pm tomorrow! I could have done today at 3, but I can't do tomorrow 3. Friday morning?

I leave my desk, buy myself a large mocha, and walk around the block until I'm certain I can be around other people without screaming at them.

TO-DO

→ *Schools' copy sign-off*

✓ *Try to figure out <u>why</u> Adam <u>hates</u> me* — *it's because I'm an incompetent fool, obviously*

✓ *Take a lunch break* — *Success! Pret soup 🥤 I'm fucking starving!*

✓ *Find two other jobs to apply for* — *other arts charity job, and I reckon I could be a PA in an insurance firm, right?*

→ *Organise school's copy meeting* 📋 — *progress made, move to tomorrow*

TO-DO

- ☐ *Schools' copy sign-off*
- ☐ *Ask Rowena if it'd be possible to move to her team instead*
- ☐ *Eat healthy lunch*
- ☐ *Organise school's copy meeting*
- ☐ *Ivy — book launch*

SIX

'Amy!' Adam barked as I came in that morning. I stopped still, my bag halfway off my shoulder.

He didn't look up from his phone when I came in. How did he know it was me? Does he just yell at random people until he gets the right one coming through the door?

'Can you go to an SEO talk this afternoon? Claire was supposed to go, but she's not coming in.'

'Sure,' I said cautiously, sliding my bag onto the desk. 'When? Where?'

'Five thirty in Hackney. I can send you the details.'

I did some quick mental calculations. I'm attending a book launch in Bloomsbury tonight. I only know the author via Twitter, where we've exchanged a few snide jokes, but Penny always drags me along to these things to try and tempt me away from Steady and to the World of Journalism and Writing – as if I'm not already painfully aware that free Prosecco and fancy crisps are a nicer prospect than fundraising bake sales and having to buy your own teabags. The launch starts at seven. I should just – *just* – be able to make it.

'Have you got sign-off yet?'

'No, we're finding it hard to get a time to all meet, and ...' *Stop talking, Amy. Just stop talking.* '... it's hard because it's Rosie Lucas rather than Joe, and so I don't know how to play her ...' *Seriously, he doesn't care.* '... but I'm chasing, and hoping to get sign-off ... um, soon.'

'Fine,' he said, still staring at his phone. I collapsed into my desk, relieved, and just as I reached for the mouse to wake my computer up, I noticed him shake his head in disbelief. Cold sickness rose up my throat. I swallowed it down, just about managed not to choke on it, and got to work.

By the time we get to 4.45pm and it's time for me to leave for the talk, my hands are shaking but I'm fairly confident in my evening's plans. I've worked out the journey from the talk to the book launch numerous times, and calculated the timings perfectly. As long as I leave at 6.30pm, I should arrive at the launch for 7.15pm – late enough that Penny will probably have already arrived and I won't have to talk to strangers, but not so late she'll be pissed off with me for being rude. And the talk won't be longer than an hour, will it? How much is there to say about Search Engine Optimisation?

The talk is being held in one of those super-cool co-working spaces. Everything is orange or white and plastic and translucent, every edge curved somehow. I had to walk round the building several times until I could be sure it was the right one. Even then I had to buy a flat white from a cafe across the road and casually hang around until I saw someone else go in so I knew which of the huge glass panes doubled up as a door.

'Hi! I'm here for the SEO talk,' I said to the beautiful, crop-top wearing woman behind reception. I tried not to stare at her tiny waist and flat stomach, and pinched my flabby sides hard in punishment when I failed.

'Name?' she replied, not unkindly but also not entirely unlike a robot.

'Amy Jones, from Steady.'

Robo-Lady ran her finger down a list, spotted my name, and highlighted it in orange before plucking a sticker with my name on it from the desk and handing it to me.

'Just down there,' she said, waving. 'And here's your goodie bag.' She had slim arms with muscles popping out at the biceps, a thin line of geometric shapes circling her elbow. As she leant back, the light caught the multiple piercings in her ear.

God, she's cool! I wish I was cool.

Clutching my coffee cup, I followed her vague wave towards the room where the talk was happening. There was a group of men with what my dad would call 'haircuts' standing outside, wearing shirts with quirky patterns on them, all chatting and laughing loudly. I pushed my way through the testosterone-fest to the door and was surprised to find that the talk was being held in a room laid out like a cute indie cinema rather than a meeting room. There weren't many people sat down, yet; most of them were women like me, sitting on their own and studiously examining their phones. I attempted to get myself, my rucksack and my enormous goodie bag into a seat without falling over or getting stuck, and (mostly) succeeded.

My cheeks were hot even though the room was cool. I checked my phone: 5.25pm. *Cool.* To pass the five minutes before the talk started, I peered inside the goodie bag, rubbed my eyes after being dazzled by the bright orange goodies within, opened my rucksack and started decanting the freebies into it. I made a note to keep the notebook, lip balm and pen, but to chuck the mug, stress toy and bright-orange man-shaped XXL t-shirt as soon as I got home. After folding the bag up, I stashed it under my chair and waited.

5.30pm. 5.35pm. 5.38pm … I shifted in my seat uneasily and looked around. The flat white, which I'd finished in a hundred tiny swigs after I'd packed my bag just so I had something to do with my body, was racing round my system and my left leg was jiggling up and down, seemingly of its own accord. The door swung open and shut as the men outside gradually came in and took their seats, but the room was still less than half full. *5.41pm. 5.43pm* …

Shit. Fuck. Ballsacks … *What do I do?*

5.45pm. I need to leave at 6.30pm. I can't be late for Penny again. *5.46pm.* Adam knows I'm here – I can't say I would come to the talk and then not go, he'll murder me!

What do I do?

5.47pm. I could just stay until it gets to 6.30pm and then leave? But then I'll have to walk past everyone in the middle of the talk and this is a *really* small room. Everyone would see me, and I bet that woman outside isn't going to leave, I'd have to go past her.

5.48pm. The room was still a third empty. *5.49pm. Fucking shitbags, what do I do? 5.50pm. 5.51pm. 5:52pm* … Shit. Shit. *Shit. How do I get out of this?*

As if someone were watching, I put on a panicked expression and shoved my phone in my pocket. As I stood up, my vision was peppered with little black spots; I ignored them and rushed out of the room, not turning so I couldn't see the looks of surprise from everyone else – even though, rationally, I knew they were probably totally ignoring me. As I flung open the door, Robo-Lady looked up.

'I'm so sorry,' I panted, the wildness in my eyes only slightly put on. 'My husband … he's been hurt at work … I have to go.'

'Oh my God! Okay, of course, no problem,' she said. She opened her mouth to say more but I was already running away. 'Can I do anything?'

'No, no,' I called over my shoulder. 'I'm *so* sorry.'

As I burst out onto the street it occured to me that to Robo-Lady, it looks like I turned up, bagged a load of freebies, and left. Guilt punched me in the stomach. I kept running until I was at the end of the street and round the corner, where I was sure the treacherous building with its glass walls couldn't betray my lack of actual emergency, and I slowed to a walk.

That couldn't have gone worse, really. Unless I'd physically vomited in front of everyone, but that's a bit much, even for me. As I marched through the streets of Eàst London, ignoring the burning in my calves and the stabbing pains in the arches of my feet, I went through my options. I needed to figure out how to stop Adam from finding out that I left early. I could email the organisers directly, maybe get the presentation and some notes from the talk? I needed to do that before the talk ended and they had time to post event admin – okay, I can do that on the bus.

I rounded the corner to the bus stop and saw a sign on it that made my heart sink: 'Bus stop not in use'.

Fuuuuuuuuuuuuuuuuuuuuck!

Okay, fine. I opened Google Maps, inputted the address of the book launch, and followed the tiny pulsing blue dot that represented my current location until it led me to a different bus stop, to the start of a different route. I'm not going to get there until 7.30pm, now, but that's still not so late that Penny can be properly annoyed – is it? *Is it?* I jiggled my legs up and down until the bus arrived, threw myself into the most secluded seat I could find, and opened up my work email.

> *Hi Ros – I'm so, so sorry I had to leave the talk tonight. I was really looking forward to it. Is there any chance you can send over the presentation or notes on the talk, please? My team were really keen on finding out what you had to say.*

I pressed send. As my inbox refreshes, three new emails come through. A cold fist closes around my heart as I see the first one is from Rosie *cunting* Lucas.

> *My meeting ended unexpectedly early. Are you around now?*

It was sent at 4.49pm, *minutes* after I'd closed my computer. The next email is from Elias, and was sent two minutes later.

> *I am! Amy, are you here?*

The final email is also from Elias, and sent at 5.03pm.

> *I think Amy's left already. Pity! Hopefully see you tomorrow. I'm in and out of meetings all day, but might be able to squeeze you both in.*

If I hadn't had to leave early to go to a panel I didn't care about and didn't end up staying for, I might have had the schools' copy signed off by now. I swore so forcefully the elderly couple in front turned and scowled. I scowled back and they looked away nervously.

Don't test me, Grandpa. I'm fully in the mood to make someone bleed, and I'm very happy for it to be you rather than me.

*

When I arrived at the independent bookshop in the heart of Bloomsbury, I was soaked in sweat. I don't mean this in the way a lot of people mean it – when they've maybe got sweaty armpits and a sweaty upper lip and need a spritz of perfume to feel fresh again. I mean, I was *soaked* in sweat. I have always been a sweaty person, but when training for a 10k a few years ago, I unlocked the ability to sweat in new and exciting parts of my body such as my shins and the backs of my hands. Having raced across London, I was utterly *drenched*. I touched my back and found my dress was sopping. My underarms would be the same, I knew. Christ, I could *smell* my boobs!

And this bookshop, though beautiful, was far too tiny to hold the 75 people that Ivy had invited to the launch of her critically acclaimed debut novel. Everyone was packed in like commuters at 8.45am on the Northern Line, only it's acceptable to be a sweaty mess on the Tube but not really The Done Thing at a book launch in an bijou independent bookshop, especially when you're a fat charity pleb rather than a fabulous new connection people can use to get commissions.

'There you are!' Penny said, sweeping down on me. 'You gorgeous girl, how are you?' As she pulled me into a one-armed hug, I angled my body so she didn't get an armful of cold sweat.

'I'm okay, how are you?' I said pulling back and holding her at arm's length – also sweat-smell's length, I hoped. 'You look *incredible*.'

I always say this to Penny at parties, but it's because she does indeed always look incredible. She'd clearly had a blow-dry because her thick blonde hair was gleaming and bouncy. She was wearing a floor-length, floral dress in clashing pastels, cut so low at the back you could *just* see a line of lace from her knickers. If I'd worn it, I'd look like a mental patient on day release. Penny resembled a character from an indie rom-com.

'So do you!' she lied brightly.

I suddenly spot Janae – who met Ivy through Tumblr back when she was starting out as an artist and Ivy was posting *Star Trek* fan fiction – walking towards me and waving. Since I saw her last she'd swapped her blue braids for violet twists drawn into an elaborate bun on top of her head. She looked gorgeous. As she hugged me, pressing me against the clingy red dress she was wearing, I felt a wave of nausea and self-hatred that was almost comforting in its familiarity.

God, I'm shit. I don't deserve to be here.

I picked up a flute of Prosecco, sipped it gamely and tried to hide the face I pulled afterwards. Penny, Janae and I squeezed through the packed shop in search of Ivy, whose novel, *We Told You So*, we are celebrating. A *Times* reviewer described it as being like if 'Nora Ephron tried to write a Wes Anderson film, but met Stephen King on the way,' and no one could tell if it was a compliment or not. Either way, the publishers were *very* excited about the comparison and had put the quote on all the posters.

Ivy was standing by a tower of books, holding court with a group of people, including a couple who must have been her parents because they were the (a) oldest, (b) most nervous and (c) the only other non-white people in the room other than Janae. Ivy wasn't listening to them, though. Instead, she was gesturing with her wine and laughing.

'… it was such a lovely weekend, but now I've got the *worst* case of cystitis, like peeing razorblades. I'm mainlining cranberry juice, but I fucking hate the stuff! Reminds me of getting pissed on two-for-one vodka cranberries at uni and going home to someone's crappy dorm room to do second-rate drugs,' she drolled to peals of laughter. Her father looked very uncomfortable.

'Did those memories make it into the book, darling?' said Penny, pushing forward through the crowd. Ivy saw her and beamed, her arms opening to embrace her like she was an old friend even though Penny had only met her once before and they loathed each other.

'Penny, gorgeous girl!' said Ivy, kissing her on both cheeks. 'Thank you so much for coming.'

'Awww, thank you for inviting me!' Penny replied sweetly, even though she was only invited because they share an editor. 'And what a fantastic book! Really, it's so thought provoking. I loved it.'

If this writing thing ever fell through, Penny should become an actress. Only last week she was WhatsApping me about how it was the biggest load of shite she'd ever read and she was going to recycle it rather than give it to a charity shop so that no one else would be subjected to it.

'You're so sweet,' Ivy purred, just as disingenuously. 'Oh, we must get a selfie with Lily.' She turned to grab the arm of the red-headed woman I knew was the aforementioned editor. 'Lily, Lily, come on, let's get a photo with Penny!'

'Let me take it,' I said, reaching for Ivy's phone. She looked me up and down, smiled sweetly, and handed me her phone. I took several photos, their heads tilting this way and that, and handed it back. Penny and Lily crowded round the phone to find the most flattering picture while Janae teased them loudly, her grin wide and completely lacking in malice. I felt suddenly awkward, in the way, so melted backwards into the crowd.

It was very hot. And there were a lot of people. Even without the sweaty back, I'd be uncomfortable. Eventually I found a place to stand, back to the wall, and watched the crowd. They were all talking, smiling and laughing like they were having the time of their lives; Plato's Form of cool, cultured, successful people.

God, how do they do it? How can they go into a room and be charming and confident and chatty? Are they all on cocaine, is that it? I know cocaine used to be big in the publishing and writing worlds, but I thought it had died out a bit now, what with the recession and everything. How did they even *afford* cocaine, along with those lovely dresses? And I know from Instagram that loads of these people have bought their own flats; how did they afford drugs *and* to save up a £30,000 deposit? I can't even save up for a new pair of Doc Martens. *Is this the level of success they're operating at? Am I really so far behind?*

When I felt a gentle tap on my arm, I turned to see a familiar face beaming at me: Claire Winters, aka Little Claire, aka the junior content producer (Youth) at Steady, who was replaced by Fee a year or so ago.

'Claire!' I said in genuine delight, hugging her tightly. She hugged me back, arms wrapping all the way round me. 'What are you doing here?'

'Amy! I'm so happy to see you.' She beamed. I noticed the gap she used to have in her teeth is slowly being closed by a pair of braces she didn't have 18 months ago. 'I work with Ivy at *Nouveau Femme.*'

'But I thought you left to go to Mind …?'

'I did, but the job at *Nouveau* came up pretty quickly so I just went for it,' she said. The longer I looked at her, the more differences I saw – her eyebrows were more neatly shaped, her lips a beautiful bright red when she always used to protest her mouth was too big to wear lipstick.

'That's great! How's it going?' I managed to keep my voice excited and happy, even though I could feel panic and envy seeping up my throat.

I am happy for her, I *am*. But fuck. *Fuck.*

'Really well, actually. I've just been promoted to senior writer.' She looked down modestly, but was flushed with pleasure. I squealed in a delight I definitely *did* feel, but perhaps not as much as I felt seething, sickening jealousy.

'That's so great! Well done you!' I said, grabbing her shoulder in what I hoped was an affectionate way.

'Thanks. Hey, how's Steady going?'

'Yeah, it's okay,' I said brightly, trying to add something that wasn't a lie or would make me burst into tears in the middle of a room full of successful people, but I was spared. Little Claire immediately shook her head.

'Yeah, that's what I thought. I saw Nish the other day ...' *When? Where? Why wasn't I invited?* '... and he said the same thing. Whenever I speak to people still at Steady, it's like I'm talking to prisoners. "Oh, you know, it's fine. The food's okay, now. Hardly any broken glass in the beans".' We both laughed, and I hoped the sound wasn't as hollow as it felt. 'Honestly, Ames, you're so good, so talented. You deserve better than that place. Are you still doing your freelance stuff on the side?'

'I haven't in a while,' I admitted. 'Just been busy, I guess.'

'That's a shame. You're such a good writer. Hey, why don't you email me tomorrow and I can put you in touch with my editor, see if I can help you out?'

Wait, what? I had to spend six months getting you to stop putting apostrophes whenever there was a word with an 's' at the end because 'it was just easier that way'. What the fuck are you doing, telling me you can help me out?

'That sounds lovely, I'll definitely do that,' I said.

At that point, Lily dinged a fork against a glass and started to make a speech. I grinned through it, and the agent's speech, and Ivy's, clapping at all the right places and taking lots of photos dutifully posted to Instagram later. Then, as soon as was decent, I found Penny and Janae, told them a lie neither of them believed about needing to be home to feed the cat, and escaped.

The cool air outside shook me out of the fuzzy blur I was in inside the bookshop – like getting into a hot bath on a winter's day, but in reverse. I gulped in its cool, admittedly pollution-ridden freshness as if I'd been drowning. I put my headphones on, switched on a podcast, and spent the rest of my journey home ignoring it. Instead, I stared at my reflection in the bus window, at the familiar angles and curves of my eyes and my cheeks, at the shadows which moved over my face as the bus drove through the night, and wondered how exactly everything went so wrong.

TO-DO

➡ *Schools' copy sign-off*

☐ ~~Ask Rowena if it'd be possible to move to her team instead~~
Why would she want me?

☑ *Eat healthy lunch — chicken katsu curry is healthy as long as you ignore everything about it apart from the chicken itself, the rice and the salad it comes with, so that's what I'll do*

➡ *Organise school's copy meeting*

☑ *Ivy — }book{ launch*

TO-DO

- ☐ Schools'. Mother. Fucking. Copy. Fucking. Sign-off

- ☐ Redo CV

- ☐ HAVE THE GODDAMN SCHOOL'S COPY MEETING

- ☐ LITERALLY, THAT'S IT

- ☐ THAT'S ALL I NEED YOU TO DO, JONES

- ☐ JUST HAVE THE DAMN MEETING

- ☐ JUST GET THIS FUCKING THING OFF YOUR LIST!

- ☐ Helen's leaving cake-and-stare, 4pm

SEVEN

When I woke up, there was only one thought in my brain: I *have* to get the copy signed off, I can't stand to see that look on Adam's face again. Last night proved I'm seriously lacking in the career department as it is, and if it turns out I'm bad at my shitty, substandard job as well, I don't think I'll be able to survive. I need a win or I'll have a full-on screaming breakdown in the middle of Steady's canteen.

At 6am I logged into my work emails to send emails to Elias and Rosie *motherfucking* Lucas to ask when they were free that day. I planned to send another one the second I got into the office, then prowl the floors, asking everyone I see – male, female, non-binary, the office dogs some people bring in on Fridays, the fancy new printers, the staplers – to find out if they are Rosie Lucas. I'll go onto every floor and yell 'Rosie? Rosie Lucas?' until someone answers. I'll stand in reception, screaming, 'Why, Rosie Lucas, why hast thou forsaken me?' until someone brings her to me. Then, as soon as I find her, I'm going to grab her by the ear, drag her up to the fifth floor to find Elias and get this copy signed off. I swear to God I'll raze this place to the ground until all that's left of Steady is me, Rosie Lucas, Elias and a charred printout of my school's copy in size 14 double-spaced Arial (all the better to make edits on). I'm getting this copy signed off. *Today.*

Adam was the only person at our bank of desks when I arrived at work, 45 minutes early. He glanced up, raised an eyebrow, and nodded in greeting. I nodded curtly back, my level of concentration on the task at hand so high it had even managed to obliterate any Adam-based anxiety, and turned my computer on. I sat down heavily, staring at the monitor in hatred for the five minutes it took Windows to wake up and log in.

I was fully prepared to send another email along the lines of 'OH HI, GUYS, NICE DAY ISN'T IT? HEY, ARE YOU READY FOR A MEETING? ARE YA? ARE YA REALLY? *ARE YOU FUCKING READY?*' However, when I opened my inbox, there was a message waiting.

Will be around at 10am, if you two are?

I reply with an emphatic 'YES' and five minutes later, Elias replied to that.

Great – see you in the Fry Room then.

It was only 8.30am, so I spent the next 90 minutes watching the clock obsessively and getting almost nothing done. When Fee came in and nattered cheerfully about last night's episode of *The Big Bang Theory*, I smiled and nodded in all the right places. When Claire came in and showed me photos of her daughter fast asleep, I cooed but gave not a single solitary shit. And when Nish came in, scowling in the bright lights and rubbing his temples and spending an awful lot of time running to the toilet, I didn't mention the incredible hangover he must have. I just sat and stared at the clock and clicked around the same few websites, waiting for 10am and this nightmare to end.

At last, 9.55am arrived. I casually stood and picked up a folder of neatly printed documents, my notebook, and pencil case. Smiling serenely at Claire's little thumbs-up, I made my way to the Fry Room.

Rosie *motherfucking* Lucas was already there. My dealings with her this week had led me to expect a six-foot-tall blonde goddess, who could unhinge her jaw and swallow me whole if

I disagreed with her, so I was not prepared for the tiny speck of a woman with a thick gingery-blonde plait, fifties glasses and fabulous embroidered cardi who greeted me. She was sitting at a table when I approached, head buried in her phone. I rapped on the door and she looked up; her eyeliner, in thick cat's-eye flicks, was *flawless*.

''iya!' she said in a broad South Wales accent when I opened the door. 'You must be Amy, I'm Rosie. Lovely to put a face to the name after emailing all this week!'

'Yes, lovely to meet you too,' I said, wrong-footed, shaking the proffered hand and trying not to knock over a chair as I squeezed round the table. 'Sorry for all the emails this week, I've ...'

'No, don't apologise, my lovely,' she said. 'It's my fault. Been mad, it has, what with Joe off and everything. Still, glad we've got it sorted now, ey?'

'Yes, hopefully this won't take too ...' I'm interrupted by Elias coming in the door, a similar amount of stationery tucked under his arm as was tucked under mine. '... long. Hi, Elias.'

'Morning, morning,' he said, nodding to us both. 'Glad we got there in the end, yes?'

'Yes, and I know copy sign-off can be an issue so I'll make this quick,' I said as he sat down. 'So you've both had a copy of what we want to put in the school's leaflet ...'

'Yeah, it was great!' said Rosie, beaming.

'Thanks, Rosie. So, um, I just need you both to tell me what changes you need doing. Doing to it, I mean. Then we can rewrite them together, see if we can make them work, and we're all happy and ... and everything.' Elias and Rosie were listening intently, nodding. Momentarily buoyed, I dove into my pile of papers. 'So, here's a copy of the, er, copy again ... Ha ha, yes, copy of the copy! So, what do you both think?'

They took the papers from me and, brows furrowed, started reading. I started getting pens out of my bag, colour coding them into Good Comments, Neutral Comments and Bad

Comments. I may not enjoy negative feedback, but I do enjoy the stationery that goes with it ...

'That's all fine by me,' Rosie announced cheerfully, handing the papers back to me.

'Really?'

'Yeah, looks great!' Elias, sitting next to her, was still reading, brow slightly furrowed in concentration. Eventually he looked up at Rosie, nodded firmly, and handed the papers back to me too.

'All good by us. Thanks, Amy, great job!'

'So there are no changes?' I asked incredulously. 'That's it?'

Elias looked at the clock and laughed.

'Six minutes from start to end. Must be a record!'

Rosie laughed too.

'I know, right! I booked in an hour for this meeting. I'm gonna have a cup of coffee, I am – have a bit of a break.'

They left the room, laughing and chattering. I stayed entirely still for what must have been five minutes, before standing up slowly and leaving as well. ALL WEEK. ALL WEEK, when they could have just read the attachment and signed off via email. ALL. FUCKING. WEEK.

Back at my desk, I sat down, placing the folder, notebook and my pencil case to the side of my keyboard, and stared ahead blankly. A notification from Claire popped up, asking if I was okay, but I ignored it. Instead, I shifted my body slightly so it was directly facing Adam, and stared at him intensely. He pretended not to notice. However, when my staring became so obvious and strange that Nish, Fee, Claire and even a few people on surrounding desks noticed and were staring at him too, he raised his gaze to mine.

'What?'

'I got sign-off,' I announced quietly.

'Eh?'

'On the school's copy. Elias, Rosie m ... Lucas ... We just had a meeting.' I paused, gathering the energy to say it again. 'And they signed off. It's ready to go.'

He looked at me blankly for a second, then his eyes flickered with recognition.

'Oh. Great,' he said. 'Make sure you prepare a presentation on that talk you went to last night for Monday's meeting.' With that, he turned back to his iPad.

That's it. After a week of stress. A week of nagging. A week of crying and emergency coffee ingestion and developing a pathological hatred of a woman I hadn't, until this morning, even met before. A nod, one word of recognition that the task had been completed, and then back to the iPad. And that, my friends/witnesses for the defence when I eventually crack and go postal on this place, is that.

I stayed motionless for a while longer, then pushed my chair back abruptly. Ignoring the flurry of messages from Claire and Fee I could see tripping over themselves on my screen ('omg, u ok?' 'What the hell?' 'where u going? do u want me to come with?' 'You've been working on that all week!' 'if ur going to Pret can u get me a chocolate croissant plz?'), I stood up, walked out of the office, down the stairs, out the front doors and into the cafe opposite. I ordered a large hot chocolate – with cream, this time – and while waiting for it, typed out a message with a shaking hand.

Need to get my CV sorted. Need to start applying for other jobs. Need to get out of this place. Now. Help, please, I'm begging you.

I sent it to Penny. I sent it to Frankie and Janae. I sent it to Garry. I sent it to a few journalist friends. I sent it to myself. Then I stared into the middle distance, ignoring the tears slipping down my face, until my drink arrived and I could smother my furious misery with sugar.

FRIDAY, 10 MARCH
TO-DO

☑ Schools'. Mother. Fucking. Copy. Fucking. Sign-off

☑ Redo CV *See note

☑ HAVE THE GODDAMN SCHOOL'S COPY MEETING

☑ LITERALLY, <u>THAT'S IT</u> ⇧

☑ THAT'S ALL I NEED YOU TO DO, JONES

☑ JUST HAVE THE DAMN MEETING

☑ JUST GET THIS FUCKING THING OFF <u>YOUR LIST!</u>

☑ Helen's leaving cake-and-stare, (4pm)

☐ Tweet Helen to apologise for eating all the millionaire's shortbread

☐ Find some kind of soothing hobby to take up. Knitting, maybe, or recreational drugs

✳ Note: get Garry to read over it, maybe have another look when you're less stressed. If nothing else, possibly want to rewrite the 'Profile' bit as 'Looking to find a new job where I don't want to kill everyone else and then myself' will probably not endear me to a potential employer

TO-DO

- ☐ Romantic breakfast in bed
- ☐ Get ready — make self look very cute
- ☐ Romantic walk in the park
- ☐ Adorable lunch in favourite cafe
- ☐ Find recipe for fancy tea
- ☐ Get stuff for tea
- ☐ Cook tea together
- ☐ Farmers' market
- ☐ Film?
- ☐ Proper Sex

EIGHT

On waking, I realised that I was so hot, I wanted to rip off my own skin. Behind me, my husband had pressed his entire body – naked save a pair of Ted Baker pants – into me, and slung his arm over my hip. His hand was resting on my lower-belly flab, the part of my body I referred to as 'the gunt' in a dramatic stage whisper, an evil so great I dared not speak its name out loud. On my other side, the cat had done the same as my husband – the entire length of her hot, furry little body pressed against my bare stomach.

I was covered in a thin layer of sweat, Garry was covered in a thin layer of sweat. Our bodies were stuck together wherever they touched. The cat, purring happily, radiated heat into my belly like one of those teddies you stick in the microwave. She was also shedding fur, which was mixing with my sweat to form a kind of *paste*, which was covering my torso. I love my little family deeply, but at that moment, I would have jabbed a finger in their eyeballs happily to get them the fuck away from me.

Wriggling dislodged the cat; she squeaked at me and jumped off the bed. Garry was less easy to lose; he snuffled in sleepy frustration and pulled me closer. I moved away, and our skin separated with a sound like a sticker peeling off a Tupperware. He flipped onto his back, still asleep, and I flipped over onto mine. I wanted to boil my brain to remove the memory of the last five minutes, but as I brushed the wet cat fur from my stomach and my sleepy brain stopped screaming silently, I realised something.

It was Saturday.
And Garry had the weekend off.

I rolled over to face him and beamed into his slack-jawed face. Garry is a police officer, which means shifts and odd work patterns, so we only really get a weekend together once every two or three months. My friends are brilliant but busy people, so my weekends are usually spent bumming around the house and refreshing Twitter until my eyes bleed and it's time to go to bed again.

But not this weekend, I thought triumphantly. *This weekend, I have my husband with me!* We were going to go to a cafe, and for a walk in the park, and snuggle on the sofa together with books and visit the farmers' market, and cook together, and have Proper Sex rather than Weeknight Quickie Sex, and generally have the kind of lovely romantic weekend I always saw on Instagram. For once, I was going to have a relationship as good as everyone else's.

But first, breakfast. *Even better*, I thought as I typed out a quick To-Do List on my phone, *breakfast in bed!* I waited until Garry took a particularly deep breath in – by that, I mean a snore – and swung myself out of bed (a tip learnt from many a situation where I've had to extract myself from bed without waking him. Try it, thank me later). The cat trilled and followed as I left the bedroom, walked to the kitchen and closed the door softly behind me. I opened the cupboard doors and surveyed the contents, much like the lead in a rom-com who has finally bagged her man and wants to impress him with her excellent, yet understated cooking skills. And I *did* want to impress him. If I was going to have a romantic weekend, I was going to have it to the high standards our patriarchal society demanded of me, goddammit!

So, what should I make? Pancakes were always a solid option, but he only liked the big American ones and I didn't have buttermilk. Shakshuka? But I didn't have coriander, or peppers, or anything that'd stop it being just a can of tomatoes with some eggs cracked in. Eggs on toast? The bread had gone mouldy. Cooked breakfast? No bacon. Porridge with coconut, honey and berries? It was fucking boiling outside, who wanted porridge? Also, I didn't have coconut. Waffles? *You don't even have a waffle maker, Jones, stop being stupid!* And so, 30 minutes later, I returned to my (now-awake) husband with two bowls of Crunchy Nut Cornflakes and a coffee with warm milk and vanilla essence to try and make it fancy.

'Hello, handsome,' I attempted to purr at him as I entered the room.

'Alright?' he replied flatly, squinting because he didn't have his glasses on. He'd stretched out on the bed, covers off, one hand on his phone, the other resting on his crotch. I beamed and handed him both his coffee and his cereal; he registered them blearily and sat up, removing his hand from his tumescent penis to take both from me.

'How are you?' I said, coming round the bed and sitting next to him. I was still wearing my PJ top but I'd taken off the bottoms so I could arrange my bare legs with the toes pointed and the knees bent, which everyone knows is the *sexiest* way for a woman to arrange her legs. Earlier, I'd also run my fingers through my hair, popped a little white spot which had emerged inside my right nostril, and wiped the black crust from under my eyes. I was going for a Meg-Ryan-in-the-opening-scene-of-*You've Got Mail*-vibe – mussed and adorable, but also so sexy I made men and lesbians round the world quiver. Garry, however, didn't seem to have noticed.

'Tired,' he said, spooning cereal into his mouth. 'Grumpy.' I paused for him to ask how I was, but he didn't: instead, he picked up his mug and took a slurp of coffee. I felt a flicker of irritation and immediately afterwards, a flicker of hopelessness: this wasn't going right at all.

'It's a beautiful day,' I said, twitching the curtain. The sun blasted through the gap and we threw our arms over our faces to block it out. 'What shall we do?'

He peered at me through half-closed eyes.

'Do we need any shopping?'

'Only stuff for tea.'

''Spose we better go to the shop.' I waited for him to say something else – *anything else* – but he didn't, so I ploughed on.

'Well, shall we go up to Edith's and get some lunch?' I asked. 'Then we can wander round, pop to the Co-op, come home, maybe have a walk in the park or something …?'

'Sure,' he replied. He'd finished his cereal now and returned to his original position: one hand on his penis, the other scrolling through his phone. I briefly fantasised about smothering him with a pillow, but instead took our empty crockery to the kitchen and started getting ready.

Already jittery, I didn't think I could cope with having to think about my naked body long enough to shower and dry it, so instead I had what my nana would refer to as a 'swill in the sink', my mum describes as a 'personal wash' and what Janae calls a 'tits-pits-pussy wash'. I hoisted my boobs into my sexiest bra (and by 'sexiest', I mean the only one that fits), dug the newly bought matching pants out of the washing machine in case we had sex later, and sprayed antiperspirant over as much of my body as I could get away with. When I went back into the bedroom, Garry was still lying in bed. He totally ignored me as I stood in front of my wardrobe to pick the day's outfit, but I put my hands on my hips and pulled my flesh down to disguise my back rolls anyway, just in case.

If I truly was the Nora Ephron-era Meg Ryan that I longed to be, I would have casually thrown on an off-white linen shift and some powder blue slip-ons. Shift dresses, however, made me look like a balled-up pair of socks, so instead I put on a skirt and top I could wear with sucky-in leggings underneath. As I was putting on my shoes, Garry threw his phone down on the bed and stretched dramatically. I glanced at him.

'Are you getting up?' I asked.

He frowned, his mouth bulging into an exaggerated pout. 'Don't bully me,' he said, swinging his legs out of bed. 'You big bully!' He walked over, kissed me cheerfully on the side of the head, and walked out of the room. The bathroom door closed and moments later, I heard the sound of his favourite YouTuber's voice. I threw myself back down on the bed and picked up my phone – it'd be a while before we were ready to leave, so I might as well make myself comfortable.

I started scrolling through Instagram. It was 9.42am, and according to Instagram Stories, most of my friends' Saturday plans were already well underway. Claire and Edie were playing with bubbles in the garden. Frankie had been to the gym and was now walking through the park – I knew she was on her way to a date. Penny and Ollie were at his parents' in Oxford; they appeared to be volunteering at some kind of village fete and were wearing matching sunglasses. Janae and Emily were on a train, heading to Brighton for a day of wedding prep and eating ice cream on the beach. I fanned my hair out on the pillow behind me, raised my phone, twisted my face into a quizzical 'I'm waiting …' expression and tried to take a photo I didn't hate so I could add it to Instagram Stories. Eight rejected photos later, I gave up and instead posted a photo of the cat lying on her back in a sunbeam. Hashtag #caturday. Send.

When Garry emerged from the bathroom, he looked slightly more like himself and less like a half-shaved bear emerging from a long winter's hibernation. I beamed at him, the cold worry in my chest warming in his presence, and he smiled back.

'Hello, you,' he said, doing up his shirt. 'You alright?'

'Mmm,' I replied. 'You alright?'

'Yeah, tired. I hate the first day after nights.' As he was talking, I was trying to take a photo of him to put on Insta Stories. When he saw, he frowned exaggeratedly – he never lets me get a photo of him where he looks anything less than furious – but the second I lowered my phone, his face went back to normal. 'What do you want for tea?'

'I don't know,' I replied, concentrating on my phone. I added the caption 'Look who I found!' to the photo of him and added it to Stories. 'Maybe pasta?'

'Let's just get some spaghetti and a jar of sauce,' he said, putting his shoes on. 'Something quick and easy we can throw together.'

'No, I want to do something special!' I protested, sitting next to him and putting my arm round him. 'We should do something nice because we're together.'

He groaned at me and I groaned back teasingly. He smelt great. We'd been together for eight years, and I was always reassured to discover that I still found him incredibly attractive. I kissed him enthusiastically on the cheek, jaw and neck, and he grimaced at me.

'Come on!' I said, leaping to my feet. 'It's Saturday, it's sunny, and we're together. Today's going to be a perfect day.'

*

Reader, it was *not* the perfect day. We bickered because I wanted to walk across the park and he wanted to get the bus. Then I was cross because we couldn't get seats together and when the seat by me freed up, Garry chose to stay where he was. Edith's was full, so we'd had to go to The Cat's Pyjamas, which didn't do French toast – which left Garry in a massive sulk because he'd been looking forward to it. We argued in Sainsbury's because I kept trying to get him to choose between two recipe cards and he kept saying he really didn't care. Eventually we'd just gone for a pizza meal deal and walked to the bus in silence. The bits in between were fine, but it wasn't the point: I wanted today to be perfect, Instagram perfect, like everyone else. What was so *wrong* with us, we couldn't have that?

At 9pm, dinner eaten, we were lounging on the sofa. There was some police documentary on TV (apparently, Garry had never heard of a busman's holiday) and I was lying with my back against his chest while scrolling through Facebook, Twitter and Instagram. Laxmi was on holiday somewhere hot, beaming and beautiful in front of various historical monuments and pretty doors. Yomi was playing with her cherubic baby, who was giggling delightedly. Ivy was home alone, like me, but had taken a photo of her balcony table with a glass of wine and a notebook and posted it with a wry caption about how she was having a 'wild night in'. I thought about the photo Garry and I would take right now, sprawled like two sacks of potatoes on a sofa covered in mystery stains and cat hair, him eating Haribo Starmix and me looking like a bowl of blancmange that'd been dropped on the floor.

I threw my phone down on the sofa next to me. Getting time with Garry was a rare delight, something I looked forward to the same way I used to look forward to school holidays. When we first got together, I'd been doing a degree with only eight hours of contact time a week and he'd been working as a private music teacher doing about the same, so we'd spent the first three years of our lives together in each other's pockets (I don't think my mum's ever quite forgiven him for being, in her mind, the reason I got a 2:1 rather than a First). Garry had been working shifts since we moved in together three years ago, and although I was absolutely fine on my own and filled my time with friends and culture and more side-projects than any one human should feasibly be able to manage, I still felt like spending time with him was a treat, a delight, a wonderful thing. So why didn't it *feel* like a wonderful treat when I was with him? Why did everything feel so distractingly sub-par?

I tilted my head back so it was resting against his collarbone and looked up at him. He was *so* handsome. His face had changed a lot in the 13 years I'd known him, but every time I looked at him I thought he was the handsomest he had ever looked, would ever look, could ever look. I could stare at him for a thousand years and not get bored. He was kind and funny and thoughtful and smart, and I loved him so much, I sometimes felt my chest would burst with it. I smiled involuntarily: who *cares* if we're not Instagram perfect? He makes me so happy.

'I love you,' I said, stretching up and kissing his jaw.

'Love you,' he replied, not taking his eyes off the TV. I stared hard at him for a little longer; eventually, he met my gaze, smiled briefly at me, and looked back at the man who was having his car searched by a copper and his enthusiastic, entirely-unaware-of-how-much-of-a-nark-it-was-being spaniel.

I rolled over so that I was on my stomach and stared at him a little longer. He didn't react. I poked him in the stomach; he frowned and swatted my hand away. I poked him again; he made a sound of frustration, like a child waking up from a nap. I kept poking him, over and over – in his stomach and on his chest and under his arms and everywhere – until he caught my hands.

'Will you behave?' he said, scowling.

'Play with me!' I said brightly.

'No, I'm watching this.'

'But I'm bored!'

'Then go read a book or something.'

'I don't want to, I want you to play with me …' I started tickling him and he jerked away so that he was out of reach. Without his body to support me, I fell belly-down on the sofa and reached over to tickle him again.

'Will you stop it!' he snapped. My hand froze where it was. 'I don't want you to tickle me, I don't want to play – I'm watching this.'

My stomach twisted itself into a sad, ashamed knot. I lay there silently for a few minutes, watching him. Then I sat back up properly, arms crossed, and pointed my face at the screen. I wasn't really watching it, I was making a mental list of all the things about him that pissed me off. How he was always, always tired and therefore always, always grumpy. How anti-social he was. The way he uses technical lingo around me when he knows that I won't understand it just so I have to ask what he's talking about and he gets to explain. The stupid thing he does with his hands and his voice and his *face* when he's ordering food at a restaurant. He's a grumpy, anti-social, stupid, smug bumhead.

But I was also thinking about all the things about *me* that piss me off. How annoying I am. How needy I am. How I manage to ruin everything, even nice cuddles, in front of the

TV. How I do things that I know will piss him off and then get upset when he gets pissed off. I'm rubbish. I'm *totally* rubbish. I know Garry's a grumpy, anti-social, stupid, smug bumhead, but I don't deserve him. Christ, I'm *worse* than rubbish. I'm a horrible, useless twat, and I don't deserve him.

When, a few minutes later, Garry shifted back over to his seat and tugged me back into his body, I was so grateful but so furious that I kept myself completely rigid. I picked up my phone, and the first thing I saw on it was a selfie of Penny and Ollie with matching face paint from the fete: little hearts all over their temples and their perfect, high cheekbones. I closed Facebook in fury, opened BuzzFeed, clicked on a quiz entitled 'The Things You Buy At Urban Outfitters Will Reveal The Dog You Should Adopt' and took personality quiz after personality quiz until it was time to go to bed.

(In case you're interested, dachshund. My secret talent based on Canadian foods I like is 'sexy kissing', my make-up preferences suggest I am emotional rather than logical, based on the salad I made, I am 60 years old and no, I can*not* guess which celebrity is taller!)

Garry turned off the TV and stretched, carefully moving so as not to dislodge my head from his chest. I moved away and he stood up, kissing me exuberantly on the head as he did so.

'I love you,' he said, as he walked out of the room.

'I love you,' I said, simultaneously meaning it from the depths of my bones and saying it entirely out of a sense of obligation. We got into bed and into our usual sleeping positions – as far over on our own sides as possible, but with feet, hands and elbows *just* touching. I was a mess, a lava lamp of frustration and discontent, a storm of misery and self-loathing; I was far too worked up to sleep. He, meanwhile, started snoring within minutes.

Prick!

I don't remember how long it took for me to fall asleep. But I do remember listening to his sleep and letting impotent rage churn in my chest. Rage at him for snoring, rage at myself for listening to it rather than disturb him, rage at how the day had gone. I listened to the cars and trains going past outside, to the cat running around the windowsills, to the people laughing as they came back from doing something wonderful in the bright lights of the big city. I listened to Garry's snoring and the jittery, uncomfortable energy racing through my blood. I felt sad, and heavy, and desperate.

And, as I lay there in the dark, I listened to the voice in the depths of my brain which explained, patiently, how I was fundamentally *wrong*. There were so many things in my life which should be wonderful – my friends, my job, my family, my happy relationship – and yet, I was unhappy about all of them. *The problem must be me*, it whispered. *I am ruining everything. My crappy life is my own damn fault, and I'm trapped in it. I'm going to keep fucking things up for myself and for the people I love most forever, and there's nothing I can do to change it.* It was this thought that held me in its arms and rocked me to sleep, and this thought which chased itself round my dreams all night: *the problem is me. The problem is me.*

Theproblemismetheproblemismeismeismeismemememememe ...

Fortunately, sleep has a wonderful way of resetting the brain, the human equivalent of restarting a misbehaving computer. When I opened my eyes the next morning, once again sandwiched between my husband and my cat, I felt a little bit more in control. I glanced at my sleeping husband and felt love rather than frustration. For now, at least, that was enough.

So, once again, there was the question of breakfast. Although we'd been shopping yesterday, we hadn't been sensible enough to think beyond the next meal, so we still had barely any food in the house. Once again, I snuck off to the kitchen and came back carrying two bowls of cereal – but this time we'd run out of coffee beans, so I couldn't even make us a mildly fancy coffee to go with it. The prickle of self-loathing returned.

God, why couldn't I just get a fucking grip?

When I handed the bowl to Garry, he smiled.

'Thank you, lovely,' he said, puckering to show me he wanted a kiss. I leant down and obliged; he smelt warm and familiar and ever-so-slightly like the food-waste bin in the kitchen. After eight years, the ripe, repulsively sweet smell of his morning breath was weirdly comforting, but let's not examine that thought too closely as I don't think it says good things about me.

I climbed into bed next to him and picked up my phone. We sat in companionable silence for several minutes, scrolling through social media and eating our cereal.

'What do you want to do today?' he asked. Without looking at him, I opened my To-Do List.

Okay, so yesterday didn't quite go to plan – there was no romantic breakfast in bed, no romantic walk in the park, no fancy tea, no adorable scenes of us cooking together in the kitchen. But there was a chance to fix all that with an item on today's list: the farmers' market. Well, not the romantic breakfast in bed, *stupidstupidstupid*, but the rest of it! We could walk across the park to the farmers' market (tick), and buy ingredients for a fancy tea (tick), which we could then cook together (tick). I turned to him with an expression of pure joy.

'Let's go to the farmers' market!' I exclaimed brightly. His smile suddenly looked more like a grimace and his eyelids fluttered closed as he took a deep, steadying breath, but didn't protest. Forty-five minutes later, we strolled, hand in hand, across the big park near our house to get to the farmers' market at the other side. Romantic walk in the park? *Tick!*

I fucking love our farmers' market! I love the cheery Welsh butcher who always has homemade Welsh cakes and whose thick accent seeps into my tongue, making me sound like an extra in *Gavin & Stacey*. I love all the stalls of fresh fruit and vegetables – I never buy anything, obviously, because it's always unwashed and twice the price of what I can get in Morrisons, but I love the fact that I *could* buy it if I *wanted* to. I love looking at all the wares which have no right to be at a farmers' market, like the secondhand furniture truck and the person who sells pencil drawings of surrounding landmarks like the old bingo hall (even though it's now a pub) and the old art-deco style pub (now a vet).

Mostly, though, I love the fact that when I'm there I can walk up and down and peer at the things on display and pretend for a few minutes that I'm the kind of person who'd be able to spend £7.50 on a tiny pot of locally sourced honey inexplicably flavoured with coffee. I can even pretend that I'm the kind of person who'd *want* to, who looks at coffee-flavoured honey and thinks, 'Oh, what a delightful and unusual treat! I must try it' rather than 'What kind of drugs have you taken to think that's a good idea?' As we approached the honey stall I could see that they had a new fizzy pop-flavoured range, and I squeezed Garry's hand in excitement. He didn't squeeze back, and when I moved towards the stall, he didn't come with me.

I looked back at him quizzically, but he just shook his head and gestured for me to go on. I did so, smiling pleasantly at the owner, and considered trying a sample of Tango-flavoured honey, but the knowledge that Garry was waiting awkwardly behind me had taken all of the joy out of the experience. I thanked the stall owner and wandered back, perplexed.

'What's wrong?'

'I don't like going up to stalls when I don't know I'm going to buy something,' he said. 'I always feel really awkward.'

'But it's fine!' I said, bemused. 'It's what they expect.'

'I just feel guilty,' he said brusquely. 'Come on, let's keep going.'

But the thing is, the joy of a farmers' market is the pottering – the trying, the tasting, the looking. More pressingly, farmers' markets ain't that big. Because we weren't stopping at stalls, we had walked up and down in less than five minutes.

'Well, what do you want to do now?' I asked. Garry shrugged. I leant against the park gates for moral support.

'Shall we get stuff for tea?'

'Sure. What do you want?'

'Dunno.'

'Did anything catch your eye?'

'Not really.'

I took a deep breath. We walked up and down the market twice more. Well, I say 'walked', we *marched*, really, because Garry's a quick walker and had no intention of slowing even for a moment. I'd had to break into a light jog to keep up.

'Well?' I asked, breathing heavily and leaning against the gates again. 'Anything?'

He shrugged.

I resisted the urge to kick him in the shin.

'There was that pie stall. We could get a pie?' he offered.

'A PIE!' I said, so delighted I almost shouted it at him. 'Yes! Let's get a PIE! What shall we have with it?'

'We've got some mixed broccoli and cauliflower in the freezer.'

'Right. Okay, we can ...'

But Garry wasn't finished yet and his mood had brightened considerably.

'And some Smash in the cupboard, actually.'

I'm going to kill him, I'll fucking kill him.

'Smash. *Fucking* Smash?' I said, teeth gritted. 'There's a whole stall just for potatoes, over there, why don't we *make* mashed potatoes?'

'Nah, Smash is easier,' he said breezily, swinging his bag for life on the end of his arm. 'C'mon, I'll get the pies.'

At this point I was hot, thirsty, tired, and completely out of fucks to give. Mutely, I followed him, picking my pie with all the enthusiasm of a posh politician trying to appeal to the proles at a football match. I didn't have the energy to argue with any more decisions that day, I would just go along with whatever he wanted. Which is why, later that night, I sat on my sofa watching the Minions movie, drinking Morrisons own-brand lemonade and eating a chicken and ham pie with soggy boiled broccoli and Smash po-*fucking*-tatoes. I use Smash all the time, but it was hardly the 'fancy tea' I had in mind. After deleting that item from my To-Do List, I studied my progress.

There was only one thing left on the list: sex. And not just sex, but Proper Sex. After such a long time together, Garry and I have perfected our routine. Not only do we get off every single time, it's so perfectly coordinated, if we ever learnt to ice-skate then we would probably have a shot of matching Torvill and Dean's score with it at the Winter Olympics. However, because he's always either just about to go to work or just about to go to bed so he can be at work within the next ten hours, it's also a rather *quick* routine – flick it, pull it, twist it, spin it, bop it, you're out, y'know? But today, we had time. Today, we could do Proper Sex, like normal couples do.

I'm a bit nervous about Proper Sex, though. For one thing, it usually involves quite a lot of your body being seen, and even though Garry has seen me naked a bazillion times before I'm always worried that a bazillion and one is when he'll go 'Urgh, no!' and/or spontaneously vomit on me. For another, we don't have a great history with trying to seduce each other. Every time he tries to be sexy – dropping his voice, giving me intense looks, that kind of thing – he reminds me of Christian Bale as Batman and I start laughing. The one time I tried to be sexy around him was a disaster: I'd been talked into buying a hot pink teddy when I got my bi – okay, *tri* – annual bra-fitting at Bravissimo and I'd modelled it for him later that night while wearing pink knickers and red heels. I climbed on his lap and kissed him, and did all the things that sexy, seductive people do on TV and films, and he was completely unconcerned. So, I just sort of sat next to him and snuggled him, hoping my nearby, nearly-naked presence would make something *happen*, only for him to fall asleep with his head on my shoulder. The sexy lingerie went back in the drawer and I haven't worn it since.

Now, we just sort of simultaneously leap on each other. We are always fine talking about it once we've *had* sex – our during and post-coital chat is *full* of explicit, healthy sex chat – but unless his penis is or has just been inside me, we act like we've never even *heard* of sex, let alone spent eight years single-handedly trying to close the UK's orgasm gap. Well, sometimes two-handedly, but only when it's *really* taking a while …

So, when the end credits of *Minions* started to roll, I wasn't really sure what to *do*. If we were to spend hours exploring each other's bodies languidly (a phrase I once read in a Molly/Sherlock fan fiction and really liked) then we needed to get a wriggle on, because it was already 8pm. I glanced over at him; he was chuckling away as the filmmakers tried to squeeze as many jokes involving little yellow creatures saying the word 'banana' into the final few minutes of the film as possible. Hushing a voice in the back of my head that said '*Really? You want to have sex with this man?*', I leant over to kiss him.

Okay, cool. Kissing … Kissing was good, a good start. He even reached up and put his hand on my face, which is *definitely* the stuff of rom-coms. I rolled over so more of my body was touching his. Should I use my tongue? We never kiss with tongues, but if we're doing this properly, maybe we should. Okay, okay, three … two … one … *Bleurgh!* No, nope, okay, nope, that's why we don't kiss with tongues, it's disgusting! I don't even like the feel of my own tongue in my mouth, let alone in someone else's. Back to normal kissing … *There we go, that's nice.*

We were now horizontal on the sofa, me lying on top of him, our legs tangled together. Everything was going brilliantly, exactly as I planned it, when I opened my eyes suddenly. The cat was sitting just behind Garry's head, staring straight at me, her head cocked in confusion. I jumped in surprise, managing to catch myself halfway through so I didn't fall off the sofa. Removing my hand from Garry's shoulder, I swatted at her. She reached out a paw to swat back, and when I kept trying to shoo her away, she sat up on her hind legs and batted at my hand with both paws. Frustrated and concentrating, I frowned so hard, I went slightly cross-eyed. Flick took this opportunity to pounce on my hand and play-bite it, and that was the moment when Garry chose to open his eyes.

'Are you alright?' he asked, alarmed.

I immediately switched on a dazzling smile, realised it wasn't the most attractive face in the world, and swapped it for a slightly more seductive one.

'I'm fine,' I lied smoothly.

We froze, me with my attempted sexy smile and him looking slightly perturbed, waiting to see if we were going to acknowledge that the cat, now in full playtime mode, had leapt over my head, landed on my shoulders and pelted down my body and out the room, skidding wildly on the wooden floors and crashing into the doorframe as she did so. We didn't, though – we just kept on kissing. I wriggled on top of him, partly from enjoying myself and partly because Garry was stroking my arms and it tickled, but I didn't want to say in case it ruined The Mood. I didn't have to endure it for long, though; soon we were getting off the sofa and moving to the bedroom.

Whenever you see people moving to the room where the Proper Sex will take place in movies, they always do it so *elegantly*, twirling around each other like they're doing sexy WWE wrestling – like Daniel Cleaver and Bridget Jones, kissing each other and tumbling onto his sofa/floor in a glorious, graceful tangle of limbs and pheromones. But that's not what happened when Garry and I tried to move the ten feet from sofa to bed. I accidentally put too much weight on his stomach when I sat up and winded him, then he needed me to pull him from the sofa because his hip was hurting; then when we'd tried to keep kissing and sexy-wrestling as we walked, we'd kept stumbling and standing on each other's toes. My legs, you see, are roughly six inches long, and it turns out it's hard to move in tandem with someone several inches taller than you, whose centre of gravity is therefore up near your nipples. Eventually we gave up, broke apart near the living-room door and separately, placidly, walked into the bedroom. We sat on the bed, and immediately smushed ourselves together again.

Okay, clothes removal time. Both of us were wearing jeans and t-shirts. I was lying flat and he had his knees either side of my hips; I did a sit-up, trying not to grunt in exertion as I did so, pulled my top off and flung it triumphantly aside. I hadn't shaved my armpits in several weeks so I immediately pressed my upper arms to my sides to hide the spiky little forests concealed within. As Garry pulled his own t-shirt off his head, I quickly undid my bra and tossed it to one side. Best he doesn't see what happens to my boobs when they go from being supported to unsupported – they brush my knees when they don't have a minor miracle of engineering holding them up.

A further interlude of kissing followed. Then it was time to get the jeans off. I went first. Garry raised himself up and I unbuttoned and unzipped them, then started pulling them down. They were stuck; my hips, arse and lower belly have a circumference so large that the gap between Garry's legs wasn't big enough to slide the jeans off through it. I struggled, wriggling frantically while simultaneously trying to look calm and poised, like Grace Kelly if she were a clumsy, 16-stone charity worker trying to bang her scruffy but enthusiastic husband. When I play the 'Who Would Play Them in a Movie?' game, I always get stuck with Garry. My mum, bless her, says he looks like a young Tony Curtis, but I can never get past David Baddiel.

Focus, Jones! Jeans ... I took a deep breath and lifted my hips up as far as I could, throwing all of the core strength built up through swimming directly into the most sensitive area of my poor husband's body. He made a sound like a beanbag being jumped upon and went slightly cross-eyed, but I managed to get enough space underneath my arse to pull my jeans out. I took my knickers off at the same time (*no way was I going through that again),* kicked them off, and pulled him down on top of me to give his poor undercarriage a rest.

'Sorry, sorry!' I murmured between kisses. He didn't say anything, just responded enthusiastically. This was going *great*. We lapsed into silence, happily getting on with the business of getting it on, and in that silence, I gradually became aware of a new sound. A high-pitched, two-beat, almost musical sound repeating erratically, but with increasing frequency, from somewhere outside our flat.

Boop, boop, I heard. I frowned, rolling over so that I was on top of Garry. What *was* that? It felt so familiar …

I tried to ignore it, running my hands over his chest and arms and enjoying the sensation of his fingers gripping my hips, my sides. *Boop boo! Boop boo!* I switched into sexy autopilot as my attention went to figuring out what the fuck was happening. Was there an owl outside? But no, it was the *exact same sound* every time. And there was music playing underneath it. Jaunty, bouncy music. *Bhoo-boo!* And it sounded … electronic? *Whoo-boo!* But so familiar. Why? Was it a TV show or something? Or was it … wait, was it …?

Whoo-hoo! Whoo-hoo!

It was Mario. *Fucking Mario*, jumping around the Mushroom Kingdom, yelling in delight each time. As if the moustachioed little bastard read my mind, the faint music paused and he wailed 'Ohhhh nooo!', a swansong to both his life in the game and the perfect night of passion I had planned.

'Aaaaaaahhhh, you fucked it!' our upstairs neighbour crowed, his voice muffled but decipherable through the thin carpets and walls of our converted pre-war house.

'Fuck you!' his flatmate replied.

'No, fuck *you*!' came the cheerful reply, and the music started up again.

Whoo-hoo. Whoo-hoo. Whoo-hoo. Whoo-hoo …

Garry snorted with laughter. Tearing my mouth away from his, I pulled his hands from my body and flopped back onto the bed, naked and frustrated. He rolled onto his side and reached for me, but I shook my head.

'Don't let those twats spoil it,' he said gently, brushing hair off my face. 'Let's go back in the living room.'

I shook my head, trying to hold back the tears.

'No, it's too late, let's just go to bed.'

'It's only, like, nine o'clock ...'

'I'm going to bed,' I said quickly. I couldn't look him in the face – I'd break if I did. 'You can stay up if you want to.'

'Hey!' he said. I could feel rather than see him looking at me with concern. 'You don't have to be upset. It's not your fault, it's fine. It's just one of those things about living in London and being so close to other people.'

'I'm not upset, I'm fine,' I replied shortly. 'Honestly, I'm fine.'

I was staring at the ceiling, my voice cold and hard, and I felt like I was going to explode with the effort of keeping all my emotions controlled. I categorically was *not* fine, and Garry knew it, but he also knew I didn't want to talk about it. His desire to look after me fought with a desire to respect my wishes, and after a few minutes the latter won.

'I love you,' he said quietly, leaning down and kissing me gently on the temple.

'Love you,' I said as he stood up, picked up his t-shirt and left me alone in the dark room. I pulled the duvet over and rolled onto my side, squeezing myself into a tight ball and letting the enormity of my own failures slide out of my eyes in silent tears until Garry came to bed a couple of hours later. He lay next to me and gently rolled my tight, miserable body into his, kissing my forehead and wet cheeks, and reminding me with his compassion and love for me, a worthless, useless toad of a woman, that I didn't deserve him.

I'd spent a great deal of time in my first lot of therapy learning that the thoughts which popped unbidden into my head about how my loved ones would be better off without me were bollocks. Mostly, I believed it, but it was hard not to take the weekend – the bickering and how annoying I'd been and our entirely failed attempt at sex and how I ruined everything, *everything, everything* – as proof that I was right: he *would* be better off without me. Everyone would – they're just too nice to say so.

SATURDAY, 20 MAY

TO-DO

☐ *Romantic breakfast in bed* ♡ — nope

☑ *Get ready* — make self look very cute (Terrible as this weekend was, I must admit that I looked very cute throughout it) ✿

☑ *Romantic walk in the park*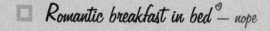

☑ *Adorable lunch in favourite cafe*

☐ *Find recipe for fancy tea*

☑ *Get stuff for tea*

☑ *Cook tea together*

☑ *Farmers' market*

☑ *Film?* (if you can call the Minions movie a film)

☐ *Proper Sex* ♡ ♡ ✗

NOTES

You know those religious marriage preparation courses?

I wonder if they do one for atheists after they've already been married for two years?

*Add it to the list.

TO-DO

☐ Buy Mum's card at Paperchase at the station

☐ 18.10 train — Euston to Nuneaton

☐ Write covering letter for DoP job on the train

☐ Ask: What's happened since I've been away?

☐ Lovely Friday night with parents — NO ARGUMENTS

☐ Lovely Saturday with parents

☐ Fortifying Saturday-afternoon nap

☐ Mum's birthday party — 6pm, Amid Palace

☐ Ask Freddy about divorce

- [ ] Don't let Taggie give you shit about job

- [ ] Say something, ANYTHING POLITE, to Andrew

- [ ] Get family photo for Facebook

- [ ] Give WICKED COOL LADIES FROM HISTORY: VOL 2 to Alice; get a photo for Instagram

- [ ] Breakfast at the Harvester on Sunday

- [ ] Lovely Sunday lunch

- [ ] 18.58 train — Nuneaton to Euston

- [ ] Check DoP covering letter

- [ ] Shower

NINE

When the train arrived at Nuneaton station Mum was, as always, waiting on the platform for me. She was wearing a big puffy coat bought in a charity shop and insisted was only for walking the dogs in, but she wore it out and about far more than I'd let her get away with if I still lived at home. She didn't particularly *smile* when she saw me, but watched me approach with an intense, slightly twitchy gaze that reminded me of the dogs staring intensely at the Bonios we were instructing them to 'sit' for.

'Hello, matey,' she said, grabbing me round the neck and pulling me into a tight, one-armed hug.

'Hiya, Mum,' I replied, my accent immediately becoming several shades Welsher. 'Happy birthday.'

'Thank you,' she preened as we walked up the stairs together, avoiding the steady stream of businessmen who had come off the same train and were clearly *much* more important than us.

'Did Mam ring and sing you the song?' I asked.

'Yep, first thing.'

'Did she cry?'

'What do you think?'

My nan, Mum's mum, had a tradition where every birthday she would ring us up and sing a special birthday song to us. We didn't know where she'd gotten this song from, but it was to the tune of 'Auld Lang Syne' and the lyrics were a mystery. By the second line she'd start crying, and her already very-screechy Cardiff voice would go higher and higher until only dogs and sadomasochists could bear to listen. Over the years we'd perfected the art of holding the phone away from our ears at *just* the right distance so that her crying-while-singing voice wouldn't deafen us, but we'd know exactly when to yell a quick 'Thank you, Nan!' before she, with the same lack of ceremony she'd started the song with, abruptly hung up. It was absurdly touching, if utterly baffling.

The drive home was filled with idle chat: the dogs, how much of a twat Mum's workmates were, how badly behaved my sister's daughter was being at the moment, that sort of thing. Occasionally, I'd remark that another shop had closed down, or a new pub had opened, and she'd fill me in with her opinion of the new development. She was glad that Beige, the clothing shop for plus-sized women, had closed down as their clothes were 'expensive, but something of nothing, really,' and she really rated the new Indian by the tip because they would use Frylight instead of oil if you asked, which made it Slimming World-friendly. I knew for a fact that before an Indian meal my parents ate so many poppadoms they rattled, probably negating any of the benefits of Frylight, but thought it wise to keep my mouth shut.

There's three whole days to go, after all. Let's not start an argument yet.

The car pulled up to the house and my parents' three spaniels went *mad* with excitement, bouncing up and down in the living-room window. When Dad opened the door, they poured out, tails wagging and tongues lolling. Taffy, the littlest one, leapt straight onto my lap as soon as I opened the car door. I'd had previous experience of her weeing all over the place in excitement, so I shoved her off as soon as my parents couldn't see me do so.

Dad, who stayed silhouetted in the doorway because he didn't have his slippers on, was looking at me with the same concentration and fierce joy that Mum had done in the station. As I grabbed my bag from the back seat, I yelled a cheery 'Hiya!'. He merely nodded fiercely and did a strange little salute in reply. When I stepped into the hall, he grabbed me and crushed me to him in a fierce hug, slapping my back.

'Ha ha ha ha!' he said gruffly, a laugh less about humour and more a general sound of delight. I beamed, trying not to wince as Mum whistled piercingly between her teeth and screamed for the dogs (now excitely exploring next door's front garden and peeing on everything in sight) to come back in. I went into the living room and collapsed in a chair, the front door slammed and, after an intense five minutes where all three dogs took turns climbing on top of me and Dad discerned that the journey had been good, I would like a cup of tea and no, I didn't want a posh coffee, a mug of tea would be lush, thank you, I was left alone.

My parents' house is covered in *stuff*. You collect a lot of stuff in 42 years of marriage (Mum was 16 when they got married. She actually went into labour with my sister, Taggie – Agatha – all their kids have names beginning with A – on her wedding day), whether that's pictures, memories, or random shit because you spent too much time watching QVC in the nineties. Alongside numerous family photos (my favourites are the ones of my brothers, Freddy and Andrew, and Taggie as teenagers, staring in bemusement at baby-me as if they couldn't quite understand why our parents would do this to them), there were paintings bought on our holidays, a genuinely enormous piece of brass wall-art like a saxophone mid-groove, and a number of little statuettes, including one of a horse so realistic that there was even horse shit in the hay. My forehead creased, as it always did when I encountered this particular piece of art. Who the hell *made* this? And why did my parents buy it, let alone have it in pride of place next to my favourite armchair?

My parents filtered back in – Dad holding a mug of tea so big, I could dunk an entire packet of McVitie's in it – and settled in their chairs. I took a fortifying swig of tea and turned my entire body to face them.

'So,' I said, levelly, 'what do you have to tell me?'

They glanced at each other nervously. Ever since I'd had that first lot of therapy, my parents had stopped telling me things until I came back home and dragged it out of them. Last Christmas, they'd told me that Mum had been made redundant. The time before, it was Freddy getting a divorce. Nan having a fall, Taggie's daughter cutting off a girl's plaits in playgroup, Andrew having a car crash – I WhatsApped my mum constantly, but never heard these things from her until I came back home. A little voice whispered in my ear that if I had any kind of decent relationship with my siblings I'd probably hear it from them; I brushed away the subsequent cold finger of shame poking at my sternum.

'Well?' I asked, probably more aggressively than I meant to.

'So, everyone's fine,' Dad began slowly, 'but you know back in April, we had that snow?'

'Yeeeeesss ...'

'Well, the dogs got hit by a car.'

I was on my feet and quite unaware of how I'd got there.

'What?' I demanded. 'They got ... what? What happened?'

'Everyone had parked along the bottom,' said Mum as I flung myself across the room and started running my hands over the dogs, looking for some sign of injury even though they'd been doing excellent impressions of gymnasts on speed not ten minutes previously. 'And when Dad was walking them in the morning, they ran between the cars and got hit by one coming down the road. It was going slowly,' she added quickly when she saw my black face. 'The dogs were fine – they got up, scrambled away and carried on with their walk.'

'I can't believe you didn't tell me!' I said as I stroked Bertie's ears.

'We didn't want you to worry ...'

'I can cope with it!' I said loudly. 'Honestly, I really appreciate you trying to take care of me, but I can cope. It's things like ... like having a shower or making a phone call, or having a tough conversation at work that stress me out.' I looked at them both, sitting on either side of their big squashy sofa, Fudge curled up between them, their faces guilty. 'Please, please tell me things like this. I can cope with the big things, and I want to know. I *need* to know. I'm a grown woman, you don't have to baby me.'

'Okay,' said Mum. 'We will, I promise.'

But they wouldn't, I knew they wouldn't. When I'd rung and told them that I was about to start therapy because I wanted to kill myself and couldn't leave the house without crying and shaking, the way they saw their youngest child had switched from 'proud as hell' to 'worried as hell'. I mean, how could it not? How could they *not* worry? How can you hear that your youngest, who lives halfway across the country from you, feels like that about themselves and *not* want to do anything you can to protect them? No matter how hard I tried to explain, to prove that I was good, I was strong, I was *fine*, I was still the responsible adult I used to be, they wouldn't do anything that might put my sanity at risk – even if it meant they drove me mad with irritation instead.

The rest of the evening passed without drama. Mum had cooked a leg of lamb for tea, because she knows Garry doesn't really eat meat unless it's chicken or between two buns with chips on the side and therefore feeds me up whenever I'm home. While we ate it, we talked about their neighbours, and Freddy's divorce, and Taggie's job, and Andrew's twins. They asked me how work was going, and I gave truthful but careful answers – I didn't want them to worry about me more than they already did, and I knew they were already confused as to why Penny's a journalist and I'm not.

After tea, we settled in front of the telly. Dad had the remote so we watched his favourite shows: old detective and crime dramas we'd seen multiple times before. When he went to bed, Mum switched over to TLC and we watched *Say Yes to the Dress* and *Curvy Brides*, tutting about the budgets that these brides had and reminiscing over the time Mum pulled a wedding dress that was the absolute opposite of what I'd planned off the rail and it had ended up being utterly perfect.

After that, when Mum went to bed and took a delighted, snoring Taffy with her, I lay in the dark in my old room with the windows open (a luxury my overactive imagination couldn't

afford in London – but nothing bad ever happened in Galley
Common) and let the familiar feelings of *home* seep into me. I
breathed in and out, smiling at the familiar peeling wallpaper
and the giant painting of a flower I'd bought at 14 and only
realised recently was actually an enormous painted vulva. It felt
good to be back. Weird – it always felt weird – but good.

The day I'd moved to London, I cried. I cried when the
car pulled away from the drive, my dad and our next-door
neighbours giving us a guard of honour and Dad openly crying
for the first time in my memory. I'd cried when we got on
the M6. And the M1. I'd cried when we pulled into the last
service station before the North Circular and while we shared
terrible, overly-sweet donuts and tried not to think about what
was going to happen next. I'd cried when we pulled up to the
flat, and when Mum produced the little jar of coffee and box
of teabags she'd hidden in the glove compartment so that we
could have a cuppa when we arrived, and when she spread the
beautiful blanket she'd crocheted over our new bed. And then,
when she'd hugged me tight, said a cheery goodbye and driven
away (only, I learnt later, to park around the corner and sob),
I went upstairs and cried until I had nothing left in me to give,
until everything I was lay on my pillow in two mascara-smeared
puddles.

Emotions are so much more complex than you give them
credit for when you're young, aren't they? Until I hit about
13, I knew you could be happy and I knew you could be sad,
and that you could be angry or excited or guilty or lonely, but
I didn't know you could feel all of those emotions at once, in
different parts of yourself. I didn't know your eyes could be sad
while your legs were so excited that they kept doing little skips,
that your heart could feel heavy while your head was dizzyingly
light. As I sat in my new bedroom, I felt sick with longing for
the home I'd known for the past 22 years and angry, almost
petulant, that I'd had to leave it. In the same breath, I was so
excited for my new life that I could sing.

I get a mini-version of that feeling every time I go on a train home to visit my family, and then again, every time I leave them to come home to London. Leaving home to go home, and then going home again, and never quite knowing which one is the 'real' home. Or do I have two homes? Maybe I have none? At what point does the home I've made for myself supersede the one my parents gave everything to make for me? When does my life stop feeling so temporary and transient? When do I start trusting myself and the life I've built to be *my* life, rather than the thing I'm just doing right now?

Coming back to see my family is exciting, because I get to 'come home'. But it's sad, too, because I'm leaving *behind* my home. And not just my home, but the person I am in that home: whenever I get on a train, I feel like I'm both returning to myself and leaving myself behind on the platform, no matter whether that train is Nuneaton- or London-bound. For a day or so I always feel awkward in my own skin, then slip back into the role I've perfected of daughter, sister, neighbour, wife. The problem is, that awkwardness lasts longer and feels more and more uncomfortable with every passing year, and I can't help but worry about what will happen when it becomes unbearable.

The best way to describe it is this: coming back to see my parents always feels like putting on an old pair of slippers. Not your slippers you've had for ages, but an *old* pair of slippers, the ones before the pair you're currently wearing. Although comfortable and familiar and lovely, they're also strange and disconcerting, and was there *always* that hole, there, just under the heel? Really? Huh. It might have gone unnoticed before, but it's rubbing you raw, now. They don't feel the same as they used to, no matter how much you wish they did, and you're really, really not sure how long it'll be before you start to bleed.

*

To celebrate Mum's birthday, we were going out for a meal at
the very same Indian restaurant she'd pointed out to me on
the trip home from the station. And by 'we' I mean me, my
parents, my siblings and their families. The birthday of one of
our parents acted as a kind of homing signal; my siblings rarely
saw or even spoke to each other, but the second either Mum,
Dad or a Nan had a birthday, we descended like locusts on a
dead buffalo – if the buffalo was wearing a party hat and saying,
'You didn't need to get me anything, love, you being here is
enough.' We might miss the occasional Christmas or look up
and realise it's been half a year since we spent the weekend with
them, but we'd never, ever miss their birthdays.

So, as I stood in front of the mirror that night and tried
to apply winged eyeliner without making myself look like Avril
Lavigne, circa 2008, I was highly aware that I wasn't just
applying make-up because I wanted to look pretty, but I needed
it to double up as armour. My stomach was a heaving mass of
eels because I was so worried about how the evening would
go. The last time I'd spoken to Freddy, he'd taken the piss
out of me for being a London wanker. And when I'd spoken
to Taggie she'd made snide remarks about my ever-increasing
waistline. I couldn't even remember the last time I'd spoken
to Andrew; I actively tried not to, the twat. If I was to survive
tonight without using my knife to either stab someone in the
face or slit my own wrists at the dinner table then I needed
to be bulletproof, and the secret to that is always going to be
perfect eyeliner.

When Mum, Dad and I got to the restaurant, Andrew was
already sat at the table with his wife, Dolly, and their twin girls,
Prudence and Sierra. He and Dolly stood up as we walked in,
and she hugged Mum effusively.

'Carole, it's so good to see you!' she lied convincingly,
smiling widely. Her hair had been cut into a sharp bob and dyed
a weird mix of dark brown with thick blonde streaks – it made
her look like a shocked tiger. 'Happy birthday, babe!'

'Hello, Delores,' Mum replied, smiling just as convincingly back. Dolly's smile didn't flicker. Instead, she presented Mum with a sparkly purple gift bag.

'It's not much – it's just so hard to buy for you, you've got everything you need already!' she said sweetly. Mum smiled just as sweetly back and peered inside the bag – which, I was willing to bet next week's Costa money on, contained a Body Shop smellies set that she'd received for Christmas and hadn't wanted. I couldn't really blame her; Mum did the exact same thing to people social convention forced her to buy presents for, too. Dad, meanwhile, totally ignored Mum and Dolly doing their very well-practiced dance of social necessity, and instead shook Andrew's hand and kissed the squirming twins on the side of their heads.

'Say hello to Nan and Bampy, girls,' Andrew said in his gruff Welsh accent. I felt a pang; one of the many reasons I theorised my siblings and I didn't really get on was that they all grew up in Wales, but we moved to England when I was seven. That's a whole cultural world that they share, but I don't share with them. It also means they have their lovely accents, but I only sound Welsh when I'm drunk, angry, or I've been watching the episodes of *Doctor Who* set in Wales.

In true Jones fashion, the twins *totally* ignored their father. Andrew shrugged half-heartedly, and gave me an awkward nod.

'Hiya, sis,' he said. 'You alright?'

'Hiya. I'm alright, ta. You?'

'I'm alright.'

And that, if I can help it, is the extent of the conversation I'll have with him this evening.

Cunt.

Taggie arrived shortly afterwards, looking as thin and beautiful as she always does. I tugged at my dress self-consciously. Her daughter Alice was trailing behind, like she'd been literally dragged from the car – which, knowing Taggie and Alice, isn't entirely unlikely. Taggie had never revealed who Alice's father was, and my nan often opined that the whole reason Alice was 'so badly behaved' was that she didn't have a strong father figure to discipline her. Mum and I privately agreed that Alice wasn't even that bad, she just took after Taggie, who in turn took after Nan; the lot of them were headstrong shitbags, and Nan was the worst of them all. We didn't say that to them, obviously. It wasn't worth the sulk. Or the bruises.

'Nice make-up,' Taggie said, sliding into the seat next to me.

'Thanks,' I replied. 'It's a new eyeliner. From Mac.'

'Suits you!' she said cheerily. My heart *soared*. 'Not sure about that lipstick, though. Is your mouth really big enough to pull off red?'

'Thanks, Tags,' I said, grimacing. 'How's work?'

'Eh,' she said dismissively, waving a hand absentmindedly and trying to get Alice to sit nicely rather than climbing under the table. 'Still there, they're still all idiots! How's the … where are you, now?'

'The charity,' I said, hoping she wasn't going to say, 'What, still?'

'What, still?' she said in surprise. 'I thought that job was a stopgap and you'd be long gone.'

'Well, I quite like it,' I said, trying to calm down the inky panic which had dropped into my brain, slowly turning everything black.

'Good for you,' Taggie said absently. 'I guess if you're happy just doing that, then great.'

Just doing that. Just doing *that*? Or *just* doing that? Either way, she said Just. Doing. That. I opened my mouth to say something, but then a pair of hands covered my eyes.

'Freddy?' I asked.

'Hullo,' my eldest brother said cheerily, plopping into the seat on my other side. All of my siblings were tall, but he was the tallest, and with age his already-broad frame had filled out so he now resembled a stuffed armchair. Add to that the same thick bushy beard and cloud of fluffy hair that all the men on my dad's side of the family had, and he looked like The Rock cosplaying as a young Santa Claus.

'How are you?' I asked politely. 'I'm sorry to hear about ... y'know, Laura.'

'Ah, thanks,' he said awkwardly. 'It's for the best, y'know? Things haven't been right for a while.'

'Yes, I remember you telling me,' I said sadly. What I didn't add was 'when you cornered me outside at my wedding reception, just after the first dance, and talked to me for 45 minutes about how your marriage was a total failure and how you wished you'd gone off with Nicola Burns from sixth form when she'd offered, two months before the wedding'.

Now the table was full, the waiters descended with menus and notepads to take drink orders. I'd been dreading this night for months, but when it came down to it, it was fine: as difficult as it is to get seven adults and five children to behave themselves, we all loved our parents so much that we would even get our horrible children/horrible selves under control if it meant that they could have a pleasant evening with us.

'It was a good night,' Dad said thoughtfully the next day, as we sat on opposite ends of the sofa and half-watched an episode of *Poirot* we'd both seen at least five times before. 'Nice to see the kids. They're growing up nicely, aren't they?'

I thought back to the interactions I'd had with my siblings' kids last night. Once I'd managed to get the twins' attention, they'd been only too happy to show me exactly how Elite Beat Agents worked, and cheered me on when they realised I was amazing at it (all those years of saxophone lessons finally paying off). Freddy's kids, Zach and Bruce, were easy to impress because they were only interested in Pokémon Go and Manchester United, one of which I could talk about for hours and one of which they could talk to me about for hours while I pretended to listen. And Alice, for all her nightmare behaviour at school and for her mum, was a sweetheart who had slipped her hot, sticky hand in mine and read to me from the book she'd brought with her.

To be honest, they'd been my saving grace. After the starters, I'd looked around the table and realised that I was the only one not talking. Dolly and Taggie were chatting earnestly about schools and what various bloggers were saying about homework debates, Freddy was taking my parents through the intricacies of the divorce and the unrealistic demands of his ex, while Andrew was occasionally chiming in to explain exactly how divorces worked even though he'd never had one himself and was, if I recall correctly from his last monologue about how successful he was, an IT consultant rather than a fucking divorce lawyer. After the mains I'd looked around and the groups had switched: Taggie and Andrew were bickering companionably about some technical thing I didn't understand or care about, Dolly and Dad were talking about Ofsted inspections, and Freddy and Mum were talking about childcare.

I couldn't join in with these conversations – I didn't have the experience, the insights, the fucks to give. I don't have the assurance in my convictions to bicker without being upset, to put forward an opinion that completely contradicts what everyone else thinks without feeling sickeningly guilty for it. Thank God for the twins and their game, for the boys' endless enthusiasm for talking about Man U, for Alice's desire to show off to someone who hadn't admonished her in the past 24 hours! Their kindnesses had been the only things stopping me from needing a quick safety-cry in the toilets, and I wouldn't have been able to stand the look on Andrew '*Depression? Just pull yourself together. Do some yoga*'s smug-fucking *face* if I'd come back to the table with wet, red eyes. I was sitting with the people who, by rights, should be closer to and more like me than anyone else in the whole world, but I might as well have been a different species.

I didn't say this to Dad, obviously. I just smiled and nodded and said, 'They are.'

'They're doing well,' he said, dunking an entire biscuit in his tea and putting it in his mouth whole. I get my eating habits from my dad, FYI. 'They all are, they've made a good life for themselves.'

'I have too, Dad,' I said, bristling. 'I've got good friends, a great marriage, a lovely flat, and my job's going really great. My boss's boss, the head of department, is really pleased with me.'

'Mmm,' he said, eyes still locked on the TV. Beat. 'Still, it's not what you thought you'd be doing, is it?' On screen, David Suchet was doing something ostentatiously pernickety with his moustache to act as comic relief from the horrific triple-murder going on around him.

'What do you mean?' I said slowly, turning to face him. 'I wanted to be a writer. I'm writing for a living, I'm doing exactly what I wanted to.'

'I know, but ...' As he tried to think of what to say, his face creased like he was in pain. Maybe he was. Maybe it was the pain of having to concede a point to me, or perhaps trying to figure out how to say what he thought without upsetting his mad, fragile daughter. 'But it's not what we thought you'd be writing, is it?'

'No?' I said.

We? I thought.

'No. What you're writing is great, but it's beneath you,' he finished. He looked at me and paused for a second. His face creased again and he shrugged awkwardly, as if about to tell me something against his better judgement. 'To be honest, I thought you would have published a novel by now.'

'Oh,' I said, turning back to the screen. I think Poirot was about to discover a tear in a skirt that, along with the fact the young ingénue was left-handed rather than right-handed, would provide the solution to the whole thing. Very important to concentrate on *that* and not the fact your father thinks you're a disappointment, yes. *Very important indeed.*

'Don't think we're not proud of you. We are,' Dad was saying, as if from far away. 'It's just not where we thought you'd be.'

'That's okay,' I said. But it wasn't okay. *It wasn't fucking okay.* It wasn't okay that he'd said it, and it wasn't okay that it was true. 'It's not where I thought I'd be, either.'

Wasn't it? Well, no, because when you're a little girl and dreaming about where your life will take you, you don't really *think* about the fact that mental health charities are going to need youth-facing content producers with some level of seniority, do you? Then you get older, and you move to London and you try to be a writer, and your first job out of uni is writing three hundred 150-word summations of white goods products for a reviews website who clearly don't care whether you live or die, let alone file on time, and you're doing it in a miserable flat share with an intimidating German couple, who keep trying to get you to go cycling with them while your best friend is off with her new friends from work and you've never felt more alone. So when you're offered an office job, you take it, because even if it's not what you've dreamed of, it's human contact and a feeling of some direction, and if you don't get that this very moment then you think you'll explode, like an over-inflated balloon, and scare the pigeons. And then you start your job and you get caught up in the endless cycle of meetings and tea breaks and avoiding post-work trips to the pub, and you somehow forget that you dreamed of being a writer and the feeling in your soul when your Year 9 English teacher said she thought you could do it.

So what if you didn't live up to your childhood dreams? Roisin Lloyd from number 34 isn't a space dolphin trainer either and we're not giving her shit for it, are we? Just because I'm not the writer I thought I'd be doesn't mean I'm a failure, does it?

Does it?

That question was the only thing I could think of all the way through the rest of the programme (it was the pretty woman with the cocaine problem and the fabulous pin-curls who dunnit), through lunch, and through the three unbearably awkward hours before I could get on the train again and leave/go home. When Dad hugged me tightly goodbye at the door and said,

'Take care of yourself,' all I could think was, *He's disappointed that I'm not the daughter he thought I'd be.* When Mum drove me to the station, waited 20 minutes on the freezing platform with me and waved until the train pulled out of sight, all I thought was, *She pities me, and the mess I've made of my life.* My parents love me so desperately; I can see it in every head ruffle and cup of tea and fierce, watchful gaze, but I wonder if they love the version of me that I could be rather than the person I actually am. The guilt for disappointing them, for being the odd one out in our family, was agony.

I wish I could be the person they wanted me to be, I thought, as I lay my hot face against the cool train window and ignored the man further down the carriage, who was talking to himself and sticking his hands down his trousers. *Could I change? Could I be the person that fits in with my siblings, that my parents can be proud of? Maybe. Maybe I could. And maybe*, I thought as the fields and houses blurred and the sky outside the window darkened, *I should start by writing that novel.*

I reached into my bag and retrieved a notebook and pen. Yes, I always have them on me. *Maybe*, I thought despairingly, *that's a sign that I do agree with Dad – I always carry them just in case I get struck by divine inspiration and start writing the next Harry Potter.*

Okay, he's right: I suck. I'm a big sucky failure, a waste of space, a smear of shit on the Jones family name. God, I hate myself! *No, don't get sucked into a hate spiral, Jones, get working!* This is what the To-Do Lists are *for* – to help you plan and improve and fix problems. You've realised that you are a problem, so, let's fix it.

What shall I write my novel about? I looked around for inspiration. Maybe a train? Thinking about Harry Potter, J.K. Rowling wrote her books with a scene in a train station and now everyone loves her, and she's linked forever to King's Cross station. And Paddington is linked forever to Paddington! Maybe I should write about a big life event happening in a train station, then, because people will always be reminded of my book when they go there. But which station? Liverpool Street? No, they had that flashmob there in *St Trinian's 2*, so it's kind of been taken. And ABBA got Waterloo years ago. Maybe … maybe Euston! It's the station I always go to and come home from – after all, it means an awful lot to me. I close my eyes and think of Euston, waiting for inspiration to strike. I think of the dark grey concrete outside and the light grey concrete inside and the … um … rectangular shape … and the Upper Crust, and … Sod it, no, it's too depressing! Euston is, categorically, the worst station. The only big life event that could realistically happen there is a suicide pact.

Okay, so write what you know. I leant over my tiny grey train table, opened my notebook and just started writing. No planning, no plot, just words. And it felt good, just to let my pen move and not think too hard about where it was going. Look at me, writing my novel! On a *train* and everything, like proper, cool writers do! I wrote solidly for the hour and 43 minutes it took to get back to London and poured all of my frustrations and self-doubt onto the page. I felt *great*, I *was* great! As the train pulled into Euston, I felt a warm rush of pride in myself – which quickly turned acidic as I re-read what I'd written and realised a book about a woman who writes a bestselling novel to get back at her father for saying 'I thought you'd have published a novel by now,' and has fabulous success with it is probably *not* going to get picked up by a publisher.

When I got into Euston I wound my way through the tunnels and down the shadowy stairways of the Underground until I arrived on my platform. I reached behind me so that my fingertips touched the wall. It's a habit I developed the first time I lost my mind a few years ago, and I still pull it out like a safety blanket whenever I need it. See, if my fingers are touching the wall then I'm grounded, I'm safe. As long as my fingers are touching the wall, I won't end up on the rails – not because of the force of the train sucking me under as it rushes in, and not because of myself. The number of times I've stood with my toes touching the yellow line and realised there's nothing stopping me from stepping forward onto the track apart from my own will is terrifying. And the thing is, when I feel like this I don't trust the force of my own will to be enough – it always helps to have a backup.

With a scream and a rush of air, the train thundered towards me and jerked to a stop. I released my breath, pulled my fingers from the wall and found a seat in the middle of the carriage. As the train hurtled into the dark tunnel and towards home, I looked around me and wondered how many of the other passengers knew I felt that a messy end underneath a train might just be preferable to the perfectly normal but seemingly unbearable life I currently led.

TO-DO

- ✓ Buy Mum's card at Paperchase at the station

- ✓ (18.10) train — Euston to Nuneaton

- ✓ Write covering letter for DoP job on the train ✉

- ✓ Ask: What's happened since I've been away?

- ✓ Lovely Friday night with parents — NO ARGUMENTS

- ✓ Lovely Saturday with parents

- ✓ Fortifying Saturday-afternoon nap

- ✓ Mum's birthday party — 6pm, Amid Palace

- ✓ Ask Freddy about divorce

- [ ] ~~Don't let Taggie give you shit about job~~ — Fail

- [x] Say something, ANYTHING POLITE, to Andrew

- [x] Get family photo for Facebook 📷

- [ ] Give WICKED COOL LADIES FROM HISTORY: VOL 2 to Alice; get a photo for Instagram (She wouldn't pose for a picture, but she liked the book)

- [x] Breakfast at the Harvester on Sunday 🍳

- [ ] Lovely Sunday lunch — Is a lunch lovely if it sends you into an existential crisis?

- [x] 18.58 train — Nuneaton to Euston

- [→] Check DoP covering letter Move to tomorrow — spent trip home writing my shitty shit novel

- [ ] ~~Shower~~ — can't face it

- [ ] Write bestselling novel to prove Dad wrong

Not a bad
completion rate,
to be honest.
Not sure why I still
feel so crap.

TO-DO

- ☐ Meet Penny at King's Cross
- ☐ Meet the hens at Paddington
- ☐ 12.07pm train to Bath
- ☐ Unpack
- ☐ Get superhero costume (try to find one that'll fit me and not make me look like Miss Piggy on Halloween)
- ☐ Go to The Club
- ☐ ACTUALLY DANCE at The Club
- ☐ Don't get too drunk
- ☐ Find a reason to escape before 1am — maybe Hannah?
- ☐ Communal breakfast
- ☐ Taxis to Bath, 10am
- ☐ Skincare treatments, 11am
- ☐ Knicker decorating, 1pm

☐ Afternoon tea, 2.30pm

☐ Taylor Swift dance class, 5pm

☐ Dinner at La Italiana, 7pm

☐ Film time — find out if there are any lesbian equivalents of WHEN HARRY MET SALLY

☐ Hen party games (drinking games edition)

☐ Communal breakfast #2

☐ Country walk

☐ Board games

☐ Pedicures

☐ 18.37pm train to Paddington

☐ Talk to at least three people who aren't Penny, Janae, Frankie and Emily

☐ Do shots, at least once, because you can handle shots and it might trick people into thinking you're cool

☐ Be normal

☐ Don't let anyone know you're having a terrible time

TEN

'Janae better fucking love me,' I muttered furiously to Penny as we dragged our weekend bags through Paddington.

'Janae *does* fucking love you,' she replied cheerfully, swiping her Oyster card and loping across to the escalator like a beautiful gazelle in leather ankle boots. 'That's why she wanted you on her hen weekend.'

'If she loved me, she'd have let me stay home this weekend and I could just like everyone's Instagram posts as soon as they were uploaded.'

'Now you're being selfish,' she said wryly.

My bowels lurched. *Fuck, am I selfish? Is that what everyone thought? That I'm an awful selfish cow?*

'No, I know she loves me and I, um, obviously, I'm so happy to be on her hen weekend,' I gabbled. 'But I just don't really know anyone, and so I'm just a bit … um … yeah.'

Penny didn't say anything. *Fuck.* Janae probably only invited me here because she felt sorry for me. I shouldn't be so ungrateful. She's so lovely, I'm trash. *Trash.*

'It's going to be lovely,' I lied determinedly.

'It is!' she replied cheerily. 'The Airbnb is beautiful, Bath is beautiful, Janae and Emily are beautiful, it's going to be great!'

'Great!' I replied brightly. 'Really great!' As I said this we were arriving into the station concourse and could easily spot a gaggle of about 20 women, all holding the handles of brightly coloured wheelie suitcases. They spotted us and immediately started whooping. Without looking, Penny reached behind her and squeezed my hand.

Janae's hen do: ten of her friends and ten of Emily's, all crammed together in a big converted barn in Bath. I recognised some of them – Janae's two sisters, Frankie, Ivy-from-the-book-launch, a couple of people from Janae's church – but the people I felt comfortable around were outnumbered by those I didn't know seven-to-one. For someone who is not great with new people, those were not good odds.

'AMMMMMMMMY! PEEEEEENNNNNNNNNYYYY!' Janae squealed, running up and flinging her arms around us. 'It's my hen weekend! I'm getting marrrrrrrried!'

'You are, you *are*!' I said, squeezing her tight and trying not to feel sad about how slim and lovely she felt in my arms. Emily had come up behind her and was shyly beaming at us, her round cheeks glowing.

'Just look at you two!' Penny said, fondly. She rummaged in her bag and pulled out two enormous, rainbow 'Bride to be' badges. 'Come here, let's get these on you …'

There was much cooing and squealing, especially from Janae's church friends, and then we all took photos of the happy couple wearing their badges. Then we decided to get a group photo, so Frankie went up to a pissed-off staff member and got him to take a photo of us together on the platform. But then there was squabbling over who had the best camera on their phone, so it took a while to get us all in place and show the guy how to use the phone, and then there was taking the photo multiple times and all poring over it to make sure that we were happy, photos of Janae and Emily getting on the train, photos of us on the train as a big group taking over a whole carriage, photos of us individually, photos of us in friendship groups …

I'd been dreading this hen party for eight months, ever since Bett, Abi and Emily's sister Imogen had invited us into a WhatsApp group entitled '#janilymarriage hens!!!', which had received 347 messages within the first two hours. And then the messages just didn't stop; I'd had to start charging my phone at work because all the buzzing was draining my battery so quickly. At first I'd muted the group for my own sanity, but then missed a crucial message from Abi about whether I had any dietary requirements for the afternoon tea we were having between the knicker decorating class and the Taylor Swift dance class on Saturday, and I hadn't replied for a whole four hours. The resulting drama (Imogen had called me up and burst into tears when I answered the phone because she was convinced I'd died) meant that I'd unmuted it, and read every single message in that fucking chat three times since.

As I smiled for photo after photo and tried to make small talk with women I was pretty sure thought I was a weirdo, I could feel my chest tighten with nerves. Not nerves that they wouldn't like me – indeed, I'm so nice and so bland that someone having strong opinions on me would be like someone having strong opinions on vanilla yogurt – but nerves for what social faux pas I would soon commit. Would I make stupid jokes that don't land and embarrass myself? Or be too quiet, then start worrying I'm too quiet so interject with a comment or opinion which is really boring or makes no sense, and end up doing calming breathing round the back of the building while stuffing my face with whatever white carbs I could find? I was 100 per cent *not excited* to find out.

As the train pulled away, I looked around the group, all unpacking cans from their bags (M&S gin-in-a-tin for Janae's church friends, craft lagers and cocktails for the brides' gay friends, Diet Coke for Penny and pregnant Hannah). Because of that WhatsApp group, despite not knowing these women I knew so much *about* these women. I knew that Bo, Ivy, Carla, Nikki and Tobi were all going to be on their periods, that Nikki got bad cramps so wasn't sure how much she'd be able to do at the dance class. Carla wanted people to remind her that she was on her period if she got drunk and started trying to pull anyone at the club, that Ivy, Katie, Iesha and Lisa were all totally unbothered by period sex while Val was positively in favour of it. I had hazarded a guess that Janae's straight church friends,

Bo, Hannah and Liz, were all slightly alarmed by this. Hannah snored and Andy would kick in the night if she had to share a bed. Ashley, Imogen, Kirsty and Frankie were gluten-free and Bett was vegan. Liz used hashtags when it wasn't appropriate and all of Emily's friends became really passive-aggressive when faced with someone sending messages like #whoopwhoop and #packingmybestbra. I put personality quirks to faces and made a mental list of who to cling to (Emily, Janae, Frankie and Penny, maybe Imogen because she at least seems as unhinged as me) and who to avoid (everyone else).

'Boris Johnson is such a cunt!' Frankie announced cheerily next to me, scrolling through Twitter. 'You okay? How's the patch doing?'

Um … How to play this? I'd switched to the contraceptive patch last week after telling my doctor that I thought the Pill was affecting my mood, so had a small square the colour of one of those dildos that's supposed to be flesh coloured but really, really isn't stuck to my upper right arm. It was not working for me. I'd jokingly said to Garry in bed on the first night of wearing it that, because it contained oestrogen, if it went onto him in the night then he'd wake up and would have grown a vagina. He'd laughed.

'Yeah, but what if you take it off at the end of the week and you've grown a vagina on your arm?'

And although I know it's a joke, although I know this would never actually happen and that's not how literally anything works, I can't get the idea of having a vagina-arm out of my head. I've thought about it constantly for 16 days. What's worse, I'm not even thinking about one vagina in my arm; the idea firmly planted in my mind is that I'll peel the patch off and underneath will be multiple holes, a perfect square of tiny little vaginas. I'm itching constantly, especially on my head and back, and feeling so uncomfortable in my own skin that I want to rip it off and start again. Old nightmares about baby carrots growing in my arms and being pulled out to reveal tiny carrot holes on my forearms have resurfaced, so I'm getting very, very little sleep, so I'm currently feeling anxious, fuzzy and stupid.

So, how is the patch doing? Not … not great? But even though Frankie knows and loves me for the insane twat I am, I think stories of vagina holes and carrots are probably quite a lot to unload, especially at the start of a hen weekend, especially when there's a chance people who've not met me properly before and only know me as That Bitch Who Didn't Tell Us What Her Afternoon Tea Preferences Are will overhear and start thinking of me as That Crazy Bitch Who Didn't Tell Us What Her Afternoon Tea Preferences Are. I need to distract her, but not lie because she'll see through that in an instant. So, I need to make a joke.

'It's so weird,' I said, pulling up my sleeve to reveal the patch on my upper arm. VAGINA HOLES, VAGINA HOLES EVERYWHERE. 'I look like I'm trying to give up smoking or something.'

'God, what a gross colour!' she said, prodding at it. I shuddered.

'Isn't it? It looks like that sex toy I found in my mum's drawer when I was a kid, the one I thought was a giant finger.'

'What?' Penny and Ivy were sat opposite and had been happily talking shit about another journalist (whose debut novel came out last week and had been universally adored) since they got on the train. At this, though, they both turned to look at me.

'Oh, yeah,' I said, slipping into the anecdote. I'd told this one before and it always got a laugh. It was Safe. 'When I was little, like, seven or eight, I was going through my mum's drawers and I found this weird thing that looked like a really big *finger* but had a battery compartment in it. I remember being really confused about why Mum would need a big, battery operated finger, but also realising pretty quickly that this was something I shouldn't be looking at, so I put it back. I only realised when I was a teenager that it was actually an enormous dildo.'

'Oh my God, that's so funny!' Ivy said with an entirely straight face. 'I remember once when I was like, 15, I was looking through my dad's drawer to find some thick socks to wear with boots and found a vibrating strap-on.' She paused for dramatic effect 'In my *dad's* drawer.'

'Oh my GOD!' Penny laughed, before telling us a story she'd seen on BuzzFeed about someone who'd used their mum's vibrator (*ew*) for years (*ew*) before somehow learning that it was actually one of those casts you can get made of your partner's penis and she'd been wanking with a model of her dad's penis for years (*so many ews*). Other hens (*ew, again!*) joined in and the resulting conversation (covering how our parents reacted when they found out we'd had sex/come out, worst one-night stand stories, weirdest things we'd found in our discharge and whether or not everyone also got the period shits) took us all the way to Bath and traumatised several middle-aged men, who'd just wanted to read their papers in peace.

The Airbnb was just as lovely as Penny promised it would be. It was a huge converted barn on a working farm, about 30 minutes from the train station. When the numerous taxis dropped us off at outside we'd opened the rickety, supposedly sheep-proof gate, walked the 200 metres to the barn and oo-ed and ah-ed loudly – loudly enough so that Bett, Abi and Imogen could all smile smugly at how great their organising skills were, anyway.

'Ooh, isn't this lovely?' Frankie said to me and Hannah.

It really is, I thought, trying not to think about how *not*-lovely it'd be when we all had to walk down it in the dark at 2am tomorrow morning.

At the barn I waved goodbye at Hannah and Frankie, now chatting cheerfully about how pregnant Hannah's areolas and vulva had started getting darker (*Christ*), and started dragging my suitcase up to the top floor. Penny and I were in half of the loft conversion together, and as I reached the first floor, I saw her at the end of the corridor, chatting animatedly to fucking Ivy-from-the-book-launch.

'That'd be *so great*,' Penny said brightly. 'I think you're, like, just the right person to do this with!'

'Oh my God, me too! Lol' – yes, Ivy said lol, out loud – 'Nothing like two hosts in direct competition to make a podcast interesting, right?' The two laughed like breaking glass. I tittered too late, *way* too late, and felt a stab of anxiety. 'I know a girl at work, well, the intern, who like, does all this podcasting stuff. We could *totally* get her to do all the, like, editing for us.'

'Great!' Penny said brightly.

'Great!' Ivy said back. They beamed at each other for a moment. I looked from face to face – *shit, were they becoming friends?* I thought Penny hated Ivy. Are they going to be friends, now? Best friends? Is she going to replace me in the group? It wouldn't surprise me. Ivy is beautiful and clever and cool and successful and I'm a slug with a Dairy Milk addiction. *They'll get rid of me and start hanging out with Ivy instead and I'm going to be left all alone …*

'I'm going to get unpacked,' Ivy said cheerily to Penny, totally ignoring me. 'It'll take me *at least* two hours to get ready to go out. See you later!'

'Bye!' Penny trilled as Ivy went into her room and closed the door. I raised an eyebrow – *keep it light keep it light keepitlightkeepitlight* – and she made a face back. We hoiked our bags up another set of stairs, waved at Tobi and Nikki through the doorway (they had the other half of the loft conversion), then went into our room for the weekend. It was light and very beautiful; the windows were wide and we could see half of the farm from them. I closed the door behind me and leant against it, breathing hard.

'Looks like you and Ivy are getting along well,' I said, trying to keep my voice light to hide the fact that my world was ending around me.

Penny chucked her suitcase on the bed and rolled her eyes. 'Such a cunt!' she said darkly. I laughed, feeling the iron bars around my heart loosen a bit. 'We're thinking of doing a podcast together, though.' She began absently chucking lacy black French knickers into a bedside drawer. 'Something on amazing women in the workplace, or the problems women face in the workplace. Or maybe women on what they do out of work, because feminism has focused too much on women in terms of their *jobs*. Not sure, yet, but something like that.'

'If you snap and murder her, I call dibs on making the true crime podcast about it,' I replied, walking over and opening my suitcase, ignoring the pang of loathing I felt on seeing my clothes. 'I can call it "Penny's Dreadful".'

'Fine, but only if you promise it's not going to be more popular than mine.'

'Ah, I can't,' I replied sadly. 'You know what true crime podcasts are like.'

'That's true,' she said thoughtfully, straightening up. She had the oversize *Ghostbusters* t-shirt she wore to bed in one hand, a PVC Batgirl costume in the other. 'Bitches do love true crime podcasts.'

We grinned at each other.

'I love you,' I said simply.

'Love you too.' She blew a kiss at me. 'Do you want to use the loo? I have quite the poo brewing, so I'd go now if you do.'

The bathroom was panelled in wood with a vase of obviously fake flowers on the toilet cistern. I made sure that the doors to both our room and Tobi and Nikki's room were locked, dragged a floral bath towel over my lap to try and stop sound escaping and had the slowest, quietest wee I could manage. When I pulled the flush, I let the farts I'd been holding in for several hours sneak out, hoping the rushing water would hide the sound.

While I washed my hands, I looked in the mirror above the sink. *Fuck*, I looked like such *shit*. My eyebags were the colour of bruises, dramatic against my greasy, pale skin. My hair was all over the place and I had a spot on my chin. I'd left all my make-up in my suitcase, but Tobi and Nikki had left a big washbag in there so I opened it, trying to see if I could use some of

Nikki's foundation. What I found instead was a *lot* of skincare products, several vibrators, and a towel covered in brown and red stains that I quickly realised was a designated period sex towel. I quietly closed the bag and settled for splashing water on my face instead. When I did, I caught a glimpse of the patch on my arm and winced.

I checked my phone: 4.47pm. Forty-nine hours left. *You can do this, Jones. Come on!*

*

The first night was exactly as bad as I thought it would be. We had ordered in pizza, drank a *lot* of alcohol, all dressed up like superheroes (or, in my case, put on a Superman t-shirt), called taxis and went clubbing in Bath. On arrival, Imogen had suddenly pulled out a huge number of deeley boppers with vulvas on the ends, and made us all put them on. She spent the night screaming 'AREN'T THEY GOOD? THEY'RE FROM ETSY!' at people who showed a passing interest, while Bett and Abi kept having pissed-off conversations in the toilets about how all the vulvas were white and considering the bride, her sisters and all but two of her hens were black, couldn't Imogen have gotten some fucking racial diversity in there?

Hannah, who at six months pregnant already looked like she was ready to give birth to a calf rather than a baby, was almost as unhappy as me. She got a fairly clear spot whenever she wanted to dance, her protruding belly clearing a circle around her, but she was hot, her ankles were swollen, she couldn't drink alcohol and whenever she tried to drop it like it's hot, she found she needed two other hens to pull her back up again. I tried not to think about the fact that even with my empty womb, I was a similar size to her. Eventually I said that I'd 'take care of her' – i.e. not drink alcohol, sit down, and attempt to chat over the music before giving up and staring miserably at the rest of the thin, beautiful hens who were all having a marvellous time. I watched Frankie spot a tall, slim, ginger man from across the room – her type, exactly her type – and gradually, over the course of an hour, attract his attention and eye-fuck him until he offered to buy her a drink. At midnight, when Hannah said she wanted to go home, we passed them outside, kissing furiously, him pressed against the wall with his hand up her dress.

'Frankie is such a slut,' Hannah said mildly as I helped her into the back of a taxi.

'I know!' I replied proudly, shutting the door behind her. I took a breath, looked around gratefully at the chaos I was leaving behind, and darted round to the other side of the car.

'CAREFUL!' someone shouted. I took a step back and a car appeared where I had been standing a second ago, its driver honking the horn loudly.

'Sorry!' I yelled after it, and to the person who had warned me, and to anyone else who was around. I got into the car and leant my head against the cool window then spent the journey making vague, sympathetic noises in response to Hannah's prattling, watching the twinkling lights of the sleeping city rush past, and thinking about the moment the car had rushed past me and wondering how painless a death being run over by a car would be.

One good thing about my brain going in a million directions at once is that I'm always exhausted. I fell asleep immediately when I got back to the barn and wasn't aware of anything else until my eyes snapped open seven hours later. Penny was lying next to me, scrolling through Instagram, her fluffy blonde hair twisted into a messy bun.

'What time did you get back last night?' I asked in a voice that seemed to have been replaced by an old extractor fan.

'About four,' she said cheerily. Her skin was suspiciously pink and glowy, especially considering the extravagant cat-eye she'd spent 45 minutes carefully applying last night.

'Did you take your make-up off?'

'Always,' she said, throwing her phone on the bed and flipping on to her side to face me. 'It's, like, the worst thing you can do for your skin, sleep in your make-up. I've only brought the basics with me, though, so I just did a double-cleanse and a quick hyaluronic mask last night. It'll be fine, I hope! I'll do an oil treatment when I get back tomorrow.'

'I honestly think if I wasn't your best friend, I'd despise you,' I said blankly. She grinned so widely I could see her wonky front teeth (she usually only smiled closed-lipped), leant forward, and kissed me lightly on the end of the nose.

'Thaaaaanks! Oh my God, so, I have to tell you about what happened when you left last night ...' she said, flinging back the covers and leaping out of bed. She was wearing tiny cotton PJ shorts along with her Ghostbusters t-shirt. I tried not to stare at the triangle of space between her bum and thighs, and failed miserably. *God, she's gorgeous. Why is she friends with a lump like me?* My hand rubbed my arm-vagina absent-mindedly.

As we got ready for the day, she told me all the gossip. One of the reasons Hannah was so grumpy was that in the taxi, Bo had taken her hand and said, with love and sincerity, 'I hope your baby looks like you, not your man. You deserve a pretty baby.' Katie spent the evening kissing two different blokes, thinking they were the same one. Imogen had burst into tears because she thought Bett and Abi were ignoring her, so Liz had taken her into the toilet and sung Disney songs with her for 52 minutes until she calmed down. But, most excitingly, Carla – who had warned us all to remind her that she was on her period in case she got too friendly with a bloke – *had* in fact ended up pulling someone: Val.

'VAL!' I squeaked and sat up, surrounded by fluffy white pillows. 'I didn't even know Carla was into women?'

'Me neither,' Penny said. 'Janae and all her church lot didn't seem to know either, so either it's a big secret or this has been a *big* weekend for Carla.'

We eagerly discussed what this would mean for the rest of the weekend – were Carla and Val dating now? Would we mention it at all, or was it going to be left unsaid? About halfway through getting ready, we were joined by Tobi and Nikki, who agreed that this was the most exciting thing to ever happen in the history of hen dos (including that time they went on a pub-crawl in Whitechapel, where they all had to dress like famous serial killers and had bumped into the sister of one of the victims – she'd thrown a pint over her head), but laughed in our faces at the notion that just because Carla and Val had had a snog and a grope in a club, it meant this was to be the start of a relationship. Before we could start arguing, there was a rap at the door; Imogen poked her head round a second later.

'Morning, morning!' she trilled. Her hair was in buns either side of her head and she was already fully dressed and made up. 'Just letting you know it's five to nine and if you look on the schedule we emailed and WhatsApped and printed out for everyone, we've got a lovely big breakfast together planned for nine, so …' She trailed off, but every woman in the room understood that she meant one thing: BE DOWNSTAIRS IN FIVE MINUTES OR FACE THE CONSEQUENCES. Nikki and I exchanged a look.

'No problem, Gin, we'll be down in a second!' Penny said beamingly. Imogen simpered and closed the door gently behind her. Penny's face dropped the second she did.

'For fuck's sake!' she muttered to Tobi, who grinned wickedly.

'Ten quid to the first person to make one of the bridesmaids cry!' she called over her shoulder as she left.

'Twenty quid to the first person to punch one of them in the tits!' Nikki added, following her wife.

'Bold of you to assume I won't do it for free, darlings!' Penny said, turning to me. 'Come on, let's go.'

'What happened to "Oh, it'll be so *lovely*, so *wonderful* and *great*"?' I said quietly as we picked our way downstairs.

'I forgot how much I hate people,' she muttered, pushing open the kitchen door and breaking into her best smile. 'Morning, ladies! How are we all today?'

Strict adherence to The Schedule was very much the theme of the day. After a breakfast of pancakes, pastries and 11 different types of tea, we climbed into taxis for 10am and by 11am, we were at our first activity: personalised skincare treatments (i.e. putting drops of essential oil into cocoa butter) and giving each other facials in a basement room beneath a McDonald's. I was paired with Frankie and tried not to laugh as I sensually rubbed her face and she enthusiastically waggled her eyebrows at Carla and Val, who had their faces far closer together than was entirely practical. Afterwards, ravenous from the smell, we all got a portion of McFries and ate them by the fistful in the street while Bett, Abi and Imogen stared at us with hate in their eyes.

At 1pm we were in the knicker decorating class. Everyone whooped with laughter as they made the rudest pants they could (Penny spelt out 'Viva La Vulva' on the front in pink sequins) and felt vaguely ashamed when, at the end, we realised Janae and Emily had quietly made each other comfy cotton shorts with cute animal patches on the front. Then, at 2.30pm, it was time for fancy afternoon tea – I was impressed and slightly embarrassed by Hannah calling for more and more sandwiches, then demanding they pack up all our leftovers so we could take them home – and onto the Taylor Swift dance class for 5pm.

Janae, despite her incredibly cool shell, fucking *loves* Taylor Swift, and for the first time that weekend, her entire face lit up as she bounced around with her friends to 'Shake It Off' and taught the instructor how to twerk properly. I hung around at the back and tried to be as unobtrusive as possible, secretly relieved when Andy started throwing up her fancy cakes and needed to be looked after.

By 7pm, I was exhausted. Not physically (I'd managed to get away with about ten minutes of half-heartened dancing and spent the next 30 rubbing Andy's back and going, 'Oh, you poor thing!') but mentally, emotionally, spiritually, giving-a-fuckally, whatever. I hated everyone there, I hated Bath. I hated weddings. I hated love. And, mostly, I hated myself. Everyone had bonded throughout the day – especially Carla and Val – but I just wanted to be alone. Turns out, it's incredibly hard to be alone at a hen do; there are 21 other women there who'll come and find you and try to wheedle whatever is wrong out of you with sympathetic words and head-tilts.

Damn women, I thought as I squeezed to my spot round the back of the table of the Italian restaurant where we were having dinner. *Damn them and their empathy.* Why couldn't I be surrounded by *men*, nice, emotionally stunted men who wouldn't ask me what was wrong even if I slit my throat with a pizza wheel in front of them? I sat down with Penny on one side, Frankie on the other. They had no problem joining in the conversations around them and so, for a while, I was safe to just listen.

'Has he ever actually said he fancies you?' Frankie was asking Imogen as they divided their shared gluten-free, dairy-free vegetarian pizza. Basically, a dust patty with tomato puree smeared on top, but they seemed to be enjoying it.

'No, but whenever we're at the pub after work he, like, always, like, always goes straight for me,' Imogen said. 'And he's nice to me. He's always watching my Instagram Stories. But he says he goes on Instagram when he's on the toilet, so I dunno if that's a good sign or not.'

'But there's never been any obvious signs he wants to shag you?' Frankie asked.

'Oh, I mean, we fucked once,' Imogen said casually as Frankie choked. 'But it was after he'd landed a big client so I dunno if it was more a *testosterone* thing, and he only came after he covered my face with a pillow ...'

'... I quite enjoy occasionally eating an entire pizza and then having terrible shits afterwards,' Katie said thoughtfully. 'Like, diarrhaeoy. It feels like I'm eating something for "free", and being cleansed afterwards.' She looked at me and Penny and went pink. 'Which, now I think about it, sounds a bit eating disordery.'

No shit, Sherlock.

'It's fine,' Frankie interrupted. 'I've done the same with Senokot before. If I don't feel properly empty, I always feel really sick. It's why I stopped eating gluten. I'm trying to cut out dairy, too, but I really love flat whites and soy milk tastes like jizz.'

Katie nodded.

'I feel so *guilty* about wanting to do all this – like, I'm being a bad feminist. But then I feel so guilty if I eat anything bad, too. God, it's so complicated, isn't it?'

'It is,' I chimed in. Now *this* is a conversation I can contribute to. 'I'm finding it *so hard* to figure out how to eat. I can't remember the last time I ate something without feeling proud of myself because it was healthy, or guilty because it wasn't, or like I was making a *big statement* by having a sandwich for lunch.' More people were listening to this conversation now and nodding encouragingly. Emboldened, I ploughed on. 'Sometimes, I wish I could be hit by a truck or a bus or something. Not so that I'd die, but just so I go into a coma and have to spend, like, six months lying in bed being fed by a tube. Think of all the *weight* I'd lose – and I wouldn't have to put any effort into it at all!' I looked around triumphantly and saw everyone's dismayed faces.

Oh, okay. Maybe that wasn't the right thing to say at all.

As Penny jumped to my rescue and started talking enthusiastically about how learning judo improved her relationship with her body, I stared hard at my plate so that I didn't cry, shoving forkfuls of carbonara in my face to try and smother the sick feeling of humiliation. I felt like ridiculous, stupid, embarrassing *trash*.

At 8.25pm, Bett forced us all out on the street and into taxis. By 9.15pm, we were back in the barn and in front of the big TV in the living room. We draped ourselves over each other, and with duvets, pillows and blankets, and loaded ourselves up with cocktails, popcorn and Bakewell Slices. Bett had gone to put on *When Harry Met Sally*, but Ashley had wrestled the remote from her and put on *But I'm A Cheerleader* instead. Half the group – let's be honest, the straight women – had sulked for a bit, but when RuPaul appeared on screen, they brightened up considerably. There is apparently nothing straight women love more and lesbians know more *about* than *RuPaul's Drag Race*. Within moments of his appearance on screen they were screaming, 'Go back to party city, where you belong,' and 'BACK ROLLS!?' at each other. Janae, Abi and Bett started doing impressions of their favourite queens, bouncing off each other with a practised rapport that I wish, I wish, I *wish*, I had with my siblings. I tried to laugh in the right places, and squeezed my hand into a fist so tight my nails made little indents in my palm.

For most of the rest of the evening I kept quiet. We played a game of Ms. and Ms., which fortunately ended up without anyone crying. Penny had been to a hen party recently where the groom, who gave his answers via a prerecorded video, hadn't gotten *any* of the answers right. The bride had burst into tears, stormed off to call him, and became hysterical when she couldn't get hold of him. She was convinced he was having sex with another woman while she was away and so had accessed their Pet Cam to spy on him. Unfortunately, he had smeared peanut butter all over his feet and was wanking merrily while their Weimaraner puppy licked it off. They didn't get married after that, surprisingly.

Anyway, after Ms. and Ms. we played Werewolf, which I am amazing at (a bonus of constantly having to exist in normal society when suicidally depressed is you become an excellent liar) and Pictionary, which I'm terrible at. And, because it's a hen do, both became drinking games: we had to take a shot every time we got killed or caught in Werewolf, or we lost a round in Pictionary. Soon, the room was pleasantly fuzzy. I laughed and teased and joined in with everyone else as best I could, but something kept nipping at my ears and whispering to me: because I'd shown I could lie, everyone hated me. Because

I hadn't managed to guess *The Sisterhood of the Travelling Pants*, everyone thought I was stupid. *Untrustworthy and stupid, as well as ugly and fat and unlovable.* Why are you even here? No one wants you here. Janae only asked you because she felt sorry for you. Janae is so good, she doesn't deserve shit like you in her life. God, you're DISGUSTING.

Fighting with my brain was taking up most of my energy and I was painfully aware that I was *not* being very good value. No matter how many encouraging smiles I got from Penny, Frankie, Janae, Emily and even Hannah and Nikki, who'd figured out at some point between my crying-in-the-toilet breaks and my announcing over dinner that I wished I could be put in a coma for a few months so I could lose a couple of stone that I was a bit mental, I still couldn't help obsessing.

I am awful. No one likes me. I don't deserve to be here.

As midnight approached, the mood turned sombre. We were still in the living room, which was entirely dark apart from the glow of *The Great British Bake Off* on mute on the enormous TV. Janae and Emily were twisted together like headphone wires in a big squashy armchair, Carla and Val were at other ends of the room but kept glancing at each other and I was wrapped in a blanket, sitting against the wall, my head on Penny's shoulder.

'I've got an idea,' Abi slurred. 'Why don't we all go round – bleurp! Sorry, little burp! – and give them advice for a happy marriage?'

'We don't need advice, Abs,' Janae said, smiling and closing her beautiful big eyes sleepily. 'I love her, she loves me. We're gonna be fine.' Everyone around the room aww'ed as she and Emily kissed, and I felt a sickening twist of envy.

'But even Anna … Anna … Annana Faris and Chris Pratt split up,' Imo said, nodding sagely. 'S'best to be prepared, right?' There were murmurs of agreement and the couple shrugged sagely.

'Go on then,' Emily said, settling her head on Janae's. 'Advise us.'

'I'll go first,' said Hannah, sitting up. 'My advice is, forgive quickly, because otherwise you're going to argue all the time. *Allllll* the time. Forgive the idiot, move on, and you'll be much happier.'

'And respect each other,' Bo added quickly. 'My mum told me on the morning of my wedding' – and here, she slipped easily into a strong Ghanian accent – '"Bo, child, respect your husband even if he don't earn it from you. Give it to him, and it'll make him want to deserve it."' She shook her head. 'I told Ike he better respect my ass and if he do, I'll respect his. It's worked out great so far.'

'Really? Because only last week you were telling me Ike was a piece of shit and you wished you'd never married him,' Hannah said coldly.

'You sure that wasn't you telling me that Stan hasn't made you come in ten months, eh?'

'My advice,' said Katie brightly, interrupting them both. 'Is never to go to bed angry. My parents always say that, and it's working out great for them.'

'Your parents are basic bitches,' Frankie muttered in my ear.

We went around the room. The advice varied *massively*, from 'Always keep a regular date night' to 'Make sure neither of you has a nut allergy before spreading Nutella on your tits'. Frankie's advice was to be honest, because a relationship is a team and you'll only work well together if you know what you're up against, while Penny quoted Nick Offerman, who said that his excellent relationship with Megan Mullally was because they 'enjoy engaging in humour, jigsaw puzzles and a regular diet of each other's genitalia'. As we all screamed with laughter, Val raised a single eyebrow across the room at Carla, who turned pink.

'And what about you, Amy?' Imogen said, finally. 'How do you and Garry keep your relationship good?'

How do we keep our relationship good? *Was* our relationship good? I loved him, but as I pretended to think, I was actually looking at Janae, who was stroking Emily's hair as Emily snoozed on her, and at Val, who was looking at Carla like she wanted to eat her; we didn't have a relationship like either of them and aren't they the goal? *Maybe our relationship was actually shit, and I just hadn't realised.*

Everyone was still looking at me. This wasn't the time or the place to start having a meltdown. I swallowed, and looked Janae straight in the eye.

'I don't think I need to tell you about mine and Garry's relationship to give you advice,' I said quietly. 'Besides, you know all of it anyway. I think I can give you better advice by saying this: be you, just be you. Brilliant, kind, thoughtful you. You've meant so much to me these past few years, and you've been such an amazing friend and ...' I swallowed again, emotion rising up my throat like a snake. '... and if you bring the love, patience and support you've given me to your relationship with Emily, she'll be a lucky woman. Just ... just keep being you, and you'll be fine.'

'Awwww, babes!' Janae said. 'That's so sweet!'

'So sweet, so sweet ...' Abi said, nodding in a drunken haze. Lisa swallowed hard and dinged a cake fork against her wine glass.

'Leshsav a toast!' she slurred, raising her glass in the air. 'To Emily and Janae!'

'To Emily and Janae!' everyone repeated, clinking glasses. We sat in companionable silence, watching Paul and Mary scrape the bottom of tarts with forks, perfectly content to not say anything and to let the moment rest.

'SHIT!' Imogen squeaked, leaping up and dashing for the kitchen. 'I forgot! We have one more Hen Party game I forgot to do – Nail Polish or Porn Film?'

Everyone wobbled to their feet and sat around the big table, still wrapped in blankets and duvets. I waited until the game was well underway, Imogen reading out phrases and everyone around the table voting on whether they thought it was the title of a porn film or the name of a nail polish (Orgasm, Half Past Nude and Lose your Lingerie were nail polish, Precious Pink was porn, as was On Golden Blonde, and, unsurprisingly, Riding Miss Daisy) and slipped quietly upstairs.

What's wrong with me? I thought as I lay in bed, looking at the stars out of the window. *I'm on a hen do with 21 women who are, if not lovely, at least normal human beings, who are managing to laugh and drink and hold conversations without resorting to panic and mild self-hate. Why can't I do that? Why am I spending this lovely, beautiful, perfectly planned weekend feeling miserable? Especially when not a single thing has happened to make me feel bad.* Everyone was being lovely to me. The worst I'd had to endure since I got to Paddington was a slightly awkward silence, and at this point, awkward silences are a big part of my personal brand.

So, why do I feel like this? Why am I like this? And, most importantly, *why can't I fix it?* I've been through therapy, I've read the self-help books and the mental health memoirs, watched the TED Talks, read and retweeted all the brutally honest blog posts and articles about how it feels to be an introverted, modern woman. Nothing has changed. What else can I do? I'm trapped here, trapped in this life and these feelings and this stupid *self*. Christ, I hate myself. I hate myself. *I hate myself.*

The booze that had made me so warm and sleepy a few hours ago was making me maudlin and brooding now. I shivered, although I wasn't cold – it was more the chill in my feelings than the one in the air. The problem with thinking like this – apart from the obvious – is that these thoughts are gateway drugs to harder feelings. To get wanky about it, they're like draughts in the ramshackle hut that is my brain: stiff, cold breezes which sneak into every corner, rattle the windows and blow the doors open to let even more cold air in. And when those doors open? All bets are off.

The next morning, eating another huge breakfast around the table, I looked at every other woman there and thought about out how fat/ugly/badly dressed and/or badly put together I was compared to them. When we went for a brisk walk in the countryside around the barn, chatting about what we had coming up at work in the week ahead, I thought about how they were all earning enough to buy their homes and go on holiday and think nothing of buying themselves a new dress or an £11 cocktail. I felt an acidic stab of loathing for my pathetic, miserable job and how little money, respect and success I had. And then my thoughts came faster, harder, sharper, uglier. Every time I spoke to someone, I was comparing myself to them.

Why wasn't I as beautiful as Penny? Why wasn't I as fit as Frankie? Why wasn't I as talented as Janae, or as clever as Emily? Why wasn't I pregnant like Hannah? Why wasn't I buying a flat like Tobi and Nikki? Why wasn't I as stylish as Imogen? Why wasn't my hair as good as Val's? Why was I failing in every single way I could? Why weren't my lists enough any more? *What's wrong with me?* And every time, every time, *every single time*, the answer was the same: because you're *bad*. I am bad. I'm bad, I'm bad, I'm so crap, I'm sosososososoo fucking *bad*. Why was I just *so fucking bad* at things? Bad at work, bad at relationships, bad at being a woman, just so *fucking bad at being alive*.

It was like a wheel, or a spinning top, or a child going downhill on a bike with no brakes. My thoughts came faster and faster, tears kept lurching behind my eyes, my throat burned. I was talking normally on the outside, posing for selfies, smiling, laughing at jokes, but inside I was a tornado, a volcano, a whirlpool, a black hole where a worthwhile person should be. My thoughts and emotions raged inside me until I felt like I was going to burst: as soon as I got a free second, I left the barn, walked until I was down the road and no one could see me, and then I ran.

I didn't need to go far – I just wanted to get away, get away from the perfect women taunting me with their happy lives and their beautiful faces and bodies and brains. Within five minutes of running, I was out of breath. I could see a lake we'd seen on the walk earlier but not gone near because it was off the main path. Without thinking, I forced my way through a gap in the hedges and started walking towards it.

This was a nice little patch of countryside, I thought in a crystal-clear haze as the lake got nearer and nearer. My brain was firing in a million directions now and I couldn't stop it even if I wanted to: my body might have been a black hole but my mind was a firework, a supernova, an exploding star, a force no To-Do List could even *hope* to control. The field. It was nice! And quiet! *So blissfully fucking quiet.* No chatting, no laughing, nothing to compare myself to, nothing to hate myself for. Just trees and grass and mud, and a big-ass lake of grey water which stretched so far it would have taken me another five minutes of running to go all the way round it. But no, I didn't. My desire to run had been for escape, not exercise, to escape the pressure and the anxiety and the context of the rest of the world showing me that I was bad, I was wrong, I was *bad bad badbadbadbadbad*. And I'd done that now: I was alone. *Blissfully alone.* I collapsed on a bench by the lake and, without any effort on my part to encourage or stop it, the entire force of my emotions exploded at once out of my face.

I'm a good crier, I think. I get a lot of practice. I cry at everything from Welsh male voice choirs to that bit at the end of *The Incredibles* when Violet saves her family and Elastigirl says, 'That's my girl!' But this was a new level of crying. My body crumpled into itself, forehead on my knees, fingers digging into my shins. My toes clung to the bottom of my shoes in white-knuckle determination. I sobbed. Snot and tears streamed into my mouth, and dribbled back out again. I shook with it, sweated with it, screwed myself up with it, and tried to stay afloat in a sea of unbearable pain – pain that, even as I buckled under it, even as it ravaged me, made me hate myself more because it was all in my own, stupid fucking head. How I moaned and wailed and screamed. Then, scared people would come. I bit my fist to stop myself making a noise. I stopped when I tasted blood and swapped to the other fist. And then my arms. And then my clothes ...

I don't know how long I cried for, but when the storm eventually passed it wasn't because I was done, it was because I didn't have any energy left. I rubbed my fist against my wet, hot, swollen face to wipe away the tears, choking as I tried to breathe normally. When I opened my eyes, I was looking directly at the smooth, pale surface of the lake.

The lake. I stood up, steadying myself on the bench with my wet fingertips. It looked so peaceful and still. I loved being near water when I felt like this – it's why I love swimming so much. No matter how I feel on the outside, when I'm in water, I feel calm. I took a few steps forward, hiccuping gently. My feet slid into the mud on the banks of the water, and I almost slipped. I thought about slipping into the water, about having to head back to the house sopping wet and covered in mud, and everyone staring at me like the stupid, ridiculous *cunt* I was as I explained that I'd gone off on my own and fallen into the lake. Another rush of misery crashed over me and I somehow found enough energy to sob a little more.

I wished I could swim, here. *God, wouldn't that be nice?* The mud was sloppy under my feet, and under my weight, it was moving. I was gently sliding closer to the still, glassy surface of the water. Imagine it. *Imagine if I took my hot, tired body and threw it into the water.* No, I don't want to throw it in. I want it to sink in, slowly, so slowly, so gently, so gradually I don't disturb the perfect surface. I could just gently move into the water until it covered me up and I didn't have to think about the world; didn't have to think about how awful and useless I was because the lake was all there was. I suddenly realised I wasn't breathing and took a deep, shuddering breath, raising my face to the white sky.

I just wanted to be good. To be successful, to keep up, to do everything right. I wanted the Instagram life – the good job, the perfect relationship, the loving family, all the things you're supposed to have in your mid-twenties. I just ... I just wanted to be good. But I *wasn't* good, I was useless and a failure, an embarrassment, and no matter what I tried, it wasn't changing. Living as me was unbearable, but I didn't seem to have any option *but* to be me. So, what should I do? *Maybe the only option was ...*

I thought of Garry. I thought of Penny and Janae and Frankie, of my mum and dad, and Freddy and Taggie and Alice and the twins. But not Andrew. The twat. A single tear slid down my cheek and tickled the end of my nose uncomfortably, but I didn't wipe it away, I just looked at the lake and at my feet, now slid so close to it that the water was stroking the soles of my trainers. I was so hot and so tired. *Maybe I could just lie down, take a few steps forward and lie down.* The cool water would catch me. It would cuddle me close, wrap itself around me, cool my hot face and hands, seep into my eyes and my nose and my mouth, calm my raging chest. As I closed my eyes, I held myself up in the stillness of the air and the water seeping into my socks and the weirdly calm resolution working its way over me. *Is this it? Maybe.* And for the first time in a while, I felt okay. I opened my eyes and looked at the surface of the water.

I breathed.

'AMY!'

I jumped suddenly, losing my balance and taking a step back to regain it. With a squelching noise, my foot wrenched itself out of the mud. I gasped in shock as I registered that I was in muddy lake water up to my knees. Then I fell backwards, my hands landed hard in the mud and soaked my clothes.

'AMY! WHAT THE FUCK ARE YOU DOING?' screamed Frankie. 'I'VE GOT HER, I'VE GOT HER! AMY, STAY THERE, DON'T FUCKING MOVE!'

But I *did* move. Panicked at seeing myself so far in the water, I grabbed onto anything solid I could, rocks and plants and roots, and wrenched myself out, climbing back onto the bank. My feet were numb and it was hard to balance without feeling them. I looked up: it was starting to go dark.

Frankie was with me in seconds. *Huh! All that gym work is really paying off.* Her eyes were wide and red, her nostrils flared. She flung herself at me and squeezed hard.

'Are you okay? What did you do? What were you doing?' She held me at arm's length, putting her phone back to her ear. 'Yeah, we're not far … I'll bring her back, she's okay. No, well, but she is for now. Can you pack her stuff? Shit!' She looked down and noticed the teeth marks on my hands and arms, my sodden shoes, how the water had soaked its way up to my thighs. She started talking rapidly, her eyes not leaving my face. 'She needs a change of clothes. Get a plastic bag, get her some new trousers, long-sleeved top … Keep Janae and Emily in their room, we'll be back soon. Yeah. Okay, bye.' She hung up, shoved the phone in her pocket and pulled me back in.

'You've been gone hours. *Hours*!' she said against my shoulder. She pulled back and stared at me, tears dripping down her face. 'What were you doing, you stupid woman? We were terrified.' She started rubbing my arms. 'You're so cold, so wet! We need to go, we need to get the train. We need to get you warm …'

'I'm sorry,' I said dumbly as Frankie wrapped an arm around my shoulders and started marching me back to the barn. 'I didn't realise it was so … I only went for a walk.'

'Why were you in the water?' she asked.

I didn't answer.

'Why were you in the water, Amy? Fucking tell me! Were you going to do something stupid?'

'What?' I said jovially as we forced our way through the bush back onto the main road. Frankie got a nasty scratch from a branch on her face and I felt a twist of guilt in my stomach. 'With a lake? God, that'd be a bit dramatic, wouldn't it? If I went to a lake to try and … um … To try and … To … to try and …'

I trailed off. Frankie didn't say anything. We walked for 60 seconds more in total silence. Eventually, terrified of what she was thinking, I squeezed her hand. She squeezed it back.

'I'm sorry,' I said quietly.

'Good,' she shot back. '*Do* be sorry. Be so sorry you never, ever, *ever* think of doing something like this again. Fucking hell! It'd destroy Garry. It'd destroy Penny and Janae. It'd destroy …' Her voice cracked and she swallowed hard. 'It'd destroy me. I fucking love you. Don't you *fucking dare*!'

'I'm sorry,' I repeated. Then, more quietly: 'Do Janae and Emily know?'

'No,' she said. We were almost at the barn now; I could see the long driveway we'd first walked down two days ago. 'The Schedule managed to distract them. Don't tell them yet, yeah? But promise me, Amy.' We were at the end of the driveway now. She turned to face me and gripped my upper arms so tightly I'd find her fingermarks on there when I showered later that evening. 'You can't do this alone, and I can't do it for you. Please, just get help. I love you, I love you so much. If you can't do it for you, do it for me. Please, please, *please* get help.'

Get help. I had a lot of help over the next few hours. Penny helped me get out of my wet clothes and into Tobi's leggings and Hannah's skirt, and her trainers. She wore her heels home, joking about being met by paparazzi when Emily questioned it. At the station, Imogen walked next to me, chatting with a determined casualness about what she was going to do with her hair for the wedding. Nikki waited with me in the Starbucks queue on the platform and barged in front of me with her debit card when it came to paying. When the train arrived, Bett, Abi and Imogen cornered Janae and Emily and made them sit with them at one end of the carriage; Penny sat with me at the other end, made sure I had a drink and headphones and some Maltesers, found a plug under the seat so I could charge my phone. Other hens wandered past on the way to the buffet car or the loo and glanced nervously at us. Penny would smile sweetly, but with a steely edge that didn't invite further interaction. And when we got back to Paddington, when we all hugged goodbye and Emily declared she wanted another group selfie, Frankie smacked a big kiss on my cheek so that I could screw my face up in mock-disgust rather than having to fake a smile.

When everyone went their separate ways, Penny took my arm and led me not towards the Tube but the little Pret in the station. Inside, Garry was waiting, two coffee cups on the table in front of him. She hugged me tight, said, 'Text me,' and disappeared. I watched her leave, her blonde hair bobbing away from me, and turned to look at Garry. He gave me a small, sad smile.

'Alright?' he said, nudging the cup across the table towards me.

Was I alright? I slowly sank down in front of him. *Was I alright?* I thought about crying in toilets, about digging my nails into my hands and my wrists, about Adam, about beautiful women in swimming pool changing rooms, about my dad saying, 'I thought you would have written a novel by now,' about my mum not telling me anything because she didn't think I could take it, about Mario screaming 'Woo-hoo! Woo-hoo!', the way I stared at myself in the mirror every morning in order to psych myself up with self-hatred for the day ahead, how I lay in bed at night thinking of everything I'd done wrong that day. I thought about being alone, even when I wasn't; about never ever being good enough, even though I had no evidence to suggest that was true, about feeling unloved even though I clearly was, about hating myself even though nobody else seemed to, about how I desperately wanted to hurt myself, even though everyone else only seemed to want to take care of me. Were these the actions of someone who was, in any way, *alright*?

'No,' I said, quietly. 'Not really.'

He nodded like this was the most normal conversation in the world.

'So,' he said, cocking one corner of his mouth at me, 'what shall we do about it?'

I paused. Living as me was unbearable. I'd tried changing me, but it didn't work. This afternoon had showed me that I couldn't – I just *couldn't* – stop the living bit altogether without hurting people I loved. So maybe I had to change the way I was living, somehow. But I didn't know where to start, and I knew I couldn't do it alone. I took a deep breath, and looked him in the eye.

'Get help,' I said, softly. He didn't say anything, just watched me with gentle, understanding eyes. 'I need to get help.'

'Okay,' he said, leaning back in his chair. He took a big swig of coffee, set the empty cup on the table in front of me and smiled. Cautiously, I smiled back.

'Then let's get you some help.'

TO-DO

☑ Meet Penny at King's Cross

☑ Meet the hens at Paddington

☑ (12.07pm) train to Bath

☑ Unpack

☐ Get superhero costume (try to find one that'll fit me and not make me look like Miss Piggy on Halloween)

☑ Go to The Club

☑☑ ACTUALLY DANCE at The Club !

☑ Don't get too drunk   *God bless pregnant women!* ←

☑ Find a reason to escape before 1am — maybe Hannah?

☑ Communal breakfast

☑ Taxis to Bath, 10am

☑ Skincare treatments, 11am

☑ Knicker decorating, 1pm

☑ Afternoon tea, 2.30pm

☐ Taylor Swift dance class, 5pm

☐ Dinner at (La Italiana,) 7pm

☐ Film time — find out if there are any lesbian equivalents of WHEN HARRY MET SALLY

☐ Hen party games (drinking games edition) 🍺🍺

☐ Communal breakfast #2

☐ Country walk 🌿🌼

☐ Board games

☐ Pedicures

(There is not. Maybe make one? Or is a problematic for a bisexual woman to make a film about lesbians? Add to Future Projects List to investigate)

✓ 18.37pm train to Paddington

✓ Talk to at least three people who aren't Penny, Janae, Frankie and Emily

✓ Do shots, at least once, because you can handle shots and it might trick people into thinking you're cool (Not sure if it gave me cool points as I was distracted by being shit at Pictionary) 😎

☐ Be normal (HahahaahahahahahahaahahahahahahaHA!)

☐ Don't let anyone know you're having a terrible time (I think being found half-submerged in a lake put paid to that idea)

☐ Call the doctor. Get. Help. ➕

SESSION ONE

Every lot of face-to-face therapy I've had has been held in the same kind of room: yellow-beige walls, with an old computer on an MDF desk on one side and two grey, comfortable, functional chairs on the other. There's always a clock on the wall, and always a small table with a box of tissues on it within easy reach. Good tissues, too. The kind that can hold a lot of snot and tears, and can be squeezed into the fist and wound between the fingers over and over without getting frayed.

The first time I was in one of these rooms, it was for a group CBT induction. It was massive – ten comfortable, functional chairs, with ten awkward, malfunctioning humans of all shapes, sizes, ages and genders sitting in them, all being led through exercises designed to keep us alive until we moved to the top of a waiting list. And then when I hit the top of that list, I went to a smaller room in the same building and met my therapist, Olu, a beautiful woman with skin so dark it was almost purple, enormously round brown eyes, and a mischievous nature entirely at odds with our conversations about how I was too scared to leave the house sometimes.

The second lot of therapy I had wasn't in one of those rooms – it was online, via chat boxes, with a woman named Paula, who said things like 'Your mind is a river, and your negative thoughts are like leaves blocking the flow'. I didn't do well with Paula. Olu made me feel like she took my problems seriously, like I was a normal person who could sort themselves out with a bit of steering. Paula made me feel like I'd been cursed, and only the right combination of her well-meaning but entirely empty words would save me. After a few weeks, Paula told me that I wasn't engaged enough with therapy and had dumped me back into the NHS's mental health system. I had cried, quietly to myself, about how I was such a failure, I couldn't even do therapy right.

Janae's hen party convinced me that I needed to try therapy again, but I felt sick with fear as I sat in my third beige room and eyed my third therapist, Bjorg. Already I'd waited seven weeks to get here after Penny had come to my GP with me and made me show the doctor the bite marks on my wrists. I'd started to see this as my last chance. *What if it didn't work again? What if Olu was a fluke and I was going to be stuck like this forever?*

Bjorg's face was unreadable as she read the Patient Health Questionnaire (PHQ) I'd filled in, the one you have to do at the start of each session, which tells the therapist exactly how mad you're feeling that day. She had blonde hair, delicate features and enormous sleepy blue eyes. Why did all my therapists have such fucking enormous eyes?

All the better for seeing into your soul, my dear.

'So,' she said finally, looking up and giving a small, measured smile, 'thank you for coming in.'

'Thank you for, um, seeing me?' I asked.

Fuck! Why did I say that? It's literally her job. Twat. TWAT.

'It's not a problem,' she said placidly. 'Now, I've read through your questionnaire ...' *Oh God, oh God, oh God, oh God, oh God.* '... and I can see a few obvious things for us to work on. It looks like on a daily basis you're feeling anxious, your mood is low, you're finding it difficult to enjoy things, you're easily irritated, and you're having trouble relaxing.'

I felt myself shrivel with shame as she spoke, but she was doing that therapist thing of talking about my horrible, private, personal secrets as though discussing the weather. It was weirdly reassuring. Like, no matter how awful I felt things were in my head, she'd seen it all before and would be entirely unfazed by anything I unleashed.

'You say you are currently self-harming daily –' I clenched my fingers into fists, digging my nails in the soft flesh of my palms. '– and think about ending your life in some way at least once a day,' she said mildly, turning over the sheet of A4. She glanced up. 'Do you have any intention of acting upon those thoughts?'

I shook my head. 'No. I can't do that to my friends, my husband, my parents, so I have to keep … I mean, not have to, it's, um, it's a good thing? Yes. I mean, uh, yes, I have to keep going.' I coughed. 'For … for them.'

'Okay,' she said, just as mildly. 'You know, you don't have to say it's a good thing if you don't think it's a good thing.' Pause. 'Do you think it's a good thing?'

'Well …' I squirmed internally. Christ, I was tense. My entire body was taut, like a horse about to bolt or the string of a bow before an arrow goes flying. 'I know, like, rationally, it's a good thing, but it doesn't really help when I feel overwhelmed. I feel trapped, and like there's no escape.'

She nodded again, looking at me thoughtfully. 'What do you feel overwhelmed by?'

'By how awful I feel.' My voice caught, I swallowed hard. 'I just feel hopeless, like I'm going to be stuck in this brain and this body, and this stupid, shitty life forever.'

'You think your life is stupid and, uh, "shitty"?' she asked curiously. No derision or pity in her voice, she was just interested.

I shook my head tightly and looked back at my clenched fists. 'No, that's the thing. I know, um, rationally, it's not? I know I'm fine. I know my life is fine. It's good, in fact! Good job, good friends, good flat, good husband …' I stared at her desperately, willing her to understand. She didn't look away. 'And I feel so guilty, like, I hate myself for feeling like this. Other people have much worse problems than me, and they don't feel like this.'

'That you know of,' she said, kindly.

'Well, if they feel like this, they … they cope. I don't cope. I hate myself so much that I bounce back and forth between feeling nothing and feeling everything, and I can't do it any more. I just can't do it any more.'

Fuck. I had wanted to spend this first session in control, and I was failing spectacularly. I gripped the seat of the chair and squeezed hard.

'Huh. Okay, then,' Bjorg said, leaning back in her chair. 'So, what do you hate about yourself?'

'Everything,' I said quietly. 'I hate my body. I hate my personality. I hate how I feel and how I think, how scared I am of everything. I hate how useless I am. I hate how my friends are all better than me, and how I'm rubbish compared to everyone. I hate that I'm not as good as I should be, and no matter what I do to try and keep up, no matter how many To-Do Lists I make to make sure I'm keeping up, I can't, and no matter how hard I try to be perfect, I always –' *Don't swear, don't swear, don't swear* … ' – I always fuck up in some way.' *Fucksticks!* I glance at her to see if she minds the swearing; she doesn't seem to.

'No one is perfect,' Bjorg said mildly.

'I know, I know. But I can't … I can forgive everyone else for not being perfect, but I still feel like *I* should be.' I gesture at myself, helplessly. 'I can't be perfect, and I hate myself for it. I hate myself for it.'

'Okay,' she said again. 'Okay, there's definitely a lot to work with here. Just one last thing: what do you want to get from these sessions?'

What a question! The truth was, I wanted to get better but I didn't think there was a 'better' any more. I thought I'd been 'better' after Olu, but everything had gone wrong again. So, if I couldn't get 'better', what *did* I want?

I thought about the last few months; about being with the friends I love most, and the heavy self-hatred that followed. I thought of laps in the pool, and the disgust I felt for my body afterwards. I thought of going to work and drowning in inadequacy. I thought of feeling awkward and ill at ease with the people I'm supposed to feel at home with. I thought of my good, strong marriage and the feelings of despair that had rotted its edges. I thought of my life, of my good, happy life, and how no matter how hard I tried, it felt absolutely intolerable.

'I just want for things not to be shit,' I said, eventually. 'I just want to be able to go about my life and not feel like everything is awful because my stupid, broken brain is telling me that's the case. I just need to be able to enjoy my life, a little bit. I just want to live and for it not to feel terrible, and exhausting, and impossible, all the … all the fucking time.'

She nodded, like this was an entirely normal thing to say.

'Okay,' she said brightly, and gave me a small, kind smile. After a moment, I smiled back. Just a little. She'd not said more than 50 words to me during our entire interaction so far, but I felt safe. It was scary to put the smoking, steaming wreck of my brain into her hands, but for some reason I trusted her with it.

'Okay. That, I think, we can do.'

TO-DO

☐ Janae's wedding: 1pm, Curtain Warehouse

☐ Reception, straight after: Curtain Warehouse

☐ Hair (half-up, half-down; show off cute pixie ears but hide weird jawline and double chin)

☐ Make-up (matte, pink lips, cat eyeliner)

☐ Buy cotton buds (to help with removal of inevitably crap eyeliner)

☐ Wear in shoes w/socks around house before wedding to avoid blisters

☐ Practise easy dance moves so don't embarrass self

☐ Write down list of worries about the wedding to get them out of head

☐ Check on venue website to see if loos are private in case of emergency crying

☐ Leave @ noon to get to wedding

ELEVEN

I have been to precisely five weddings in my life. Two of them I can't really remember: I was a bridesmaid at Freddy's and Andrew's weddings, but I was five for one, 12 for the other. The only memory I have of Freddy's is via photos of me in a floofy lilac dress with wide, confused eyes, and how I threw a tantrum when we had to leave but was asleep before we left the car park. What I mainly remember about Andrew's is that I'd just read *Bridget Jones* and was insistent on wearing white tights because *she* wore them as a bridesmaid, not realising the white tights were supposed to be godawful. That's the problem with reading satire too young, the jokes go right over your head. It's only recently that I realised Adrian Mole *wasn't* an intellectual, and I *swear* my misconception about the poetic merit of 'The Tap' is the reason that, to this day, I can't appreciate poetry.

Anyway … Next up was Penny's wedding. She got married in the church she'd been christened in, in the village she'd grown up in, where her parents lived, and the reception was in a barn so full of candles, I'm not entirely sure how they got it past Health and Safety. Ten months after came Laxmi's wedding, back up in the Midlands: a beautiful, secular ceremony and three-course meal full of white roses and classical music in the day, followed by an enormous Indian dance party in the evening. Have you ever watched an 81-year-old white woman who has never been out of Solihull attempt bhangra dancing with a beautiful young man with eyelashes so long, he blew the chairs over every time he blinked? Because I have. It's *brilliant*.

And the final wedding, sandwiched almost perfectly equally between Penny's and Laxmi's, was my own. Once I'd gotten past the crippling fear that everyone would think it was shit compared to my beautiful friends', I'd had a great time. Basically, your wedding day is the one day of your life people *have* to be nice to you, partly because you've paid for their dinner and partly because if they're not, you have two sets of families and an entire bridal party who'll beat them up. It's amazing how much the guarantee of a drama-free day can relax me, and apart from a 45-minute period where I wandered the venue like a ghost, asking everyone if they were having a good time, I was entirely *un*-mental all day.

Janae and Emily's wedding was not, I feared, to be quite so drama-free. Sitting on the bus to the ceremony with Garry, I was so nervous not even the double layer of support tights and Spanx I was wearing were enough to squash the sick feeling in my stomach. Garry glanced across, saw my frozen face, and squeezed my hand.

'You okay?' he asked quietly. I nodded, paused, then shook my head. 'What's going on?'

'I haven't seen anyone from the hen apart from Penny, Janae and Frankie since that weekend,' I replied, resting my forehead against his temple and whispering in his ear. 'They're all going to think I'm insane.'

'No, they won't.'

'They will. And it's fine, they're right, I'm bonkers, but I don't want them to judge me for it.'

'No one's judging you for anything, except you,' Garry said gently, squeezing my hand again. 'It'll be fine, don't worry.'

Don't worry? Oh, you know, no one has ever told me to just not worry before! I'd never thought of it that way. What do you know, Garry? I'm fixed, no more anxiety for me! I thought furiously, then immediately felt terrible for being such a dick. I know he's just trying to be kind, and it's not his fault that he doesn't know what to say in the way that Bjorg, my therapist, would. But also, *why* isn't he a qualified shrink who knows exactly what to say, no matter what my mood is? It's not *fair!*

Walking towards the warehouse where Janae and Emily were getting married, we spotted a few more people, clearly on their way to the wedding, and the nerves started bubbling more viciously. I hadn't really been out much for the past four months; I figured being found halfway through becoming a bargain bucket Virginia Woolf was as good an excuse as any to hibernate, so apart from work and the occasional coffee with Penny or Frankie, I hadn't really seen anyone or done anything. I'd thought a social event where the focus would be on someone else would be a good re-introduction to the world, but as we found our seats in the ceremony room I realised that the wedding was going to surround me with people who'd know, either first-hand or through gossip, what a nutcase I was.

My stomach lurched ominously. I left Garry to guard our seats, found the bathrooms, wrestled out of my many layers of finery, did the first of what would eventually be many nervous, slightly squitty poos, and tried not to meet the eyes of the traumatised-looking elderly woman next to me as I washed my hands.

'Congratulations on your niece's wedding, dear. Lovely day for it, isn't it?'

When I got back, Penny and Oliver were sitting in the seats directly behind Garry and I. Penny looked beautiful in a blue floral dress and enormous matching fascinator, her hair in some kind of long plait, like a sexy version of Elsa from *Frozen*. She hugged me tightly and held me arm's length, searching my face questioningly.

'How are you doing, my darling?' she asked.

'I'm okay,' I said, trying for a smile. She raised her eyebrows. 'I am! Promise.'

'Good,' she said, giving me a little squeeze. 'I'm so glad you came.'

'Hello, love,' Oliver said, kissing me on the cheek and beaming. 'Good to see you.' Roughly translated as 'I'm sorry you went mad, I am here for you but don't really know what to say without making things really awkward' in the language of the male romantic partner of your best friend. I beamed at him. After the complicated feelings of love, guilt and gratitude I had for everyone close to me, it was nice to feel pure, uncomplicated affection for someone.

The room was filling up. Emily's Irish Catholic family – the ones not too scandalised by the idea of a lesbian wedding, at least – were all in big hats and suits and carefully modest pastel dresses. Janae's side, meanwhile, were gorgeously colourful in a rainbow of traditional Nigerian outfits and fabulously bright dresses. Frankie was wearing a bright red bodycon dress and matching lipstick, her tiny afro highlighting incredible cheekbones and drawing admiring glances from men and women alike. Then came the brides' friends, most of whom were queer: there were sharp velvet suits on the men, the women *and* the otherwise defined, androgynous haircuts, more like art than hair, dramatic eye make-up, and a *lot* of glitter. Finally, Emily's lawyer friends from work: well-put-together men and women in whatever was in Zara/Ted Baker that season, eyeing the smorgasbord of diversity around them with a mix of suspicion and longing. As a congregation we looked like nothing more than a United Colours of Benetton advert. It was perfect.

The music swelled, and everyone stood up. 'At Last' by Etta James played on the speakers, and the bridesmaids came down the aisle, each carrying bouquets of pink roses and violets. Bett was freely weeping, Abi had matched her lipstick to the roses and was pouting and tilting her head to better show off her jawline, and Imogen looked, as always, like she wasn't entirely sure what planet she was on, but was happy about it nevertheless. And then, Janae and Emily appeared, holding hands and beaming, to a collective sigh at how lovely they both looked.

Emily was in a fifties dress of cream lace, violets twisted round the plaits in her gingery hair and a matching violet sash at her waist. Janae, meanwhile, had done her hair in purple crochet braids a few weeks ago; these were now twisted into an enormous bun on top of her head. She was wearing a black, shapeless dress that would have made me look like a 4x4 but looked *incredibly* elegant on her, with intricate patterns of gold sequins on the shoulders and a matching flick of gold liquid eyeliner.

I pressed my lips together, willing myself not to cry at how beautiful Janae was. I'd been shopping with her for the dress, obviously, and enthusiastically agreed with her decision to buy it, but the last time I'd seen her in it, she wasn't glowing with joy and love, her eyes soft whenever they rested on her bride's face, her smile wider than I'd ever seen. She spotted us and grinned, and I grinned back, a delighted laugh bubbling out of me even as happy tears dribbled down my face. Garry squeezed my waist; I put my hand on his and squeezed back. *God, I love love! Isn't it the best?*

The ceremony was lovely – they'd done the admin bit the day before and a celebrant was doing *this* ceremony, so it was full of personal details and charmingly free of religious and/ or legal bollocks. When the celebrant introduced the new Mrs and Mrs Watts (Janae had taken Emily's name) and they kissed, we all whooped and cheered, and filmed them dancing out of the room together to Ani DiFranco's 'If It Isn't Her'. The bridal party followed (Bett now physically supported by Abi and Imogen because she was crying so hard), and we started milling out behind them.

'Well, that was lovely,' Frankie said, beaming and trying to wipe away tears without smudging her mascara.

'They're such a great couple,' I said feelingly. Garry glanced over; I smiled reassuringly and followed the crowd out to the reception area, not knowing if I could put into words how I was feeling or keep it together even if I did.

Do you ever get it where something is so lovely or so happy, it makes you feel sad? In the warm glow of your joy there's a cold, painful spot you can't ignore, a place in your chest that feels the beauty so intensely it's almost unbearable. Is this normal, or am I a psychopath? Because I get it all the time. I see friends laughing together on a bus or across a cafe, and I feel a sharp pang in my heart. Someone I truly like and respect raves with delight about their job, or kisses their sleeping baby's forehead, or posts smiling photos of themselves in the flat they've just bought with their partner, and I feel a bit sick. And I look at Janae and Emily, look at them hugging their family and their friends and bursting with joy, so in love that the very air around them is shining with it, and it's so beautiful, all I want to do is cry.

It's not that I don't want them to be happy. I really, honestly do. I just wish I could be that happy, too. So often I feel like the true delights of being alive – those feelings of pure happiness, the moments of connection with others, loving something so deeply and knowing for certain you're being loved in return – are out of my reach, now. I'm not good enough to get them, and even if I was, I don't think I could appreciate them properly any more. The worst part about my depression isn't how it makes me feel when I'm sad, but how it makes me feel when I'm happy, how it's numbed the corners of my emotions and made my feelings foggy when they were once crystal clear. I'm not sad that others get to experience joy, I just wish that I believed, even for a second, I'd get to feel it as well.

But then … I glanced over my shoulder at Garry, who was laughing at something Penny had just said. I loved him so much I could drown in it. How could I feel this any more intensely? How could I love him any more? How much of my worries about not being able to connect with people are justified, and how many are in my head? Maybe I'm not numbed to the world. Maybe I'm so worried that I'm missing out on things, that I'm becoming a self-fulfilling prophecy – spending so much time worrying that I'm not feeling things enough that the edge gets taken off the good in my life anyway.

'COME HERE, YOU EXCELLENT WOMEN!' Frankie screamed from behind, making me jump. She launched herself at Janae and Emily, who grabbed her and screamed back, rocking back and forth in joy. Penny and I rushed up to join in, wrapping our arms around them all, squealing, and congratulating them for doing the seemingly impossible task of finding someone to love in a way that makes you happy rather than miserable, stuck on the sofa, eating garlic dough balls and refreshing Instagram to see if they're with that *twat* Charlie again tonight.

'Show us the rings!' Penny said. The brides raised their hands in unison to display delicate rose-gold twists, and we cooed in appreciation.

'Emily's mum picked them – they're Irish gold, just like she is,' Janae said, kissing Emily on the cheek and wiping off the lipstick mark. We aww'ed anew. 'I can't believe I'm bloody married. Married! It's so grown-up.'

'Yup, and everything just gets worse from here,' Penny deadpanned. 'We would have told you, but the Secret Marriage Alliance swore us to secrecy. There'll be no more wild sex sessions. It's twice a week, now, with the lights off, one perfectly satisfactory orgasm each before you get into your PJs and watch *Newsnight* together. Weekends won't be spent at exhibitions or going clubbing, you'll be down IKEA, coming back and building a wardrobe, then cooking a roast and pruning your rose bushes. And unfortunately . . .' she said, her composure breaking as she started to giggle, 'that last bit's not even a euphemism.'

'We're gay, Pen! Going to IKEA and building furniture is, like, our ideal weekend,' Janae snorted. Emily, who hadn't seen me since the hen, had caught my eye and was holding it for a little longer than was normal, smiling softly at me and searching my face. I smiled back, my stomach dropping out from underneath me. *Shit . . . Shit!* So much for the attention not being on me being enough to distract people from my mental state, even the bloody bride was thinking about me being mad.

So, wait – does that mean everyone was thinking about it? I drifted back to Garry, letting his and Oliver's conversation about Assassin's Creed wash over me as I searched the room for people I recognised. Bett was still crying and wasn't Abi watching me over her shoulder as she comforted her? Nikki and Tobi came over to say hi, but their voices were just a little too bright, their heads just a *little* too tilted to be entirely natural. *Oh, no. Oh no, oh no, oh no!*

People, in the main, are awful. Like, genuinely awful. Especially when they're drunk or high. They've got stupid opinions and wear stupid clothes, and do boring, stupid things with their boring, stupid lives. Apart from my friends, obviously, who are all wonderful angels and I hate myself for not being as good as them and for forcing them, in all their perfect goodness, to hang out with me. These two facts are linked, actually – I realised recently that the reason I'm so effusive and overly loving to my friends is that I think 90 per cent of people are fucking awful, so when I find someone I like, I'm so grateful to them for not being a cunt that I go a bit overboard. Anyway, the point is, these awful people all know what an enormous fruitloop I am, and what are they going to do with that information? Are they all going to circle me and point and laugh? Will they blank me every time I start a conversation in case whatever mental thing I've got going on is catching? Big crowds are hard enough, but when they've got ammunition to use against you there's no telling what they can do.

On my way to the loo for another nervous poo, I brushed past a group which included Bo and Ashley and heard someone say, 'a lake, for *hours*, yeah, nobody knew.' I flushed red and hurried past, locking myself in the stall and pressing my hot palms against my cold face and making involuntary mooing sounds of misery. Everyone knows. Everyone *knows*. *Oh God, this is bad. This is so, so bad!*

After ten minutes, my phone buzzed in my pocket (why yes, this dress *does* have pockets! Plus-size retailers have to throw in extras to justify their extortionate prices, you see). I pulled it out, sniffling quietly.

GARRY: You okay?
GARRY: Food is ready, I've got us a table.
AMY: Yeah. Coming.

I stood up, wiped my nose with the back of my hand, shoved my phone in my pocket, and flushed the toilet. When I opened the cubicle door, my face was red and my lipstick had been rubbed off. One of the lawyer friends, judging from her dress, which I saw in the window of the big Next in town, stood at the sinks, reapplying hers, and looked at me appraisingly.

'You okay?' she asked.

I nodded. 'Yeah, just … you know, emotional day,' I said, my voice wobbling.

She nodded, watching me as I dried my hands. 'Here,' she said as I turned to leave. 'Put some of this on. I always use it after a toilet cry, it's a wonder. And this, it's not quite the same as the one you had on, but it should match.' She was holding out a compact of pressed powder, and the bright red lipstick she was just using. I smiled gratefully, powdered my face until it was less obvious I'd been crying, then reapplied a smile on top of my smeared, washed-out mouth.

'Thanks,' I said, handing them back. 'That's really, really kind of you.'

'Don't worry about it,' my new guardian angel replied breezily, putting them back in her tiny clutch and squeezing my arm. 'Look after yourself, yeah?'

'Yeah,' I said, holding the door open for her. 'You too.'

When I found Garry, he was sitting at a table with Frankie, Penny, Oliver, Hannah, Carla, Val and a man holding a tiny baby that I assumed was Hannah's. Hannah looked incredible – her boobs were even bigger than the last time I saw her, and her bright yellow low-cut dress was definitely trying to emphasise rather than hide that fact.

'Amy!' she said with a toothy grin, standing up and holding her arms out.

'You look fucking *amazing*!' I said, hugging her. 'How old is Maya, now?'

'Just over a month,' she said, beaming. 'She's a good bean.'

'I can't believe you had a baby a month ago,' I said, marvelling. 'I thought you'd be still covered in sick and leaking everywhere.'

'Oh, I am,' Hannah said, airily. 'It's amazing what baby wipes and nipple pads can do though.' *Someone stitch that on a pillow, stat.* She tilted her head kindly and I tensed up. *Uh-oh. Here we go …* 'Are you okay? After, um … after …'

'After going a bit mad on the hen do?' I said with an entirely humourless laugh. She nodded awkwardly. 'Yeah, I'm fine. Had some therapy, upped my medication, all that kind of thing. Feeling much better now, thank you.'

'Ah, okay, good,' said Hannah, looking relieved. 'Well, you know, if you need anything, I'm here for you.'

'Thank you, Hannah,' I said. 'I appreciate that.'

And I do, I really do. Thing is, I'm also painfully aware there's fuck-all you can actually do to help. But the fact people are so eager to try, to say nice things or lend me their make-up? It really is lovely, and it means a lot, even if it doesn't necessarily make things better.

I slid into the seat next to Garry, waving hello to Carla and Val. They smiled back, with none of the cautious 'Is she going to start being mental at me?' energy I've been getting elsewhere – possibly because they're far too interested in each other's mouths, hands, legs, necks and other areas of bare skin that can be kissed, nuzzled or in any other way touched. I smirked at Garry, who was keeping his eyes fixed *very firmly* on my face and not on the two gorgeous women acting out the opening scenes of 'Wedding Gone Wild Pt 3' across the table from him.

'Hey girl, hey!' said Frankie, sitting down next to me with a fluorescent pink cocktail. She sipped it, pulled a face, and leant in to rest her head on my shoulder.

'I can see right down your top,' I remarked.

'Good, someone might as well!' she said, yawning and taking another sip. 'Hey, you doing alright?'

'Yeah,' I said breezily. *Not breezily enough.*

'Don't believe you!' she said in a sing-song voice, sitting up and taking another sip of cocktail.

I laughed.

'How many of those have you had?' I asked.

'Not so many that I can't tell when you're bullshitting me,' she replied smoothly.

I laughed again, rolled my eyes and groaned, tipping forward and resting my forehead on her shoulder. She put an arm around me. 'What's going on?'

'I don't know,' I said, truthfully. 'I just feel so awkward and out of place, and like everyone's talking about me.'

'Well, soz to say, love, but you're a bit of a hot topic,' Frankie said. 'But I don't think it's malicious. Most people are just genuinely worried about you, and want to know that you're okay.'

'I know,' I sighed, scanning the room miserably. A few more faces quickly turned away from my direction. 'But that doesn't make it any easier to cope with everyone staring at you and thinking you're batshit.'

'Tsk, who cares?' she said, shrugging. 'Most people are arseholes, you know that. Who cares what they think?'

'I do,' I said, quietly. 'Knowing they're arseholes doesn't stop it hurting that they think you're a fruitloop.'

'And what's wrong with fruitloops?' Frankie demanded, cheerily. 'They're a delicious start to anyone's day!'

I didn't bother to reply. After a few seconds, she sighed. 'Look,' she said, and the tone of her voice made me turn to face her. 'I've never been in your situation. I don't know what to do or to say to make it better, or even if I, like, *can* make it better, you know? But I love you, and I'm here for you, and I want to do whatever I can to help.'

'Thanks, Franks,' I said, nudging her gently. She nudged me back.

'I mean it. I think you're bloody great. You're clever and you're funny, and you've got fantastic boobs.'

'I *do* have great boobs,' I laughed, looking down at my cleavage. It had been slowly escaping my party dress. I stuck my hand down my dress and hoiked my boobs back where they were supposed to be.

'Good! You believe one out of three, we can work on the rest.' She pulled me into an exuberant hug with one hand, noisily finishing her drink with the other. 'I'm getting a refill. Want one?'

And although I don't usually drink alcohol – because I'm usually too scared of what will happen if I let my guard down in front of people and I'm not *technically* supposed to drink on my meds – I did. I had one of those viciously pink cocktails, followed by one that was sweet and purple, followed by the special 'bridal cocktail' – gin in a glass of milk. Utterly disgusting, but I didn't want to waste it so I chugged it back and got myself another purple one to make up for it. I was becoming increasingly woozy; the food was delicious, but sliders, halloumi fries and macarons were not really substantial enough to soak up all the spirits. *Oh well*, I thought as I went up to get my fifth. *In for a penny, in for a pounding headache tomorrow, eh?*

It was getting dark outside and gradually the room became lit by only the neon signs covering the walls. The faces I'd thought were harsh and judgemental looked softer and more approachable glowing in a hundred shades of riotous colour, and the warm fuzz of spirits in my brain and belly meant I wasn't worrying so much about what I was saying to people – or, indeed, *how* I said it.

'I just wouldn't want my daughters absorbing those ideas, you know?' Lisa was saying, her face full of righteous concern even with half her lipstick smeared across her chin. 'Like, Snow White spends her life being pretty, cleaning up and being rescued. Cinderella spends *her* life cleaning, being pretty, and being rescued. And whassername … the tired one?'

'Sleeping Beauty?' Ivy offered.

'YES! Sleeping Beauty,' Lisa half-shouted, punching the air for emphasis. 'She's pretty, then she's sleepy, then she's a queen, she doesn't *do* anything!' She shook her head ruefully. 'They're just not good role models, you know? Not good role models *at all.*'

'Yeah, but they're boring, who cares about them?' I said airily, swaying gently from side to side. 'The others are alright.'

'"Alright"? *Alright?* Lisa said in disbelief.

'Yeah, I mean, they're not perfect, but if you're trying to find a perfect role model for girls in classic media, you'll be looking a long time,' I said, hiding a little burp behind my hand.

Lisa's eyes narrowed unevenly. 'Who's *your* favourite princess, then?' she asked unsteadily but fiercely, like a wolf that has tripped over and banged its head hard on a rock but is still determined to catch its prey.

'Ariel, obviously,' I replied, yanking at my freshly dyed bright red hair.

'HA!' Lisa said triumphantly. 'So, you think it's okay to have a heroine who tells girls that it's – hic! – that it's okay to give up everything for a *man* and has a whole *song* about how men don't care about what women say, just what they look like?' She attempted to roll her eyes, but went a bit squinty. 'Yeah. That's an "alright" message, isn't it? Chuh!'

'When it's the *villain* singing about how men just want a pretty face, yeah, it is,' I said, more evenly than I felt, considering the room was gently tilting from side to side. 'And that Eric falls in love with the person who has Ariel's *voice*, not Ariel's face. *And* she and Eric rescued each other.' I shrugged, taking another sip of cocktail, vaguely aware of having the attention of the whole group and quite enjoying it. 'If I had a headstrong, brave daughter like Ariel, I'd be pretty pleased. Although less pleased if she stinks of fish and her best friend is a seagull, obviously.'

'Disney best friends are always a bit weird, aren't they?' Ivy interjected as Lisa opened her mouth again. 'My favourite's Mulan, and her best mates are a cricket, a horse and a tiny, sassy, lying dragon.'

'Belle for me,' Ashley piped up. 'And her best friend's a teacup.'

'An *underage* teacup,' I said, laughing. 'And a clock that hates her, a candelabra that kinda wants to shag her – oh, hush, he *totally* does – and, like, a bunch of other people cursed to live as inanimate objects because a witch got annoyed by an 11-year-old being worried about stranger danger.' I snorted, pausing to let everyone laugh. 'When you really dig into Disney movies, lack of feminist representation is the least of their problems. They are seriously fucked up!'

Even Lisa was laughing by this point, and I glowed a little inwardly. *This was ... fine? This was fine!* I was being myself and I hadn't been chased out of the room with pitchforks, I was making jokes that people were laughing at, I was interacting and it was okay. *I was being okay.* I grinned and excused myself to find Garry, coming up behind him and rubbing his shoulders just as Janae's dad tapped on the microphone and announced the first dance.

Everyone pushed themselves to the sides of the room to make way for the happy couple, who walked, hand in hand, to the dance floor. Emily's hair was falling out of her plaits; her round cheeks glowed pink in the neon lights. As 'Stay With You' by John Legend started playing through the enormous speakers dotted around the room, Janae twirled Emily around and pulled her into her arms, swaying with her peacefully. Garry slipped his arms around my waist and cuddled me close as we watched them – so wrapped up in each other, they were completely unaware of the perfect vignette they made. I opened up my Camera app and took some photos, trying not to get any of the other hundred people taking photos and videos into the frame.

'You okay?' he asked, kissing me on the temple.

I sighed happily, and leant back into him.

'Yeah,' I said, honestly. 'Yeah, I really am.'

People were starting to join the brides on the dance floor now. I took a mental inventory of the guests. There were their families, Emily's impressive lawyer friends, BAFTA award-winning game creators from Janae's company, authors and journalists and filmmakers and artists, Penny and Oliver, Frankie and a devastatingly handsome stranger who couldn't stop staring at her – and then Garry and me. Janae and Emily were surrounded by incredibly impressive people, yet they still invited me to their wedding, like I'm just as important as the shiny people are. On this most special of days they could have surrounded themselves with the shiniest people in London, but I mean so much to them that they wanted me here, too. I may not be shiny, but I'm worthwhile in their eyes, at least.

And in fact, it's not just that I'm here, it's everything. Janae has been friends with me since the very first night in that flat when we bonded over the BBC *Casanova* series and how Sainsbury's own brand ice cream is nicer than Waitrose's. In the past few months she's been planning her wedding, but still found time to check in with me, and send me those spot-squeezing videos everyone else hates but we both love. Penny is putting together a book proposal, planning her new podcast with Ivy, keeping up her relationship with Oliver and having her kitchen done, but still video calls daily and treks to the other side of London to hang out with me on the Saturdays Garry is at work. And Frankie has talked to me after every therapy session, discussing what we'd covered and how I felt about it and finding ways to help. *They put the effort in, they wanted to help me.*

By now I was getting teary, and John Legend was fading out to be replaced by some electronic-sounding, upbeat music that I knew we were going to be expected to dance to. I muttered something about needing to get some fresh air in Garry's ear and squeezed my way through the crowds of people to get to the door. As I burst out onto the main road, cars and buses roared past, sending sprays of puddle-water perilously close. I breathed in the smell of engine fumes, and exhaled in a rush. *Ah! Fresh air. Nothing like it.*

'You alright, kid?' said someone behind me. I turned; Ivy was leaning against the wall, a roll-up in her hand. She took a drag and blew the smoke out exuberantly in my direction. I smiled fixedly and stifled a cough.

'Yes, just – hot in there, you know?' I said, coming to stand awkwardly next to her. 'Are you alright?'

'I'm fine,' she said, blowing another mouthful of smoke my way. 'But I meant … you know, in general. After you went all Lady of the Lake on us, back in Bath.'

'Oh!' I said, and laughed awkwardly. 'Yes, I'm okay. I've had therapy and … yeah, I'm okay. Much better. Thank you.'

'Yeah, sounds like you had a bit of an emotional enema,' she said. She tilted her head to one side, crossing one leg over the other, and surveyed me appraisingly. 'I read your newsletter, you know.'

'Oh, God, what?' I said, panicked. 'You're not subscribed!'

'I know,' she said, taking another long drag. The glow of her cigarette gleamed in her black eyes. Most smokers I know looked dried-up and faintly yellow, but Ivy makes it look incredibly sexy. 'But you always tweet it, and so I always read it from the archive.' She threw her fag on the floor and ground it out under her stiletto. 'I should just subscribe, really.'

'Oh. Well, I'm sorry …' I said, the laugh I didn't really feel already in my throat.

'Why?' Ivy interrupted.

Oh.

'Well, just … I do it weekly so it's always a bit of a rush, and it's not very good, and …'

'It is, though,' Ivy said placidly. She turned so that she was looking at me, face on. I tried not to recoil from the booze on her breath. 'Look, listen to me, now. I know you really struggle with anxiety and stuff, and I don't know what that's like because I don't have it, but you write about being worried about making a twat out of yourself and stuff like that, and you don't have to. You're great. You're really fucking great!

I wouldn't have even known you had any problems with new people until you went missing, you know? You're fine with new people and you're smart and clever and funny, and you need to start believing it. Okay?'

I didn't say anything. She stood up straight, hands on hips. 'Okay?' she demanded.

'Okay, okay!' I said, mainly because I knew if I said anything else she'd go back to shouting at me.

'Good!' She kissed me on the cheek and smiled, just a quick twitch of the mouth that was only noteable for how rarely she did it. She pushed the door open to go back inside and was momentarily battered by the light and music that poured out of it when she did. I leant against the wall and closed my eyes, waiting until all was quiet (apart from the traffic, obviously) before opening them and taking a deep breath.

Now, I know people are always nicer when they've had a few cocktails, but I truly don't think Ivy would piss on someone that was on fire if she didn't like them, let alone provide unprompted emotional reassurance. I always worry people only put up with me because they're nice – but Ivy *isn't* nice. She can be a bit of a bitch, to be honest. So, maybe she's telling the truth.

So, maybe, I need to accept that people like me. That people even enjoy spending time with me. After all, Penny is friends with some of the coolest people in London, and still wants to watch Marvel films and eat pizza with me. Frankie could have a date – platonic or otherwise – with a different person every day for a month, and frequently does, but still makes time to hang out. And Janae invited me *here*, despite having loads of other cool people she could invite instead! Why would they do that if they didn't actually *like* me? If I wasn't likeable? It doesn't matter that I'm not successful or thin or cool or incredibly clever because I'm likeable as I am, mental brain and all. I'm likeable. *I'm likeable!* Christ, that's a life-changing revelation, and not one I expected to have at 10pm on a rainy Saturday while Frankie and her handsome stranger, who don't know I can see them, fumble in the beer garden behind me. Least someone is going to get a look at her boobs, then.

I exhaled, tears dribbling down my cheek. I'm fine. Not just fine, I'm likeable. *Likeable!* People like me. Even scary people, like Ivy. I'm so bloody grateful for my friends, but maybe I don't have to be quite so pathetically so. There are still lots of things I need to worry about, but I think this may well be the first step towards accepting my brilliant friends aren't one of them.

As I heard the opening bars of 'We Are Never Getting Back Together' from inside the wedding, along with Janae's scream of excitement and Frankie's yelp from the beer garden, I laughed, wiped the tears from my cheeks, and held out my hand to Frankie. Together, we launched ourselves back into the wedding, darting between chairs and bemused relatives, and right into Janae and Penny.

'AMMMMY! FRAAAAAANKS!' screamed Janae, grabbing my shoulders with both hands. She still looked as perfect as she did at the start of the day, the highlighter on her cheekbones picking up the neon and shimmering in a thousand shades of lovely. 'IT'S OUR SONG!'

'I REMEMBER WHEN WE BROKE UP ...' I yelled in her ear.

Penny yelled the next line back at the two of us. We made a circle, performing the songs to each other as we'd done in a hundred living rooms and birthday parties and cheese-nights at clubs and pubs before, and as I hoped we'd do a thousand again.

I beamed round at my friends, at Frankie and Penny vigorously shimmying at each other, at Janae, who never broke eye contact with me as she leapt up and down and screamed the words to the cheesiest pop there was, and at Emily, who was laughing so hard she could barely stand up. My heart glowed with love for them all, for my brilliant, beautiful, utterly ridiculous friends. We danced to that song, and then the next, and then the next, snaking round the room to 'Uptown Funk' and doing an impromptu conga to '500 Miles' and making a whooping circle round the brides as they lip-synched 'Crazy In Love' to each other, taking it in turns to be Beyoncé. It was glorious! By the end of the night, I was soaked in sweat, my feet ached, and I was giddy with joy – and, let's be honest, the cocktails.

'Enjoy yourself?' Garry asked as we stepped out of the door. I was leaning on him *very* heavily for support.

'Yeah,' I said moonily as he held the door of the waiting taxi open for me to slide in. 'I love my friends, I do. They're brilliant!'

'They are,' he said, getting in the other side and doing up his seatbelt. He grabbed my hand and kissed it, his beard tickling the sensitive skin. 'But you're brilliant too.'

I am, sometimes, I thought, leaning against the cool car window. We didn't say any more for the rest of the journey: he was on his phone and I was staring at the bright street lights as they leapt out of the dark night when we whizzed by. I smiled. We'd been like those lights, tonight, like the stars shining in the dark night sky. No matter how dull and dark I felt, my brilliant friends could make me gleam. *Be friends with shiny people*, I thought as my eyes drifted closed and my breathing got slower. *No matter how bad you start out feeling, they'll make you feel shiny, too.*

SATURDAY, 18 NOVEMBER

TO-DO

☑ Janae's wedding: 1pm (Curtain Warehouse)

☑ Reception, straight after: Curtain Warehouse

☑ Hair (half-up, half-down; show off cute pixie ears but hide weird jawline and double chin)

☑ Make-up (matte, pink lips, cat eyeliner)

☑ Buy cotton buds (to help with removal of inevitably crap eyeliner)

☐ Wear in shoes w/socks around house before wedding to avoid blisters

☐ Practise _easy_ dance moves so don't embarrass self

☑ Write down list of <u>worries</u> about the wedding to <u>get them out of head</u>

☑ Check on venue website to see if loos are private in case of emergency crying

☑ Leave @ noon to get to wedding

SESSION TWO

'You do quite a lot, then,' Bjorg said, her hands folded in her lap. She'd just asked about my week and I'd haltingly taken her through all the things I did at work, all the side projects I had, and my hobbies. 'How do you cope with that?'

'What do you mean?' I asked, scrunching and unscrunching my toes in my shoes.

'Well, you said here ...' She leant forward and rested her fingertips on the PHQ on the table. 'That you're having trouble concentrating, that you're easily irritated, that you feel bad about yourself constantly, that you're so anxious it's hard to sit still ...' She sat back in her chair, while I tried to subtly press my feet hard to the floor to stop my legs jiggling. 'And you've said before that you often feel overwhelmed by your own feelings.' She cocked her head to one side, her crooked smile a little rueful. 'That's a lot to deal with, along with all your work and your hobbies and everything, isn't it?'

'Well, it is, but I just get on with it. I *have* to,' I replied, every inch of me uncomfortable. It's so fucking annoying that to get to the good bit of therapy, i.e. not being mad any more, you have to go through this horrible painful bit first. Like childbirth, but you don't get a lovely baby at the end – and there's only mildly less shit, tears and vomit to deal with. 'And it's okay in the day, to be honest. I mean, in the day I have to keep going, there isn't an option. It's at night when it feels like everything falls apart.'

'Mmm, okay,' Bjorg said slowly, nodding seriously. 'And what happens then?'

'Um …' *Be honest, Jones. She can't help unless you're honest.* 'Sometimes … crying. Sometimes I, uh … I eat until it hurts. Sometimes I just get stuck, staring at a wall for hours, or at my phone without really doing anything, and then I get wound up and frustrated.' I gave an awkward bark of a laugh, even though nothing felt funny. 'Okay, maybe "fall apart" was an exaggeration.'

'Do you find it hard to relax?' she asked, ignoring me.

I nod. 'Garry – uh, my husband – he gets frustrated because he just wants to curl up and watch TV, but I get restless if I'm not doing something productive.'

'Oh, really?' she said, sitting back in her chair and cocking her head again. Although she spoke English perfectly, her voice was melodious in an entirely un-English way. It reminded me of the way people spoke in Wales, the way my family spoke – it was soothing. 'Something productive, like what?'

'Um … Cleaning up? Exercising? Reading the news, baking, writing, learning songs on the guitar, knitting, sewing … I have these big lists of all the things I want to do, and if I'm not doing anything that gets me towards ticking things off those lists, then I feel really panicky and uncomfortable. And then I feel so panicky, I get paralysed by it and can't do anything, and it just becomes a big tangly mess.' Pause. 'I'm not good at doing nothing worthwhile.'

'Huh,' Bjorg said. 'That's really interesting.' *Christ, either she's very kind, or she's a fucking simpleton.* 'And what makes you uncomfortable, in this idea that you're "doing nothing worthwhile"?'

'Because everyone else does things that are worthwhile all the time!' I burst out. 'God, everyone else always does so much. Everyone else is always going to the theatre or speaking on panels, or using their amazing artistic skills to make these incredible things, or … or travelling, or reading ten books a week, or doing all these amazing fitness things, and I'm just sat at home watching telly or doing nothing, because I'm pathetic.'

'Don't you think you might need some time to sit at home and do nothing?' she asked placidly. I frowned. She smiled brightly in response, absolutely no fucks given. 'You spend all day worrying about things, right? And then thinking all these things about how you're not good enough, how you need to be better, work harder – despite working very hard, on lots of different things – and then having to recover from thinking all these things, and keep going, and doing what you need to get through the day.' She exhaled dramatically, shaking her head. 'Whoof! Sounds pretty exhausting, right?' I nodded begrudgingly. 'So, doesn't it make sense that you might need to rest?'

'No one else seems to,' I grumbled.

Her face twitched; I feel like she would have grinned, if she could.

'Okay,' she said, settling herself more comfortably in her chair. 'So, why don't you try something new this week? Why don't you add two things that involve looking after yourself a bit more to your list? That way, you're still being productive, but you're also giving yourself the downtime you need.'

'What kind of things?'

'Like, going for a walk. Just a little one, for ten minutes or so. Doing some yoga. Having a shower, or at least washing your face, or reading, or something like that.' She looked at me, head on one side, eyes sleepy but smiling. 'Do you think you can do that?'

'Uh, sure,' I said. *No. Be strong in your intentions, you weakling.* 'I mean, yes. Yes, I can.'

'Great!' Bjorg said, sitting up straight and beaming at me. Cautiously, I smiled back. 'And you said you like to keep lists to track all the things you need to do – do you think you could keep another list, too?'

'What kind of list?'

'A list of all the things you've done in a day.'

'Isn't that just a completed To-Do list?'

'Well, no,' Bjorg said, leaning back in her chair. 'I mean, all the things you wouldn't necessarily put on a To-Do List. Washing your hair, picking out a nice outfit, having conversations that were difficult, that kind of thing. We do a lot in a day, and we don't give ourselves credit for it. Maybe it's time you did.'

'O–kay,' I said slowly, thinking that this sounded like the stupidest thing in the world. 'I can give it a go.'

'Good!' Bjorg said brightly. 'And you've said on your form that you're still having daily thoughts of wanting to hurt yourself, or that people would be better off if you weren't around. Are you going to act on those feelings?'

'No,' I said. 'I can't. Garry, my parents, my friends ...'

'That's good.' She stood up and opened the door for me. 'And remember, two things a day to take care of yourself.'

'Two things a day. Yes, okay.'

TO-DO

- [ ] Train, Paddington to Cardiff, 08.43
- [ ] Leave house at 07.30
- [ ] Don't forget Christmas cards for everyone
- [ ] Don't let Nana Meryl and Nana Addy kill each other
- [ ] Don't let Mum kill Laura or Dolly
- [ ] Don't let Dad kill himself
- [ ] Don't kill Andrew
- [ ] Make sure Mum has a good time

TWELVE

Chocolate croissant, or mango pot? I dithered from one foot to the other, staring at the pot of shiny orange fruit and *willing* myself to want it as much as I wanted a lovely, crumbly croissant with a delicious streak of chocolate spread down the middle. A slender woman politely said, 'Excuse me,' and leant past to get a fruit salad and a bottle of water. I stared longingly at her pert bottom and slim thighs as she went to pay. *She hasn't got any problem choosing the healthy option over the delicious one*, I thought miserably. *That's why she looks like that.*

'The oh-eight, forty-three, to, Cardiff Central, will be departing, from, platform four,' said a disembodied voice from above. I swore, abandoned my fruity ideals, and got myself a chocolate croissant and a flat white from the counter, shoving the former in my handbag and balancing the latter perilously in the crook of my arm while I retrieved my ticket, fed it into the barrier and found a quiet seat on the train. The journey was almost three hours long, so I had plenty of time to sip my coffee and nibble at the croissant while flicking through the book I'd bought specially, which had just been nominated for the Baileys Prize. I'd consumed both before the train pulled away, obviously, and the book never made it out of my bag. Instead, I found my phone and opened WhatsApp.

AMY: On the train!
AMY: It's just left. I'll let you know if there are any other delays but I should be on time

Mum: ok baby. C u soon xx
Amy: Safe drive!
Dad: OK

I opened up Facebook to see if any of my siblings had posted about today, but nothing yet. Hmm … I spent ten minutes scrolling through Instagram, posted an obligatory 'On a train!' selfie, then abandoned my phone in favour of a much more productive pastime: staring out the window and worrying about the day ahead.

Today was the annual Grandmothers' Christmas Meal. Every year my mother, who is a saint, drives down to Wales and takes both her mum and Dad's mum out to a lovely carvery up at Culverhouse Cross. She does this even though both my nanas are frustrating if you're being kind, and total fucking nightmares if you're honest. Dad, whose attitude towards doing anything that isn't sitting in front of the football or a detective drama is one of the reasons I fully expect Mum to be canonised one day, doesn't even always come to these bloody meals. For a couple of years, she did them all on her own, with teenage me tagging along and about as useful as a wine gum against a case of industrial-strength cystitis. But a few years ago, she realised she hadn't been using the power of maternal and spousal guilt to *quite* its full advantage, so she upped the ante with Facebook posts about how lonely the two nanas said they were and an increased number of phone calls to us all about how stressful it was to do all of this, on her own, at her age. So now, we all come along.

Today's table is booked for an impressive 15 people: Mum, Dad, me, Nana Addy, Nana Meryl, Freddy with Zach and Bruce, Taggie with Alice, Andrew with Dolly and the twins, and even Freddy's soon-to-be ex-wife Laura. *I know.* The nanas have some kind of vortex around them, and once you get sucked into their lives, you can never truly leave. One of Andrew's ex-girlfriends from a decade ago still visits Nana Addy once month, I shit you not. Garry only got out of today because the Metropolitan

Police don't see 'inexplicable maternal power vortex' as a valid reason for a day off. *Gits*. Bet the Heddlu would've understood.

When you've that many people sitting around one table – particularly that many who are all members of the same family – there's every opportunity for fireworks. The previous night, Mum and I had been on the phone, talking through all the possible seating arrangements and the barriers between people sitting together.

'Andrew can't sit next to Laura, because of that one time on Facebook ...'

'... I can't sit next to Andrew either, or I'll call him a twat and it'll upset the nanas ...'

'... and the nanas have to sit next to each other, but they hate each other, so your dad and I need to sit next to them to keep things friendly ...'

'... and then that means you can't have Andrew near you, because you know how Sierra winds up Nana Addy ...'

'... but then if we put Zach next to Alice, they're likely to start fighting ...'

'... and we can't have Alice and Taggie next to Laura and Dolly, because they'll say something about Alice's behaviour and Taggie will deck them.'

'... I'd quite like to see that, to be honest.'

'Yeah, me too. Shall we?'

'Amy!'

We'd eventually figured out a seating plan, fully aware it was all academic, anyway. If Dad was in a bad mood, or one of the kids threw a tantrum, or the nanas managed to piss off Taggie to the point where she actually *said* something about it rather than bitching with us afterwards, the whole thing would come toppling down like the pile of chocolate orange profiteroles I planned on stuffing myself with for dessert.

I swallowed, trying to dislodge a lump in my throat. Although Mum had seemed reassured, or at least resigned, when we'd hung up last night after an hour of making plans and contingency plans, I couldn't really plan my way out of what I was worried about. Other than my parents I hadn't seen anyone coming today since I'd had another mental breakdown. In fact, apart from a few messages about the latest Marvel film with Freddy, I hadn't spoken to any of them, either – and I had no idea how things would be. *Did they know? Had Mum told them? What would they say?*

And ... ugh, forget how they'll react to me, how will *I* react to *them*? According to our seating plan, I am sat as far away from the nanas as possible (I had little patience with Nana Addy's nonsense when my brain was well, let alone now that it's held together with twigs and spit), but because my parents are sat with them, that means I'm not near *them* either. I'm going to be set adrift in the sea of wankers that is my siblings and their families. What are they going to say? Is Taggie going to be mean about my job, or how I look? Will Andrew make me feel small and stupid, like he usually does? Is Freddy going to be really awkward and intense until I'm really awkward back, and we just sit next to each other for four hours being awkward until one of us snaps and drowns themselves in their free-refill of Diet Coke?

And how will my mum – my bloody lovely mum, who just wants to do something nice for the nanas and maybe also have a nice meal with all of her kids on Christmas – react when this goes down? I know that she's the one who organises this and strong-arms us all into coming and so it's irritatingly bizarre that she gets so stressed, but if I'm allowed to have contradictory emotions that make no sense then so is she, and I will defend them with my life. As the train pulls into Cardiff Central, I run through all the ways my shitty family could ruin today for her and feel sick to my stomach. I don't want that to happen. I *can't* have that happen. I need to make sure today goes well, no matter what.

When I arrived at the carvery, I spotted my parents' car immediately. *But were the others here? Shit, was I the last one?* I paid the driver and got out, sprinting across the car park to the front door – less impressive than it sounds, because it was only about five metres and I was still out of breath when I got there. I opened the door and saw Mum at the bar. Sidling up behind her, I put my hands over her eyes.

'Gimme yer money!' I said in a fake growl.

She gasped dramatically. 'Oh no, oh no, you got me!' she said in a deadpan panic, a performance Anne Hathaway would be proud of. I moved my hands and she turned, hugging me tight. 'Hello, matey. How're you doing?'

So anxious I've already scoped the room out to find the nearest loo in case my tummy explodes, exhausted having already travelled five hours to have a three-hour meal, uncomfortable because I'm gaining weight on my upped-dose of tablets so my skirt is digging in, and already planning to spend my journey home Googling GIFs of Tom Hiddleston dancing in preparation for a relaxing evening wank, actually, Mum.

'Fine, thanks!' I said brightly. 'How about you? How've they all been?' For a second she dug her teeth into her bottom lip, crossed her eyes and wrinkled her nose in a snarl. Then everything relaxed and she beamed at me with artificial, painful sunniness. I laughed. '*That* good?'

'Yeah,' she said evenly, slumping forward to rest her elbow on the bar and cradle her head in her hand. 'They're driving me up the wall already, but I didn't expect anything else, really.'

'Who's here other than you, Dad and the nanas?'

'Just Andrew, Dolly and the girls.' The barman approached, three soft drinks balanced between his hands. 'Do you want anything?' As she paid for the drinks, I looked behind me surreptitiously for the table. When I spotted the back of Andrew's head, my stomach clenched. *Deep breaths, Jones. You can do this.*

'Hiya!' I said brightly, putting the drinks down on the table. Andrew looked up in surprise and nodded in greeting. I mentally gave him the finger and smiled back, sweetly.

'Oh, iyer, love!' Nana Addy said, blinking up at me in surprise, her already enormous eyes magnified to the size of saucers behind her glasses. She nudged Nana Meryl next to her. 'Look, Meh, it's Amy!'

'Hello, Amy,' Nana Meryl said primly. I kissed them both on the cheek, their skin like lily-of-the-valley-scented dead leaves under my lips.

Judging by our carefully figured-out seating plan, I should be sat right at the other end of the table, away from the people liable to make me explode. However, there's no one else here yet and it'd look really odd if I went and sat there on my own. I glanced at Mum (who had clearly thought the same and was trying not to let panic roll too obviously across her face) and sat down next to Dad.

'Hiya,' I said. He didn't reply, just gave me the close-lipped, dead-eyed smile that I knew meant he was annoyed, but not yet at boiling point. My stomach lurched again. I waited until Dolly had everyone distracted by telling them about the holiday they had planned to the Costa Brava next year, and opened up my Notes app to re-read my recent To-Done Lists.

I'd managed to get through five days at work without crying in public. I'd gone swimming three times. I'd showered three times. I'd read a book. I'd cooked proper food twice. I'd cleaned the house. I'd done a skincare routine. I'd watched all of *Brooklyn Nine-Nine* S3 on Netflix. I'd had several good meetings. I'd gone food shopping. I scrolled back further, reminding myself of the good things I'd done in the past few weeks. I smiled. Look at all the good conversations I'd had! I'd been entirely normal and fine with lots of different people – if I could get through interacting with them, surely I could do the same with my own family?

'What's that?' asked Dad, leaning over.

'Oh! Um, just my To-Do List,' I said hurriedly, scrolling back up to today. I didn't think now was the right time to explain the whole To-Done List concept – his bullshit tolerance is very low anyway, and it drops dramatically when he's in a bad mood.

'Ah,' he said humourlessly, staring into the middle distance. 'I had a To-Do List, but my mate used it to spliff up.' He paused while I tried to discern if I was having a stroke or he was actually saying this. 'He's now high on my list of priorities.' He waited a beat, then flicked his eyes to mine. I smirked, and he grinned like a naughty child.

'That's terrible,' I chuckled.

'I know. Here, I hope there's never a scandal involving Tesla. Elon-gate could go on for a very long time.'

'Oh my God …'

'Did I tell you that one of my colleagues broke his arm?' he said, looking serious again.

'Wha … No! Is he okay?' I stammered, wrong-footed.

He nodded grimly. 'He's fine. He invited us all to sign his cast. I wrote "You fat bastard".' *Beat.* 'Talk about adding insult to injury, eh?'

'DAD!' I yelped, swatting at his arm while he giggled gleefully. And he was on a roll, now, telling me brilliantly crap joke after brilliantly crap joke until my sides hurt from laughing and the rest of the family had arrived. Everyone sat down in completely the wrong place, warring faction up against irritant up against idiot, but it was too late now – at least the fireworks would entertain the other patrons.

We went up in shifts to get our food. I went up with Taggie and Alice in front of me, Laura with the boys behind me. Not entirely sure what I should say to Laura, especially considering Freddy was staring mournfully over at her, like Flick would stare at her pouches of wet food when I put them away into the cupboard, so while we waited to be served, I turned my attention to my sister.

'How's it going, Tags?' I asked brightly.

'Oh, same as always,' she droned, before snapping to attention as her daughter kicked the heels of the man in front of her. 'Alice, stop it, *stop it!* Sorry, sorry … Um, yes, nothing much has changed. Same shit, different day. How about you? Where are you working now?'

'Still at Steady,' I said, bracing myself.

'What, *still?*' she replied, incredulously.

'Yes, still,' I said, and this time there was an edge to my voice. I thought about the list of things I'd done that week, all the meetings I'd had and the scripts I'd written and the videos and webpages that had gone out because of me. A surge of something hot and powerful went through me. 'I've not really been there that long, actually, and even if I had, it's a good job and it's nice to do something that's *actually* helping people.'

'Yeah, but it's a bit of a waste of your talents, isn't it?' she said over her shoulder as she stepped up to be served. 'A waste of your brilliant writing.' *Wait, what?* Is she trying to *compliment* me, here? I've always thought whenever she asks about my career or my life or whatever, she's snidely saying she thinks I'm useless. Has she been saying the opposite, that she thinks I'm good? If so, is she shit at communicating, or am I too broken to recognise a compliment when it's given? Either way, I still deserved to be recognised for the brilliant job I was *actually* doing, rather than be praised for the one I could be if I just tried hard enough. I waited until we'd all been given our meat and Yorkshire puddings and Alice had been badgered into having at least two types of vegetable on her plate ('Peas! You like peas! And look at that, cauliflower cheese, mmm! Oh, come on, you can eat that, it's more cheese than cauliflower . . .') before replying.

'I don't think it's a waste at all,' I said carefully, pouring gravy over a plate that was 90 per cent potato. *Ah, it's good to be a grown-up.* 'I'm really happy there, I think it's a really good use of my skills, and I've done so much there. I've got three interviews coming up in February, and I feel good that I'll be able to talk about all the great things I've done at Youth Steady in them.'

'Fair enough,' she said as we headed back to the table. 'As long as you're happy. Where are the interviews?' I briefly told her about the other charities and websites I was going for, but then

Alice started poking her fingers in her gravy and finger-painting on the tablecloth, so she had to go. I sat down, flushed with the success of dodging my first bullet of the day. Unfortunately, there were many more to come. The nanas were in full flow, and Mum had gone up to get their plates so there was no one there to deflect them.

'Tom Jones, that's the one. He used to walk up and down my street,' Nana Addy was saying. 'And I worked in the bakery with Shakin' Stevens! I sat on the bloody Duke of Edinburgh's lap in that ... what's it called? Hall? Royal Albert Hall? I got shot off, though. I met the Marquess of Bute, the Duke of Edinburgh, the Queen ... I used to go every Sunday for my tea after church.'

'There's lovely,' Nana Meryl said, although from her tone it was very clear that when she said 'lovely', she actually meant 'shit'. 'I was down the Bay when they were filming that *Touchwood* (she means *Torchwood*) a few years ago, and I got talking to John Barryman. Lovely chap, he is. Lovely voice ... Did you see him in that *Maria* show a few years ago, Ad?'

'Oh, no, I don't watch much telly,' Nana Addy said, pulling a face like Meryl had just presented her with a poo on a plate. 'Just the news, and *Songs of Praise*, and *Emmerdale*, and *Corrie*, and *EastEnders*, and any time Boys Allowed or the Saturday Girls are on, you know? I can't afford the 'lectric, otherwise, so I just sits by myself.'

'Oh, there's a pity you don't have no one to come see you, so you have to stay all on your own,' said Nana Meryl, smoothly.
Ouch!

'Well, you know what it's like when everyone's getting older, Meh,' said Addy. 'And we can't all pay to have people come in and see us three times a day like you does, can we?'

'BOYS!' Laura snapped, distracting me from the bitch fight going on to my right. I turned to see Zach and Bruce punching each other in the head. Freddy leant over the table and pushed them apart with a fist the size of a bear paw.

'Oi, knock it off!' he said. 'That's not how we behave in restaurants, is it?'

'That's not how we behave at any time, Alfred,' Laura said testily.

'Oh, don't start! You know what I meant ...'

'Oh, the poor things! It's so stressful on the children when there's disruption with the parents, isn't it?' Dolly interjected, stroking a wiggling Prue's hair. 'It must be so hard for them, having all this *upheaval*. There's this parenting blogger I love, Mummy Of The Heart, and she says ...'

'The boys are doing *fine*,' Laura said with a smile that showed too many teeth to be entirely unthreatening. 'They're just energetic after being in the car for so long.'

'Oh, I see,' Dolly said, pressing her lips together. 'Of course. Well, we're lucky the girls aren't that energetic aren't we, dear?' She turned to smile at her husband, but he wasn't listening – he was telling Taggie all about a mystery lump in his armpit and the strange things that leaked from it when he was in the shower.

'There were no cars in the old days,' Nana Addy proffered down the table. 'Used to fit 14 or 15 girls in a Mini Cooper to get to a concert!'

No one really knew what to say to this, so we just smiled at her and moved on.

As the enormous piles of food on our plates diminished, the little battles around the table raged on. Mum played referee between the nanas as they sniped at each other; Taggie split her time evenly between keeping Alice under control and talking about the smart-arse comments Alice had made to her teachers that term ('It's not white, miss, its's transparent. And it's not a square, it's slanty, it's a rhombus!'). Andrew and Freddy talked about work and had subtle games of one-upmanship, with Dolly jumping in to compare house sizes or talk about their solid marriage or how great their kids were whenever she thought Freddy had the upper hand. Would she be so smug when she realised that Prue and Sierra were carefully tipping forkfuls of food onto the floor underneath the table because they didn't want to eat their carrots, I wondered. I checked my phone to see a text from Garry, asking how things were going, and replied with the skull emoji.

'Here, Cah, give me that,' Nana Addy was saying, waving to Mum's leftover roast potatoes. 'I'll take them home with me, have it for my supper.'

'Mam, you don't want these, they're all soggy ...' Mum protested as she reached over and grabbed the gravy-soaked potatoes off her plate. 'Mam!'

'Look! I can have them for my tea, later,' she said, dropping the potatoes into the middle of her napkin and wrapping them up into a parcel. The gravy immediately soaked through the thin layers, but that didn't stop her from dropping them into her handbag and looking very pleased with herself. Meryl tutted and rolled her eyes melodramatically.

'Pass me my bag, there, won't you?' she said primly. Mum reached behind her and passed the enormous blue shopping bag to Nana Meryl, who started digging around in it. 'I've got presents for the children, here. Amy, will you help me pass them round?'

'And mine!' shrieked Nana Addy, desperate not to be outdone. Well, I say 'shrieked', she's lived in Cardiff her whole life so has an incredibly high-pitched voice with a Cardiff accent so strong you could stand a spoon up in it. Anything she says above a whisper is, to a normal ear, a shriek, especially compared to Meryl's gentler Valleys' accent.

The two nanas started pulling out little packages and passing them to me. It soon became clear that by 'for the children' they meant everyone apart from each other and my parents. I handed out brightly wrapped presents to Taggie, Freddy, Prue, Dolly, Laura, Sierra, Alice, Bruce, and ...

'Jack?' I said, staring at a label. 'Who's Jack?'

'Jack!' Meryl said impatiently. 'You know, Freddy's boy.'

There was an awkward pause.

'You mean Zach?' Andrew said slowly.

'Oh, it's *Zach*, is it?' Nana Meryl asked in surprise. 'Yes, Zach! Zach and Bruce. I knows, it's for him. Zach. Happy Christmas, love.'

'Say thank you to your nan,' Laura said, nudging Zach as I handed him the present.

'Thank you, Nan,' Bruce and Zach chorused politely. Freddy looked like he was about to burst out laughing. He met Laura's eye, and she smiled despite herself.

'Yeah, thanks, Nan. Maybe next year you'll get their names right, too. It's been only a decade, you know, no pressure,' Andrew muttered. My stomach sank; there's no way Mum hadn't heard that. I glared at him as I went back up to the top of the table and he looked surprised.

'Can we open them now, please, Nana?' Sierra asked.

'Go on, then, that'll be nice,' Nana Meryl said.

We all ripped open our packages: scarves from Nana Meryl, which I recognised as the ones her friend Gertie sells down the market for £2 a pop. The kids got chocolate coins from Nana Addy, which they immediately ripped open, but the collection of presents the adults got was far more diverse.

'Thanks, Mam,' said Dad, holding up a large square of blue material. Not a scarf, or a tea towel, or a tablecloth, you understand. A square of material.

'Yeah, thank you!' I said delightedly, while holding up my bar of Fruit & Nut for everyone to see and smirk at – they all knew that I absolutely hated nuts. Laura had ripped open a bundle of black tea towels with skulls on them, while Taggie was holding two Reader's Digest nature books with 'NOT FOR RESALE' stamped clearly across the front.

'Oh, I'm glad you likes 'em,' Nana Addy beamed, sitting back in her chair with satisfaction. 'I gets 'em from the Wednesday Club. When I wins 'em in the raffle, I save 'em and gives 'em out as presents at Christmas, but I don't open 'em first so I don't know what's in 'em.'

That explains it, I thought, looking at Freddy, who had just opened a bottle of hair-minimising cream.

Mum signalled for the waitress and scrawled her hand through the air, the universally recognised signal for 'Can I have the bill, please?' She nodded and, a few minutes later, slid a saucer with a folded receipt in front of her. Mum went to get her purse, but Nana Addy stopped her.

'I'll pay for this,' she said primly, reaching behind to retrieve her purse with all the grace of a hippo trying to get out of a paddling pool full of jelly.

'No, you won't,' said Mum.

'Yes, I will. Don't you try to stop me, I'll hit you with my stick!' Nana Addy said in that shriek-not-shriek, her voice rising sharply as she started crying.

Nana Meryl rolled her eyes. 'Don't shout, you stupid bugger! Everyone's looking at us,' she said scornfully.

Nana Addy, whose voice was now so high only dogs, dolphins and the female members of my blood family could understand it, turned the full force of her furious misery onto her. 'Don't you start n'all! I'll hit you too! I done it loads of times, down with the boys, by the bakery.'

'No one's going to hit anyone,' Mum said firmly. 'Mam, put your stick down and your purse away. No, I'm not taking your money. Put it away! Meryl, shut up!'

'Oh, there's charming!' Meryl said snippily.

I'm pretty sure either me, Mum or Nana Addy would have gone for her throat, had the waitress not turned up at that precise moment, holding a card machine.

'Ready, love?' she asked, hair falling out of her ponytail, face red and sweaty, the circles under her eyes dark.

Nana Addy took one look and the tears evaporated straight off her face. 'You looks awful tired, come sit down a minute,' she said. 'Take the weight off your feet, love. Here, my daughter will get up, won't you, Cah?'

'Oh, no, that's ...'

'No, here you go,' said Mum, standing up and gesturing for the waitress to sit down. She slumped into the chair gratefully.

'Thank you. I'm rushed off my feet today, it's terrible busy.'

'It's like that, isn't it, though, when you're working?' Nana Addy said sagely. 'I used to work 100 hours a week for £6 a month. No one works for £6 an hour now. I used to do 36 hours on the trot.'

'I used to do four days, with only half-hour for lunch!' Nana Meryl jumped in eagerly.

'No, you didn't, you worked in the council! I was doing the toilet, up by the castle – you know the ones, with the Mormons on the top? Aye ...' She thwacked the waitress on the arm and she visibly winced. 'I saw Father Christmas in the toilet, 'cos I went in the wrong toilet. I said "Oh!" then he buggered off after five minutes!' She and Meryl roared with laughter, while the waitress's jovial expression froze. I turned to Dad, who was staring straight ahead, chin resting in his hands.

'What the fuck?' I muttered quietly.

He nodded slowly, then sat back in his chair to look at me, folding his arms across the dinner stains on his shirt. 'What the fuck indeed!' he said, not bothering to lower his voice. I glanced at the nanas and Mum, but they were all far too absorbed in their conversation about the toilets and what Santa may or may not have been doing in them to pay attention.

'Are our family insane?' I asked.

He glanced around the table: Taggie and Dolly were enthusing about positive parenting while Alice made mashed-potato handprint stars on the table, Zach and Bruce were hitting each other with their scarves while Freddy and Laura whispered to each other and giggled, Andrew was on his phone and ignoring Prue and Sierra, who were playing some weird game on their phone where they seemed to be operating on a pregnant Princess Jasmine. He looked back at me and shrugged.

'Probably,' he mused. 'Everyone's a bit mad, though, aren't they?'

'Yeah, but this ...' I gestured around the table. 'This is next-level weird!'

'Nah, it's not,' he said placidly. 'You're just young. The more you see of the world, the more you'll realise everyone is insane and some people do a better job of hiding it than others. But this?' He nodded round the table. 'This is family. You don't have to hide your weird when you're with family.'

I paused for a second, watching this group of people: the people closest to me in the world, the ones who shared my blood and my bones and my background, who'd known me since I hadn't even known I was a 'me', who'd taken care of me, no matter what. The people who knew me best: my good bits, my bad bits, my *everything*. I took a deep breath.

'Do you all think I'm weird?'

'Yep,' Dad replied instantly. 'But like I said, don't worry about it. We *all* are.'

'But I mean, do you all think I'm ... okay?'

'What do you mean?'

'I mean ...' I wriggled in my chair. 'Do you think I'm okay? As a person, like? You have to love me, I'm your daughter, but would you like me even if I wasn't? Am I an okay person or ...?'

'You're magic,' Dad interrupted. 'Absolutely magic. I know you worry about things and I know you've had some ... some problems, but you needn't worry. You're brilliant, and we're so proud of you.'

'Thanks, Dad.'

He beamed, ruffled my hair, then finished off his third pint. I made the decision not to think too much about whether or not the Guinness was contributing to him being so effusively lovely – and hey, if alcohol is what it takes to get my emotionally stunted family to open up to each other, then vodka shots for all! – and instead thought how lucky I was to be raised by a man as unashamedly himself as he was. It might be a pain in the arse to deal with sometimes, but in terms of role models for radical self-acceptance, you really can't get much better than my grumpy, nonsensical father.

Nana Meryl's attention was caught by the sound of Dad's empty glass hitting the table, and she started rummaging in her purse.

'Here you are, Dai,' she said, holding up a £20 note. 'Go get yourself another drink.'

'Hang on, hang on ...' Nana Addy said – although it was hard to hear her, because the second she'd seen the money in Nana Meryl's hand, she had whipped round and was digging on the back of her chair for her handbag. 'Get us all something. Do the kids want anything? Do you want a coffee or something, Amy? Cah?'

'I'm alright, thanks, Nan.'

'David? Do you want another drink?' Nana Addy asked.

'No, Adalynn, I'm getting my son a drink,' said Nana Meryl, a touch of steel in her voice.

'Oh, don't you bloody start!' Nana Addy snapped back.

'Oi! Less of that at the table, please,' Mum said.

'Don't you start n'all, you're not too old for a hiding ...'

'There's a nice way to talk to your daughter ...'

'I SAID, DON'T YOU BLOODY START!'

I excused myself and scurried off to the loo before Nana Addy's voice reached such a pitch that it shattered the windows. As I stood up, I glanced down the table at my family: at Freddy and Laura glaring at each other like they couldn't decide whether to fight or fuck; at Alice demanding Taggie and Dolly watch her as she sang 'Old MacDonald' while doing the Macarena; at Bruce, Sierra and Prue kicking each other under the table while Zach solemnly worked through an entire age-inappropriate Paw Patrol colouring book; at Mum shushing Nana Addy, now crying, while Nana Meryl primly drank her tap water and Dad looked straight ahead with a thousand-yard stare, his bushy eyebrows so far up his forehead they were doubling as a fringe. A strange rush of despair and love overtook me; I rode it to the toilets, through my entirely unnecessary wee, and through washing my hands with the cheap pink hand soap you find in every chain carvery toilet in the UK.

When I'd finished, I put my hands on the cool porcelain of the sink and stared at myself in the mirror. Christ, my family are annoying! Like, *incredibly* annoying, to the point where it's a skill. My grandmothers, who talk absolute bollocks and aren't letting their game of maternal one-upmanship slip just because it's been 42 years and they'll probably be dead soon anyway, are annoying. My parents, who were ridiculous human beings in the first place and are slowly turning into *their* parents, are annoying. My siblings, who can't get together without having massive willy-waving contests *even when one of them doesn't even have a willy*, are annoying. My sisters-in-law are, perversely, annoying for all the things they do that mark them out as being not part of our family. And my niblings are annoying because they've been raised by us idiots, so really, they had no fucking chance, did they?

And I'm annoying too. Hell, I'm *so* annoying. I'm needy and I try too hard to make everyone happy, and I hate not being right and I'm not living the life my parents hoped I would, and I get anxious over nothing and throw tantrums when I don't get on with my crappy siblings, and I'm living a wanky London life that doesn't really make any sense. But in this context, in this restaurant with these people, that absolutely doesn't matter. Because – and this realisation hit me with such wonderful force that I laughed out loud at my own reflection in the mirror – my annoying, ridiculous, *insane* family love me anyway.

I want my family to be perfect. It isn't. It's fucked – a big, tangled, complicated mess full of complicated people – and that's okay. I wish I got on with my siblings. I wish I had the relationship Garry has with his brother, or that Janae has with her sisters, or the Kardashians seem to have whenever they're not bickering over clothes or supposedly unflattering selfies. I wish my nanas lived on the same bloody planet as the rest of us. I wish my parents thought everything I did was perfect and wonderful and exactly what they'd hoped I'd do, but they don't, and that's fine too. It doesn't mean I'm a bad person or that they don't love me. After all, they may be annoying and frustrating and utterly insane, but I love them with all my heart. It stands to reason they feel the same about me, too.

My eyes – the eyes that mirror those of Nana Addy, Mum, and all of my siblings – were wet. I wiped the tears away with the back of my hand, blew my lips in a raspberry, and shook myself back together. Then I grinned at myself in the mirror – a grin I see in my dad's face every time he delights himself with a bad pun, or on the faces of the twins whenever they're naughty – and smoothed down my thick, frizzy hair, the hair I can still see on Nana Meryl's head, although hers is white and short and stained gold at the front from endless cigarettes. I took a deep breath, and went back out to join everyone.

Mum was standing at the bar again when I passed, so I snuck up behind her.

'Boo!'

'Hello,' she said, turning to face me. Her hair was sticking straight up at the front where she'd been running her hands through it in frustration.

'You look like a parakeet,' I said, flattening it down for her. 'Is it safe to leave them alone?'

'Yeah, Meryl's talking to your dad and I made Andrew talk to Mam before I left,' she said. 'They're slagging each other off merrily. It's fine. They're in earshot, but too busy insulting each other to hear the insults the other is making.'

'Oh, God!' I said, laughing, putting my head in my hands. 'What even is our family?'

'They drive me mad, the lot of them,' said Mum, exasperated, handing over money for the drinks. 'If it's not the nanas sniping at each other, it's Andrew whining about Laura or Taggie being high-and-mighty about Alice when she's being a shit, or Andrew being a pushover with his bloody wife, and your dad sitting there in silence, leaving me to deal with them all. It's Christmas and everything, but I just wish they'd all sod off!'

I laughed. 'At least you've got me,' I offered. 'And I'm a *delight*. I don't cause you any problems at all.'

She laughed mirthlessly. 'Yeah, alright,' she said. 'Keep telling yourself that.' I'd be hurt, but she had a wicked grin on her that let me know she was joking so I grinned back.

'Excuse me, lovely, can you make us two gin and tonics, please?' I said, turning to the bartender.

'Doubles?' she asked.

'Oh, yes!' I replied emphatically. 'I think we need them.' Mum raised her eyebrows at me, and I shrugged unapologetically. 'Why not?'

'Yeah, why not? ' she said, leaning against the bar. I smiled, drinking her in, feeling warm and fuzzy all the way to the tips of my toes. See, one of the awful things about realising your parents are people is that you see their flaws and realise they see yours, too. But if you can get past that, and you're very, very lucky, sometimes you realise they're people you actually like and get on with. If I'd known my parents when I was younger, I think I would have wanted to be their friends. While that's impossible – at least until Doctor Who gets her arse in gear and comes to pick me up to be her companion – I can at least try to be their friend, now, right?

I paid the bartender, handed Mum her drink, and we chinked glasses.

'Cheers!' I toasted.

'Cheers!' she said, and we downed them in one, snorting and gasping at the bubbles fizzing in our throats. 'Shall we?'

'If we have to,' I sighed.

We picked up the two drinks (only the nanas had wanted another in the end) and walked, hand in hand, back to our table just in time to hear Nana Addy do an ostentatious burp, which drew the attention of half the restaurant.

'Mam!' Mum exclaimed, putting her glass down in front of her. Nana Addy ignored her, and patted her chest with a wrinkled hand.

'Ooof!' she said, looking round at her horrified descendants. 'I got the hiccups!'

'Like hell you do!' Nana Meryl muttered darkly.

TO-DO

☑ Train, Paddington to Cardiff, 08.43

☑ Leave house at 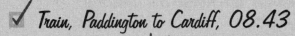 07.30

☐ Don't forget Christmas cards 🍃
for everyone (ah, shit!)

☑ Don't let Nana Meryl and Nana Addy
kill each other

☑ Don't let Mum kill Laura or Dolly

☑ Don't let Dad kill himself

☑ Don't kill Andrew

☑ Make sure Mum has a good time
(I think I did this? I gave her gin, which at
least helped)

TO-DONE

- Left the house on time ✓✓
- Got the train on time ✓✓
- Got myself breakfast for the train
- Did my make-up nicely ⚊⚊◯
- Gave the nanas a nice time at the meal
- Had a nice conversation with Dad ♡♡
- Had a nice conversation with Mum ♡ ♡
- Defended self against Taggie ⚡

- Defended self against charges of being London Wanker 🖕

- Entertained the kids while Freddy and Laura had <u>A Talk</u>

- Got the train back <u>on my own</u>

- Read some of my book

- Went food shopping

- Cooked a nice dinner, even though it was just for me

- Took my make-up off before bed

SESSION THREE

'I can't even look after myself as well as everyone else can,' I said, arms crossed, scowling.

Bjorg – wearing a green dress and boots I would absolutely wear if I were six stone thinner – nodded thoughtfully.

'But you weren't trying to look after yourself as well as everyone else, you were just trying to look after yourself,' she said levelly. *Fuck her, with her rationality and her calmness and her perfectly fucking functional fucking brain.* 'And you were just trying it out, to see what happened. It doesn't matter that you didn't manage to do it every night.'

'Yes, it does, because it's such a simple task, and I can't even do that right.' I shifted in my chair awkwardly, I couldn't get a position that felt natural. 'Everyone else manages to have a shower and do some exercise every day. Why can't I?'

By the end of that sentence I was struggling to talk. The self-loathing was rising, hot and painful in my throat, making it hard to breathe and stinging my eyes. Bjorg didn't say anything as I fought with my feelings. She just watched, hands folded neatly on her lap, eyes sleepy, face entirely unmoved as if I were telling her how to make a Victoria sponge. I swallowed hard.

Come on, Jones.

'I feel so useless compared to everyone else in my life, all the time. Everyone is so much better than me.'

'Okay,' Bjorg said. 'I'm interested – why does it matter to you so much how everyone else is doing?'

'Because that's the only barometer I have for how well *I* should be doing.'

'And how do you know how well everyone else is doing?'

'Well, I see them doing it. All the time,' I said.

She cocked an eyebrow.

'As well as your job and your newsletter, and seeing friends and having a husband and baking and sewing and reading and all your other hobbies, you're spending all this time with all these other people and seeing how well they're always doing?' She exhaled lightly, shook her head and sat back in her chair, arms flopping into the armrests. 'I don't know how you do it.' Her eyes met mine, and she cocked an eyebrow challengingly.

You sarcastic bitch, I thought with a smile. If she wasn't my therapist, I'd really love to be her friend. She and Janae would adore each other.

'Yes, yes, okay,' I said, rolling my eyes at myself. 'But I see it online. They're always twee – talking about it on Twitter, or posting photos on Instagram, or things like that. There are hundreds of women my age in London, and whenever I go online, all I can see is how well they're doing.'

'Huh,' she said, watching me curiously, again. 'And no one ever puts things online that aren't entirely truthful, or don't show the whole picture of how they're feeling, right?'

I opened my mouth. I thought of the photos I'd put up of the hen weekend – all of us grinning at Paddington, selfies with Penny, Janae and Emily gazing at each other dopily – or of my family looking like a perfect Christmas card after the meal. I try to be honest about my life online, so I'd mentioned on Stories that I was having a rough time mentally, but there'd been no mention of lakes or bruised forearms studded with half-moon indentations or having to neck gin just to get through things. I closed my mouth again, and shrugged. Bjorg smiled like a cat that had just managed to pounce on its prey.

'So, when do you think you started caring so much what other people were doing compared to you?' she asked, re-crossing her legs and rearranging her skirt over her knees.

'I can't remember a time when I didn't,' I said cautiously.

'Even when you were a child?'

'No, I guess ... from secondary school? I went from a small primary to a big secondary school. I'd been bullied at the primary school for being Welsh and a bit of a ... um, a bit of a swot ... but when I got to the bigger school, it got worse.'

I paused and glanced at Bjorg. She was listening intently, but didn't say anything. Can't decide whether I hate her silence or those worryingly innocent questions more.

'I had these ... these friends, who were in all my classes and everything, and they didn't like anything I did. It was all wrong,' I said, slowly. 'My body was wrong, my hair was wrong, the things I liked were wrong, how I behaved in general was wrong. They used to do things like ... um ... like, take my bus and lunch money, and make me skip meals and walk home to try and lose weight. They got me to cut my hair, and then made fun of me because I'd cut it wrong. They wanted me to be right, and everything I did was wrong.' I stopped, clenching my hands in and out of fists – I didn't trust myself to keep going.

'And what happened?' Bjorg prompted after a minute or so when I'd calmed down a little.

'Well, eventually I think we fell out. I didn't really have many friends for a year or so, and I eventually got some who still didn't ... who still thought I was wrong, but didn't seem to mind so much.' I shrugged.

'Do you think your friends think you're "wrong" now?' she asked steadily.

My gut lurched. I nodded. 'Yes, but they're too nice to say anything about it.' My voice was shaking. I took a deep breath, which shuddered as it went in, every atom of my being focused on not crying.

'And do you think that you were "wrong" back then? That 11-year-old Amy was "wrong"?'

I didn't say anything. Neither did she. The moment hung awkwardly, until ...

'No,' I said, my breath coming out in a whoosh. I stared hard at the floor, right between my feet. I couldn't look at her. 'She was weird, sure, but she was bright and funny and smart and just doing her own thing. She wasn't wrong, she just wasn't what everyone else was. And that's okay, she was still great.'

'Okay,' Bjorg said suddenly, clapping her hands and standing up. She took the chair from the desk and dragged it round so that it was facing me. 'We're going to try something ...' She settled back in her chair, hands once again neatly folded in her lap, delight positively radiating off her. 'Sat in that chair is your 11-year-old self.'

'What?' I stared at the empty chair and back at Bjorg, scowling. *What bollocks was this?* I was here for scientific analysis and extraction of bad thought patterns, not talking to empty chairs like they were my past selves. I trusted Bjorg and was starting to feel that strange combination of hatred and utter adoration that I'd had for strict teachers, Olu, and anyone else who had forced me to sort my shit out, but if she was going to make me start doing wanky visualisation exercises then that was going to change.

Bjorg, meanwhile, was beaming at me with serene sunniness.

'Sitting in the chair is your 11-year-old self. She's at school with these, uh, these friends, and they're all telling her she's wrong and she's stupid, and she needs to change everything.' Pause. 'What would you say to her?'

Sceptical, I turned to the chair, toying with the idea of saying something like, 'Will Young wins *Pop Idol*, not Gareth Gates – put your bet on now,' or 'Bitcoin really is a thing, you should get some,' but I didn't want to disappoint. I didn't think this was going to work, but Bjorg was trying so hard, I should try, too.

So, 11-year-old self ... At first, all I can see is the chair, but it doesn't take long to imagine myself as I was almost two decades ago: pale, round face, neat little teeth in a wonky grin, waist-length hair, enormous blue eyes. I think of myself as I was when I started my school: happy, carefree, excited to make new friends and learn new things. I think about how I loved singing out loud to myself, how I was convinced I was going to be an author, how I knew I was crap at things like sport and art, but I'd give them a go anyway, because why not, what's the worst that could happen? And then I think of myself as I was when I left school: awkward, unhappy, uncomfortable in my own skin. I force myself to look into the imaginary face of the little girl who felt she could do anything, into the face of the little girl I was before I felt like I was worthless.

'Don't listen to them!' I said, quietly. 'You're brilliant, you're absolutely brilliant! And you don't deserve what they're going to do to you.'

And then I exploded into noisy, snotty tears.

TO-DO

- ☐ Say happy anniversary to Garry

- ☐ Hot chocolate, by self, in town

- ☐ Go shopping to kill time

- ☐ Pick up stuff for anniversary meal

- ☐ Clean kitchen

THIRTEEN

As I woke with a start when the front door slammed, I checked my watch: 7.45am. I would have grumbled at the early start but was quite relieved that the dream I'd been having, where I had to repeatedly escape through a maze from a werewolf who would bloodily tear me apart only for me to find myself at the beginning of the maze again, was no longer playing in Ultra HD behind my sleeping eyes. As much as I relied upon my medication to, you know, not feel like I wanted to die, the nightmares it gave me were horrible.

The cat trilled and leapt off the bed, where she'd been curled up beside me for warmth against the cold February morning, to investigate the noise.

'Hello, Flicksickle,' Garry whispered – although when I say 'whisper', I mean something loud enough to be heard from across a football pitch in the howling wind. 'Hello! Good girl, you *good* girl! Come on, let's go in here.'

I dozed, listening to the familiar bumble of Garry coming back from work, dumping his coat and bag, giving the cat a fuss, changing into the PJs he always leaves in the living room when he's on nights, and generally letting go of his work brain and settling himself back into home. When his footsteps approached the bedroom I opened my eyes again, just in time to see him coming through the door, clutching two takeaway coffees and a brown paper bag, patches of warm butter seeping through it. His hair was fluffy, his eyes soft with fatigue, the bruises from previous shifts turning purple on his arms. I smiled.

'Good morning,' I said, sitting up and reaching for one of the coffees.

'Morning,' he said, handing it to me before sitting on the side of the bed and kicking off his shoes. 'Happy anniversary.'

'Happy anniversary, love.' He swung his legs up onto the bed and settled back into the pillows next to me. I leant over and kissed him sleepily. His beard was scratchy and familiar against my face. 'How was your shift?'

'Fine,' he said noncommittally, opening up the bag. There were two fat chocolate croissants inside; he handed one to me and I started tearing it into pieces. 'PC Rain made sure everything was q.' Or, for those who aren't in the police, it was raining and so that meant it was quiet. I rolled my eyes at this use of technical jargon, and he stuck his tongue out at me. If it were any other day or situation I'd be mildly annoyed, but it's really very hard to be annoyed at someone waking you up with coffee and croissants.

But Garry was still talking. 'I got off on time, which was nice. And it means I get to see you for a bit today, at least.'

'Yeah,' I said, nudging my foot against his calf from underneath the covers. 'It is.' He nudged my leg with his knee in return, going silent for a moment.

'Sorry I can't be home all weekend on our anniversary,' he said quietly.

I shrugged. 'Is what it is. And it's only a three-year wedding anniversary. And it's not like we do presents or cards or anything.'

'I know, but it would have been nice to spend the day with you,' he insisted. 'I miss you.'

He took a long swig of coffee, watching the cat as she jumped up on the windowsill to glare at anyone who dared walk by. He wasn't just tired, he was sad. My heart twisted itself into knots with love for him.

'I know, sweet,' I said, pausing in my croissant massacre to rest my head on his shoulder. 'I miss you too.'

And I did. I hadn't really seen him for almost a month. He'd been working early on New Year's Day, so had to be in bed by 10pm the night before, and then a combination of birthday parties, work events and bad shift patterns meant that I hadn't seen him for longer than a few hours for three weeks. We were on WhatsApp constantly, obviously, and tried to have one FaceTime a day, but it wasn't the same. It wasn't talking to him that I missed, just being near him. And to be honest, it was nine years to the day since we went on our first date and we were now such an old couple that our favourite thing was to sit in silence, side by side, while he watched TV and I read a book. Talking was superfluous, I just needed to be with him.

I sat up again, making sure that as much of my body was squished against his as possible. We chatted about nothing for a while, both of us doing a cursory scroll through all our social media platforms, and in the grand tradition of long-term couples, updated each other on people in our lives that the other person didn't really know or care about. It was lovely. Eventually, though, Garry started to droop.

'You need to go to sleep,' I said when he yawned so widely, I could see his back teeth.

'You need to stop bullying me,' he grumbled, giving his thumb another flick on the screen and making Instagram whizz past at a dizzying speed.

'You need to stop being a grumpy bum.'

'You need to go away.'

'Fine,' I said, pulling back the covers and moving to get off the bed. He threw his phone down on the bed and grabbed me, pulling me back into his chest.

'No. Cuddle first.'

'Get in bed, then, and I will.'

He got under the covers and pulled his sleep mask (the pretty, velvety blue one with a white lace trim I'd received in a gift set one Christmas and he'd immediately nicked for night shifts) over his eyes. I slid back into bed and nestled against him, my back against his chest, his arm tucked around my stomach. I unlocked my phone and started reading the day's news. I wasn't even three articles in before his breathing got heavy – which is the nice way of saying 'before he started snoring in my ear'.

I grinned and stayed in bed a while longer, texting and looking at memes and generally enjoying the cwtch, before gently extracting myself and tiptoeing out into the living room. Garry didn't stir.

Forty-five minutes later, I was sitting in Costa in our local shopping centre, a book on the table and my phone in my hand. Garry had been working these odd shifts ever since we moved to London so I'd spent a lot of weekends and evenings alone, and soon realised that I was going to have to get over the social awkwardness of being by myself in public if I didn't want to go completely stir-crazy. He wouldn't wake until about six – eight long hours to fill without making enough noise in his proximity to wake him up. Going out and having a hot chocolate by myself would fill at least one of those hours, and wandering round the shops and planning what I'd buy myself when I stop drinking hot chocolates and lose four stone would fill another.

I opened Instagram, and flicked through my Stories. As always, my friends and follow-ees were all having picture-perfect weekends so far. Frankie had been to the gym and was now having pancakes with a guy she'd been seeing for a while. Janae and Emily were in IKEA. Penny was having avocado toast and a coffee with intricate latte art on the top, gurgling niece on her lap. Hannah was still in bed, doting on a very grumpy Maya. Imogen had got a parkrun Personal Best. I sighed, and took a photo of my already-slurped hot chocolate and battered book, hoping no one was going to ask what I thought about it because it was only battered as I'd been carrying it round for a month, not because I'd actually read any of it yet. Put a filter on it. Caption 'I know how to do Saturdays alone, right?' Feel crap about self. Send.

The book lay untouched, again, as I went through the various apps on my phone, liking and commenting and retweeting, as necessary. I saved Facebook until last, the same way I used to save my carrots when I was younger, hoping I could truthfully say I was full before I had to eat them, and when I opened it up, there was a little red bubble on my notifications tab. I clicked: 'You have memories with Garry Jones, Carole Jones and 6 others to look back on today'.

I don't usually look at Facebook Memories – they make me feel sad as it's usually just photos of me when I was thinner and prettier, hanging out with people who eventually revealed themselves to be total shitbags – but it'd only been 20 minutes and I'd exhausted all other apps, so I did. It wasn't until I saw the first photo of me in my big white dress that I remembered today was my wedding anniversary, and so all my Facebook Memories were actually going to be memories of that brilliant, ridiculous day.

The photos made me beam. There I was in my enormous white dress, self-consciously climbing into a local minicab to take me round the corner to the registry office. I laughed out loud at the photo of Janae and Frankie throwing up gang symbols in front of the 'FUCK BITCH FUCK OFF' graffiti scrawled on a pillar in the garden where we had our official photos. There were pictures of my dad solemnly delivering the pub quiz he wrote especially for the reception, Penny and Ollie doing their practised dance routine, Garry and I beaming at each other as we posed for official pictures, me and my bridesmaids cracking up because Penny said, 'I just farted' just before the photographer pressed her shutter. I kept scrolling down, a warm glow that was only 10 per cent from the sugary hot chocolate filling me from top to toe.

God, what an amazing wedding it was. I can't remember ever having felt as relaxed and happy as I did that day – which was ironic, because in the run-up, I'd felt anything *but*. When I'd gotten engaged, I'd been cheerfully relaxed about the whole thing. I'd never wanted a big fancy wedding, so we'd decided to do the whole thing on the cheap. But then Laxmi and Penny had gotten engaged, and planned their weddings for six months before and six months after mine, and we all started talking wedding planning together, and suddenly I felt an enormous amount of pressure to make my wedding live up to the standards of theirs.

Penny's was elegant, traditional, dripping with an effortless class that I just didn't have because I was too working-class to ever be able to really achieve it. Laxmi's was beautiful, Pinterest perfect, polished and glossy, and just the right levels of quirky to be interesting without being irritating. In comparison, my ramshackle wedding in a registry office and a pub afterwards seemed ridiculous. And the further we got into wedding planning, the worse it got.

Their budgets were four, five times the size of mine – partly because they're better paid than me, and partly because I refused my parents' offer and we saved up for everything ourselves. They spent weekends painstakingly picking out invitations and table decorations and musicians; we made everything ourselves, right down to Garry's in-depth Spotify playlist covering every second of the day. They read the wedding magazines and the blogs and pored over photos of what celebrities were doing; I shoved a few pins on Pinterest and promptly ignored everything on it. They did it properly – basically, like grown-ups – and we didn't. I didn't care about the concept of a wedding enough to spend any more money or time on it, but I definitely cared what people would think of me because of it. At night I'd lie awake, worrying about what people were going to say about my stupid, cheap, pathetic little wedding and the stupid, cheap, pathetic little woman I was because of it.

The thing that broke me was a sheep. Specifically, a five-foot statue of Shaun the Sheep painted to look like a Chinese dragon, which the venue informed me, nine weeks before our wedding day, was to be in the middle of our dance floor. Our dance floor was outside in a covered market, which is a public space, and the statue was for a charity statue trail. It was too heavy to move, there was no way to get rid of it. No matter what I said, thought or did, there was going to be a statue of Shaun the Sheep painted to look like a snake off its tits on LSD in the middle of my wedding, for everyone to see.

I lost it. Not at the poor manager from the venue – it wasn't their fault – but my bridesmaids. Frankie assures me no matter how many times I ask that I wasn't a Bridezilla, but even she can't lie convincingly enough to convince me this wasn't a serious Bridezilla moment. I was WhatsApping them all about my last conversation with the venue while on my lunch break at work, and Penny said something about how really it wasn't *that* big of a deal that there was to be a demon sheep statue in the middle of the wedding. I thought about her gorgeous church and her beautiful barn and her classy wedding, mercifully free of five-foot possessed sheep statues, and a red mist descended. How could she understand this? How *could* she?

'Honestly, it's fine,' I typed furiously while crossing the road, half-hoping I would get run over because that would *really* show them. 'Once I get over my own damn pride, seething jealousy of everyone else who manages to have a wedding that is elegant and gorgeous and doesn't have a fucking cartoon sheep in the middle of it, and my disappointment that the one thing possibly in my entire life I was going to have that wasn't going to be a bit silly or require me to be self-deprecating is no longer going to be like that, I'll be fine. It will be fine and my wedding will go ahead as planned and all will be great. It's not what I've been looking forward to for ten months, but I'll get over it. It's *fine*.'

They didn't reply. I can't really blame them.

But I wasn't really fretting about the wedding: I was fretting about our relationship in general. Not because I didn't love Garry – I've loved him with a certainty that astonishes me from the moment I got to know him properly – but because it seemed like a sign of what our relationship was going to be like for the rest of our lives. *Silly*. Something which requires me to be self-deprecating. A bit shit compared to everyone else's. Not what anyone in their right mind would choose to have.

See, I'd always fretted about how our relationship wasn't as glorious and perfect as everyone else's seems to be. There was no meet-cute or perfect first date: we had known and hated each other for four years before we started dating, and when we eventually went to the pub together, it was because I was bored during my gap year and he was looking for a rebound shag after a messy breakup. Not really a story you want to tell at the wedding (although, actually, I did, during my speech – after Sheepgate, I really stopped giving a fuck).

For the first few years of our relationship, he'd been incredibly ill with ulcerative colitis and I'd had to be his carer as much as his girlfriend, helping him in and out of the shower and waiting on his bed while he spent hours in the toilet, painfully ejecting anything he'd tried to eat to give his skeletal, bleeding body some strength. I'd been at university and he'd been a freelance musician during those first few years, so we'd had no money for expensive gifts or fancy holidays – and that didn't change when we moved to London and supported ourselves on starter salaries. And then he worked all the time, and then I was depressed, and then we were saving for a wedding, and although I was deeply, completely happy with him, our relationship never looked as grown-up or proper as everyone else's seemed to.

That lack of show, of *shine*, made me worry. Mindy Lahiri once told Danny that she wanted a relationship she could show on Instagram: it's deliciously mockable as a sentiment, but I get it. If a tree falls in a forest and there's no one around to hear it, does it make a sound? If a relationship is happy and fulfilling but there's no visual evidence, is it *really* a good relationship, or is something lacking that you're too close to realise isn't there?

In the end, of course, it hadn't mattered that our wedding wasn't as shiny and perfect as those of our peers: it was brilliant. It was brilliant despite the fact that Penny and I were locked outside my flat in our pants on the morning of the wedding and Janae had had to get a bus up to get the keys off Garry, and despite the fact the taxi company had called to cancel both our car and the car for Garry and his groomsmen 20 minutes before the ceremony, and despite the fact that a troupe of bagpipers turned up during my dad's pub quiz so Mum, Andrew, Taggie and Freddy hadn't been able to hear or join in. The 'non-weddingy' things that happened throughout the day, like me dancing to 'Happy' with a total stranger who just happened to wander through the market, or Frankie chasing two passing police officers down the street and trying to get them to do the conga with her, or the people taking selfies with the giant demon sheep were fond memories rather than marks of shame. Our personalities had run through that wedding like a streak of sauce in a decent sticky toffee pudding. Sure, it wasn't perfect and glossy and shiny, but it felt 100 per cent ours. That's what made it special. Not what it looked like, but the way it felt and the fact that it could only feel that way because it was ours.

It was 11am. Seven hours until I could go home and wake him up. I smiled involuntarily, set my phone down on the table, and picked up my book, trying to distract myself from the warm fizz of excitement in the pit of my belly that the thought of being with my husband still inspired.

*

There are many ways to wake a sleeping person. You can gently stroke a finger on their cheek. Put on the TV or the radio. Take them by the shoulder and softly shake them awake. My mum's preferred strategy with her kids was always to yell at them a few times, then stand over their peaceful, slumbering faces and wring a cold, wet flannel out over the top of them.

With Garry, I usually chose the Cat Alarm method. I scooped up Flick, who squeaked to convey her deep annoyance, carried her into the bedroom and held her over my sleeping husband, dropping her lightly onto him again and again while speaking in a high-pitched voice.

'Wake up, Daddy!' I cheeped, like Mickey Mouse with his balls trapped in a vice. 'It's time to wake up. Time to wake up and play with me. Wake up, Daddy, wake up!'

Yes, we refer to ourselves as the cat's Daddy and Mummy. No, I'm not entirely sure how it started. Yes, I know it's weird. No, I *definitely* do not wish to discuss it any further.

Eventually Garry groaned and rolled over. I dropped the cat onto his chest; she crouched there for a second, then sprang off and onto the windowsill, hiding behind the curtains and, I imagine, plotting our gory murders. I sat on the side of the bed and fussed Garry's hair energetically, as loudly and annoyingly chirpy as possible.

'Good morning! Did you sleep well?' I trilled.

'Mmm, until some prick came and woke me up,' he said, pulling his eye mask onto his forehead and glaring. I tutted and shook my head.

'That Flick, she's a nightmare,' I pronounced solemnly. He made a noise like a displeased Marge Simpson, and I beamed back. 'What time are you leaving?'

'Eight. What's for tea?'

'Bangers and mash.'

He groaned, rolling his eyes in a mock ecstasy that Ron Jeremy would be proud of. 'God, I love you!'

'Yeah, you better!' I stood up, slapping his thigh through the covers as I did so. 'Get up, I'm putting it on now and you need to shower – you stink.'

'No, *you* stink!' He pouted.

'I know, but I've not got to go to work in two hours.' I blew him a kiss and headed into the kitchen, opening the fridge to retrieve the best pack of own-brand sausages Morrisons had to offer, bought specially for our anniversary meal.

Penny's anniversary dinner this year had been in Clos Maggiore, frequently voted the most romantic restaurant in London, which served French cuisine and had flowers and fairy lights dripping from the ceiling. The photos had looked beautiful, and I'd had conversations with at least three people about what a gorgeous, romantic evening it was. Laxmi and Tom used their anniversary every year to go on a weekend break: Edinburgh the first year, Amsterdam the second, and this year, they were going to Vienna. They always had a special photo taken together in each city, and because their wedding was so near Christmas, they used them as their Christmas cards to everyone. Two photos of them with snow photoshopped over the top beamed at me from the front of my fridge as I retrieved the sausages.

I sighed. Bangers and mash in front of the telly before he went to work wasn't going to look quite so good on Instagram – and, I thought, as he wandered out of the bedroom totally naked, taking a moment to pull a silly face at me and waggle his hips so his penis went flying in all directions before he went into the bathroom, I probably wouldn't want to share memories of the whole day anyway.

But fuck it, I thought when we sat down together to eat, carefully balancing gravy-sodden plates on our laps and laughing through mouthfuls of slightly lumpy mashed potato at an episode of *The Inbetweeners* we'd seen at least four times before. Nobody would ask my friends about my amazing romantic anniversary weekend, and if you were to ask me in 30 years' time what we'd done for our third wedding anniversary, I probably wouldn't be able to tell you. But who cares? That stuff doesn't really matter. Not really. Life can't be a continuous series of perfect, memorable moments, and as Garry took my plate out to the kitchen, booping me on the end of my nose as he went, I realised that I couldn't be happier anywhere else than I was now, in my living room, with him, right now.

Well, I could not have a huge gravy stain down my top, but no one would see that apart from him and at this point, I think he's given up hope I'll ever be able to feed myself like an adult.

'Right, my lovely!' he said in an fake, highly exaggerated West Country accent, coming back into the room and stretching. 'I've got to go.'

'Noooooo!' I protested, rolling over on the sofa to face him. 'Don't go to work. Stay home instead.'

'Got to,' he sighed, walking around me to get his bag from the chair. 'The little shits won't arrest themselves, will they?'

'Okay. Anniversary selfie before you go?'

'Fiiiiine.'

I scrambled up and stood next to him, holding my phone at arm's length. He crouched down next to me, pressing his face to mine. I crossed my eyes and stuck out my tongue; he raised an eyebrow dramatically and gave the camera a smouldering look. Click. Photo saved.

'Thank you,' I said, putting my arms round his waist and cuddling him. 'I love you.'

'I love you too,' he said, kissing me. 'Happy anniversary, you.'

'Happy anniversary,' I said, walking him to the door and opening it for him. He kissed me again on the forehead and booped me again on the nose as he walked by; I wrinkled it back at him. 'Be safe, don't die.'

'I'll try.' He waved at me and headed down the steps and across the road. I watched him disappear into the night, then closed the door, leant against it and sighed.

Saturday night. Home alone. What to do? I know my friends delight in evenings home alone, watching TV and films their partners don't like and eating food combinations they'd be embarrassed to see their beloved witness and having long, luxurious bubble baths with the door open. It's a lovely thought, but when you spend as much time home alone as I do, it feels appallingly hedonistic to have a completely lovely, indulgent evening to yourself every time. So, instead, I take another step towards metamorphosing completely into my mother and do chores. I blast my favourite true crime podcast (*Nothing Rhymes With Murder*, FYI) and clean the kitchen till it's sparkling, put a load of washing on, tidy the living room ... and then, yes, I climb into a tub more bubbles than bath. Well, all work and no play, and all that.

Soaking in the hot, perfumed water and looking disturbingly like a peeled Doctor Zoidberg, I opened my phone to look at the photo we'd taken. I choked on bubbles in shock: it was truly hideous. Garry overshot his 'smouldering' expression slightly and had instead landed squarely on 'serial killer'. I went for it a little too hard with the stupid face and instead looked like I've got something seriously wrong with me. In fact, rather than being an adorable anniversary selfie it looks like something detectives would find when they broke into a murdering pervert's house and discovered all the trophies kept to commemorate his victims. For a second I stared at the photo in disbelief, then broke into a wide smile. *I love it!* I uploaded it to Instagram, along with a similarly hideous picture from our first year of dating and a beautiful, posed shot from our wedding day. Caption: 'Year nine. Year one. Year six. Happy anniversary, Garry. I hope we take terrible photos together for many years to come'. Send.

By the time I got out of the bath, it was time for bed. After pulling on my ugliest but comfiest PJs (the Little Miss Chatterbox ones with holes on the bum), I headed to the bedroom, Flick trailing behind to make sure I'm not doing anything exciting without her. I pulled back the covers and stared blankly at the space where I was supposed to lie for a moment. Bed always feels empty when Garry isn't there, pushing me to the very edge of it while insisting I'm stealing all the duvet and draping himself over me until I'm so hot, I give it all to him and shiver myself to sleep. So, every night I'm alone, I try to think of the best way to make the most of the extra space. I lay in the very middle of the bed and built myself a nest of pillows and duvet, rubbing my feet together to warm myself up and soothe me to sleep. Either it worked, or they put Rohypnol in Radox nowadays, because the next thing I was aware of was the cat leaping neatly off my chest and heading to the front door as it opened. I jerked awake in a panic, only for the front door to slam and Garry to poke his head round the door.

'Hello, lovely,' he said gently.

'Hi. Ugh! What time is it?' I asked, thrashing my arms and legs to free them from the duvet, which I'd managed to wrap around myself like a snake in the night.

'Eight,' he said, pulling off his top and throwing it in the wash basket. I eyed the fluffy hair on his soft belly appreciatively; he faux-scowled when he saw me looking. 'Perv!'

'Absolutely,' I said, yawning and rolling onto my back. As he was putting on his PJs, Flick came back in the room and started winding herself round his legs, purring seductively. 'You little hussy!'

'She can probably smell François on me,' he said, bending down to scratch her head. I frowned.

'Who the hell is François?'

'Station cat,' he replied, straightening up and tugging his top over his head. 'I was waiting in the yard and François came up to me, meowing like he was pissed off. When I looked over to his food bowl, there was a fox there, eating it. François basically walked me over there, meowing and rubbing up against my legs the whole way, in what was obviously cat for, "Get this big ginger bastard to fuck off".'

'What did you do?'

'I shooed the fox away and gave François some more food. He gave a little happy trill, like Flick does when you give her a Dreamie, and basically stuck his whole head in it.' He'd been wandering round the bedroom and getting ready while telling me the story, but as he finished, he glanced over and saw me looking at him with what must have been a strange look on my face. He cocked his head quizzically. 'What?'

'Nothing. Just … that's a really sweet story. That's really sweet, *you're* really sweet.'

'Why?' he asked, climbing into bed next to me.

'I don't know,' I replied – and I really didn't. The thought of my husband, in his uniform with his baton and handcuffs and all the other scary stuff he carries around with him at work, chasing away a fox so the station cat could get his dinner was making my chest feel like it was filled with warm golden syrup. In a nice way, not a 'Dear God I'm about to die' way.

'I love you.'

'I love you too,' he said.

He kissed me, pulled his eye mask down and lay next to me. I shuffled back under the covers and twisted my leg and arm around his, scrolling through my phone as I climbed towards wakefulness and Garry sank into sleep next to me.

After a while, I felt uncomfortable. I let go of Garry's limbs and flipped over onto my side, facing away from him. Still snoring, he followed my movements and lay directly behind me like he was going to spoon me, but instead of wrapping his arm round my waist like he usually did, his hand slid down my side and perfectly cupped my arse.

I jolted in surprise, waited a second to see what he'd do and then, realising he was still snoring and was in fact groping me in his sleep, started laughing. The shaking of my body woke him up.

'What?' he said, groggily.

'You just goosed me in your sleep,' I said, still laughing. 'Talk about being a pervert!'

'Did I?' he said in sleepy surprise. He wriggled his hand experimentally and found it trapped between my bum and his crotch. 'So I did.'

'I know it's been a while, but just how randy *are* you?' I teased.

He shrugged, shuffled closer, and put his lips to my neck. 'Clearly more than I thought,' he murmured, kissing my skin gently. I wriggled as his beard tickled me but he didn't stop, and suddenly, I found myself very keen to join in.

I rolled over to face him and pressed my body, in my ugly, hole-ridden PJs, against his. I cupped his scratchy, bearded face in my hands and kissed him, but he clearly had other ideas because soon he moved from my mouth to kiss my face, my neck, anywhere he could reach. None of this was elegant, but I didn't care: our hands roamed, grabbing onto each other like we were drowning and only the other person could keep us afloat. I don't know whether my brain was addled because I was still sleepy or the sudden rush of oxytocin, but suddenly our PJs were off and I had no idea how. I shivered, so Garry paused to pull the duvet over us both before his hands resumed their detailed study of the precise curve of my waist and hips.

Through the blood rushing in my ears, I slowly became aware of another sound: a banging. A rhythmic banging. I pulled my face back, trying to figure out if it was us making the noise – it shouldn't be, things were moving fast but not *that* fast – when another sound joined in. A small, high-pitched voice was singing.

'... got mud on your face, you big bum face, somebody better put you all over this place ...'

'WE WILL, WE WILL, ROCK YOU!' screamed another little voice. And all of a sudden, the banging stopped

'Muuuum, I didn't say he could sing with me, he got it wrong ...'

'Muuuuum, that's not faaaaaaiiiir ...'

'Muuuum!'

'MUUUUUUUUM!'

Garry pulled his head up from my neck with a sound like a plunger being removed from a loo. He turned to better listen to the sound of Muuuuuuum herself coming down and shouting at the kids, before turning back to me, aghast.

'It's the kids next door and their fucking drum kit,' he murmured. There was a pause. Boy 1 was still shouting at his brother, Boy 2 was crying with a loud, piercing whine. We looked at each other in silent horror for a second, then Garry cocked an eyebrow.

'You're still on the Pill, right?' he whispered, bringing his mouth back to mine. 'I can't be doing with this shit yet!'

I laughed and kissed him back, rolling us both over so we were on our sides as the banging started again. It wasn't the sexiest soundtrack, but that's okay. Who cares what our relationship sounds like, or what it looks like? All that matters is what it feels like, and whether we're eating cheapo meatballs in IKEA because that's all we can afford for our dates, getting married next to a giant demon sheep, or having sex to inappropriate background noise, it feels WONDERFUL.

And hey, at least the drums gave us a good rhythm to stick to!

TO-DO

✓ Say happy anniversary
to Garry

✓ Hot chocolate, by self,
in town

✓ Go shopping to kill time

✓ Pick up stuff for
anniversary meal

✓ Clean kitchen

TO-DONE

- Lovely breakfast in bed
- Got dressed
- Walked into town rather than getting the bus
- Read 150 pages of book
- Bought self new PJs
- Meal planned
- Had a conversation with Frankie; going to meet up for a walk in the park
- Bought food from Morrisons

- Cooked
- Spent lovely time with Garry 😍
- Cleaned kitchen
- Had bubble bath
- Had <u>excellent sex</u> ♥
- Had shower
- Coffee with Garry
- Made a roast dinner
- Had excellent sex <u>again</u>, albeit very full excellent sex
- Had another shower
- Early night z z z

SESSION FOUR

'I didn't realise how hard I was on myself,' I said the next week. 'Every time this week I thought about how stupid or ugly or useless I was, I imagined myself saying it to me when I was 11 and it broke my heart.'

'How often do you think those things?' Bjorg asked. She was wearing jeans and jangly earrings I could just see poking out from behind her hair – they gave me something to look at when I couldn't quite meet her eyes.

'Nearly constantly,' I replied. 'And they're always such awful things. I make one tiny mistake that I wouldn't even notice if someone else did it, and I tell myself I'm pathetic and worthless and yeah, I'm horrible to myself.'

'Do you think they're true things?' she asked.

'Huh?'

'The awful things you usually say to yourself.' She looked up at me suddenly, her pale blue eyes like searchlights. 'Do you think they're true?'

'Well, yes,' I said, hesitantly. I knew I was being led into a trap, but I couldn't quite see how to get out of it. 'And I know, I know, bad thought patterns, making assumptions, all the stuff that CBT tells you, but CBT tells you to find evidence for all your thoughts and I can find evidence to back up the fact that I'm stupid and embarrassing and no one likes me.'

'And do you think they're true about the little girl you spoke to in the other chair last week?' she asked chirpily. I closed my mouth, pressing my lips together to try and stop the choking feeling in my throat.

'No.'

'Huh,' Bjorg said. She furrowed her brow, gently puzzled. 'But if that little girl is you, and she's not all those terrible things, then how can you be all those terrible things?' She twisted her mouth and frowned, looking for all the world like she was genuinely trying to figure out how such a thing could be true. Unwittingly, I barked with laughter. *She's such a dick!*

'Yes, okay, I take your point,' I said, dryly. She quirked the corner of her mouth in satisfaction. 'And it's interesting, trying to think about little Amy as being inside me, as someone I still am. It's made it easier to look after myself this week.'

'How so?'

'Well, making sure I get enough sleep, enough rest, that kind of thing. I thought about how I'd want to look after an 11-year-old and, kind of, did that. Although –' My stomach started squirming. '– I still find it hard to eat properly.'

'What do you mean "eat properly"?' Bjorg asked.

'I still feel so much … uh, so much guilt over whatever I eat,' I explained falteringly. 'I can't remember the last time I just ate, a time when I wasn't trying to eat healthily or purposefully trying to eat unhealthily to … I dunno, prove a point … Or trying to comfort myself, or punish myself or something. And it all feels so, excuse the pun, weighted. Whatever I'm doing, I feel terrible over it because I know that I should be better.'

'Says who?'

'Says everyone!' I exploded. 'The NHS, the news, my friends, my parents … No matter how much I try to listen to the people who say it's okay to say I'm okay at whatever size, there are always 100 more people talking about how that's wrong and it's bad to be fat, and that my stupid fat body is disgusting and bad and probably going to kill me one day.'

I took a handful of my dress and started squeezing it, twisting it round my fingers. 'And I'm reminded of it constantly – whenever I eat, whenever I get dressed, look in the mirror, see someone wearing an outfit I like, and realising I'd never be able to pull it off, all the time. It's constant. And especially ... especially when I'm feeling so miserable.'

My eyes and throat were burning again. I took a breath, pushed the pain back down to my chest once more, where I could cope with it. 'I got a handle on my eating and my body, and then I got fat again when I was depressed, and now I can't shift either of them. I feel trapped in this body, trapped in my depression. I hate that I'm so obsessed with my body, when realistically I know that it's, like, the least important thing about me. I hate that I gained weight when I was depressed. I feel like ...' I swallowed. 'I feel like I destroyed my own chances of being happy.'

'Okay,' said Bjorg, mildly. Leaning forward, she plucked a tissue from the box on the table and handed it to me so I could press it against my wet cheeks. She settled herself back in the chair and, when I managed to clean myself up and look at her through red, swollen eyes, she smiled softly at me.

'You know, I see a lot of people, and they deal with their low moods and anxieties in all sorts of ways,' she said. 'Some people drink alcohol, some people take drugs. Some people look for ways to distract themselves, like gambling or having an affair, or something like that. And not always, but sometimes, these things become an addiction.

'As well as having to cope with their depression, they have to attend meetings to help them cope with alcoholism, or go to rehab to break their addiction to drugs. Some people break up their families, get into debt. By the time I see some people, they've hit rock bottom and destroyed the lives they had before. And it's terribly sad, and they have to do some really hard work to get out of it.' She looked straight at me and smiled more gently than I think she'd done in the past four weeks. 'All I'm saying is ... Amy, yes, you over-ate to cope with your depression, and it changed your body in ways you don't like, but believe me, there's worse things you could have done than get fat.'

The words hung there in silence, and a few more tears wriggled free of my eyes. I didn't wipe them away, they fell into my lap and made two damp spots on my crotch. We both pretended not to have seen them.

'Yes?' Bjorg prompted.

I nodded, not entirely sure I could speak.

'Okay,' she said quietly. 'I think, let's leave it there this week.' She glanced at the questionnaire I filled out at the start of the session. 'So, just to confirm – you've said you're still having suicidal thoughts, but do you have ...'

'I have no intention to end my life or hurt myself. As always.'

'Good. See you next week then.'

'See you next week.'

TO-DO

☐ *Job interview: Tuesday @ 10am, Foreign Office*

☐ *Job interview: Pret @ 8am, UPSTART*

☐ *Prep for interview #1*

☐ *Prep for interview #2*

☐ *Hear back from Safeguard interview*

☐ *Draft letter of resignation*

☐ *Disordered eating piece (suppose I should do my actual job even as I'm trying to leave it...)*

FOURTEEN

As I was drying my hair after my morning swim and glaring into the mirror at my nemesis, who had spent the morning lapping me and was now manoeuvring her tiny body into even tinier knickers, my phone buzzed. I picked it up, glanced at the notification and made a noise of fury – something between an angry rhino and a happy Brian Blessed. The woman on the hairdryer next to me shuffled over to the next mirror along, studiously avoiding eye contact.

'Sorry,' I said. She nodded, still looking resolutely into the mirror like she was in the middle of a staring contest and the prize was one night with Idris Elba. Usually that kind of thing would send me into an anxiety spiral, but I was lucky enough to be in the midst of a rush of misery so all-encompassing, it blasted any other emotions out of my brain. I typed out a text and sent it to Garry, my parents, and my 'Best Girls' WhatsApp group.

AMY: I didn't get the Safeguard job :(

I put my phone face down on the ledge in front of me and started drying my hair again, scowling into the mirror and muttering profanities. My mirror buddy physically angled her body away from mine. When I picked up my phone again, a flurry of messages was waiting for me.

GARRY: Fuckers
PENNY: Oh love, I'm so sorry

JANAE: Balls. I'm sorry
FRANKIE: Cunts. There is someone out there who will
    be LUCKY to have you
MUM: That's poo :(
DAD: Bastards. I thought you said it went really well?

I thought it had. The job was for a senior writer at a homeless charity – a bigger team, but the title and responsibilities were the same. I'd spent all of the weekend before last preparing for it, looking up the latest laws and legislations around homelessness, reading their website and all their online materials over and over, and making notes on what I thought was good and what could be improved, going back through the Safeguard social channels for at least a year so I knew the tone, finding the team on LinkedIn and stalking their individual social profiles so thoroughly, I could have made a decent stab at writing them a dating profile. And then made sure I looked the part. I'd found the perfect outfit – a demure top tucked into a navy circle skirt with a bright yellow blazer and Doc Martens – that said I was someone who could be taken seriously, but who had personality and creativity to go with it. I'd agonised over my make-up, looking up several YouTube tutorials and articles on *Femme* with titles like 'Make-Up To Make You Look Like A Badass Boss Bitch Even Though You're Actually An Insecure Mess' and applying, removing and reapplying liquid eyeliner until I had the *perfect* level of flick – enough to show that I was fashionable and cool, not so much that I looked like I was more interested in looking fashionable and cool than helping homeless people. A tricky balance, but I like to think I'd nailed it.

And the interview! I'd arrived half an hour early and done Power Posing in a cafe toilet for ten minutes beforehand. I'd been kind and friendly but also assertive and confident, and given a firm handshake with a slight smile and good eye contact to anyone who introduced themselves to me. During the interview I'd sat up straight and smiled and mirrored the interviewers' body language. I'd given examples, said 'Oh, that's a good question!' if I needed time to think. I'd said 'I did this' rather than 'We did this', like men supposedly do, so that I took ownership of my own work, even though there is absolutely no way I could have re-launched an entire website on my own.

I'd done everything right! I mean, I'd been so nervous and riding such a big wave of caffeine-induced anxiety that afterwards I'd had absolutely no idea what I'd said or how I'd said it – but that's fine, right? I'd done all the things the books and articles and TED Talks said you needed to do to impress at an interview and that was the really important bit. *So why didn't I get the fucking job?*

PENNY: Remember, it doesn't mean you weren't good
       enough for the job. You definitely were. It just
       means there's someone out there more qualified
       than you, and there's absolutely nothing you can
       do about that
AMY: I know, you're right

But she wasn't right. If I was good enough for the job, why hadn't I *got* the job? There was clearly something I could have done better, *should* have done better. I stepped out of the lift, heart sinking as I saw Adam at his desk, his scowl visible from 20 paces away. I walked over, chirped an unanswered 'Good morning!' in his direction, and sat at my desk. Resisting an urge to put my head down on the desk and sob, I pretended to be rummaging through my bag for something so he wouldn't see my teary eyes.

I was trapped here, bloody trapped. Trapped in this stupid, frustrating job that was somehow incredibly hectic and incredibly boring too. I'd been doing the same thing for two and a half years. Two and a half years without a pay rise or any real promotion or any kind of progression, or even any kind of indication that I was doing a good job. I could do it with my eyes closed at this point (I really could, I can touch type pretty well) and I was so *sick* of doing the same thing over and over for people who really didn't seem to give a shit whether I handed in something worthy of Shakespeare or a literary poo on a plate. I'm clever! I'm talented! I'm good at my job! I *deserve* more than this.

A rush of righteous anger surged through me before I glanced around the same sad old office and despair overtook it again. *Yeah, right, Jones. Sure!* You deserve more than this. That's why you can't even get a job doing the same thing at a different charity. That's why all your friends are doing brilliantly and you're not. That's why even people who used to be your underlings are off working in fancy magazines and getting promoted above you. You're *obviously* useless. You don't deserve this job, let alone a better one.

My computer limped to life; I stared at it like a madwoman, hands gripped into fists so tight my knuckles went white. Fuck it. *Fuck. It.* Claire arrived at her desk and shot me a quizzical smile. I pulled an exaggerated sad face, and she nodded sympathetically. She knew I was trying to leave – in fact, at the work Christmas party in November, she'd gotten plastered on two-for-one cocktails and had slurred at me for a good 45 minutes about how I *should* leave because I had the spirit of a majestic cow inside me and I needed to let it roam free – and had had high hopes for this first interview.

We *all* had.

Unconsciously, I sighed miserably and then froze in case Adam noticed. He obviously hadn't, because that would involve noticing I was still alive, so I was free to sulk in silence. I had two more interviews that week – one tomorrow at the Civil Service and one on Thursday for a magazine – and I needed them to go well, or I might just lose my mind.

The first was with the Foreign Office, writing tweets for social media and their website, and my ego was thrilled at the idea of doing something so *worthy* and clever. Screw you, Taggie, and your judgemental 'Are you *just* doing that?' comments. Working for the Foreign Office, even just doing their tweets, was as far from 'just' as you could get. But the second was where my heart really lay. A magazine and website aimed at teenage girls, *Upstart*. It had only been going for a few years and was growing so quickly, it needed someone else to take on the management of the YouTube channel and writing some features. Feminist as hell, it was brave, open, honest, and talked to teenagers about the things they were actually interested in, in the way they liked to be talked to. It was the kind of place I could have a lot of fun, but also do some good.

My favourite part of the Youth Steady job was reading the message boards, listening to what these passionate, ridiculous, brilliant teenagers were saying and steering them in the right direction. A job where I could do that and also talk back to them using personality rather than the terribly 'safe' tone you have to use in the third sector sounded like a dream. But, if I'd done everything right for the first job interview, a job that I was basically already doing and still hadn't got it, what hope did I have of getting a job that made me as happy as this one would?

I glanced over at the adult Steady content team. Rowena was there, chatting to Iesha and Will animatedly, and they were all laughing brightly with each other. At that specific moment, the sun peeped out from behind a cloud and golden early-morning sun beamed in through the windows and surrounded them in a halo of light. I dragged my focus back to my own pod of desks. Fee and Nish weren't even in yet – the clock said they were five minutes late – Claire was absent-mindedly adjusting her boobs in her top, and Adam was glaring at his phone. He sensed me watching him, and looked up.

'What?' he asked.

I shrugged.

'Nothing.'

I looked back at my desk, cheeks and neck burning. I dashed off the work I had to do in a couple of hours, and spent the rest of the day researching Cabinet members, reading the Foreign Office's latest press releases and fantasising about strangling

Adam to death with a shoelace. I couldn't stay in this role for a second longer, and if that meant I had to kill someone – Adam or myself – then I was very, very willing to consider it.

Tuesday, 13 March

I got off the bus at Trafalgar Square and walked towards Whitehall, thighs tensed to try and stop my knees shaking. I was an hour early, even while factoring in arriving 15 minutes early in order to appear punctual – much too early, really, but after not getting the Safeguard job, I was extra-keen to make sure this interview was perfect. Hoisting my bag back onto my shoulder, I tried to ignore the fact that my hands were shaking and nervously looked around for an empty cafe to hide in for 45 minutes. Instead, I spotted a Waterstones and my heart lifted.

So excited was I that I didn't properly look left and right before I crossed the road and got a beep from an angry taxi driver for doing so. I ducked into the Waterstones and leant against the wall, breathing heavily. Holly Golightly felt safe in Tiffany's, but for me it's bookshops. Especially big ones like this, where I'm surrounded by thousands upon thousands of books and I can run my fingers over their glossy spines and let the cool calm within seep through my fingertips and into my raging brain, where no one wants to talk to me or even really pay me any attention because they're drinking in the magic in exactly the same way. Nothing bad could ever happen surrounded by this many books – it would go against the laws of nature. I feel the same way in John Lewis, too – how can anything go wrong in a building that contains Le Creuset eggcups and its own haberdashery department? It's simply not feasible.

By the time I had to leave for the interview, I'd spent enough time browsing the Cookery and Arts & Crafts that my pulse had resumed to a normal level and I could breathe without feeling like I was going to be sick. Walking down towards the building where the interview was to take place, I focused on breathing deeply to keep myself calm and tried to ignore the pollution poisoning me from the inside out as I did so. I got to the office, stepped aside for two armed police officers to go through the door first and checked in at reception. I had to show my passport and driving licence to prove my identity, first. Now I know it's shallow to be thrilled by all the security, but I was. I really, really was – I'm basically James Bond.

I was directed to wait on some squashy chairs, which I knew would inevitably make farting noises when I sat on them. As I walked over to them, I subtly checked my appearance in one of the windows. The Civil Service is far more formal than the charity sector and my outfit reflected that. I was wearing a navy and white dress last worn to a christening, with black tights and navy ballet pumps with smart little buckles. Still got the yellow blazer, though. For one thing, while it's a formal organisation, it's also a creative role and I don't want to come across as boring. But mainly, it's because I've gained a lot of weight since my last round of interviews and my other smart blazer doesn't fit.

'Amy?' said someone in a broad Scottish accent. I looked up, a confident smile already stretched across my face, and saw that the voice belonged to a tall woman, who was peering at me quizzically.

'Jean?' I asked, standing up already. It was a rhetorical question: thanks to all my LinkedIn and Twitter stalking, I knew damn well that this was Jean Young, the HR manager who'd been emailing me for the past few weeks. 'Nice to meet you!'

'Nice to meet you too,' she said, offering her hand. I shook it firmly, keeping eye contact, keeping a smile. *Make a good first impression, Jones. That's what really counts.* 'Shall we go through?'

'Absolutely!' I replied brightly. I followed her through reception, through a couple of security scanners (*so cool!*) and into a depressingly normal meeting room. Jean told me to sit in a lone seat on one side of the table; she sat on the other side next to an Asian man with dark curly hair and a young woman with a perky blonde ponytail. I smiled at them all with a breeziness I absolutely didn't feel and they smiled politely back.

'So, Amy, nice to meet you—' the man started.

'Nice to meet you too!' I blurted out, keen to be friendly, approachable and assertive.

'My name is Rama and I'm the head of the new Digital and Social Content team,' he continued as though I'd never said anything. I blushed. *Keep it together.* 'And I will be interviewing you today alongside Jean, our HR manager, and Leanne, my deputy.' Leanne smiled warmly and waved her pen absently at me, and I nodded gratefully back.

Rama shuffled through the papers in front of him and cleared his throat. 'So, what's going to happen is we'll ask you some questions and then we'll be writing down notes based on our core competency framework. We might ask you some further questions, to really delve into your answers, but don't worry about that – we're just trying to make sure we get everything we need.' He met my eyes and smiled his first proper smile so far; my stomach lurched. 'Does that sound okay?'

'That sounds great!' I said brightly, so brightly I was in danger of sunbeams bursting out of my eyes and melting them. Internally, I cringed. *That sounds great.* It's a fucking job interview. No one has ever described a job interview as *great*, you pathetic, try-hard *wassock*! I swallowed hard, trying to keep my nerves under control.

Across the table, Rama, Jean and Leanne didn't seem to notice my anxieties. Jean smiled at me encouragingly as Rama took the lid off his pen and held it ready.

'So, Amy, what experience do you have with creating content for digital platforms?'

'Well, I've been doing it for the past three years,' I said with a small laugh. No one laughed back. I cleared my throat and shuffled in my seat. 'Right, but what I mean is, as senior content producer for Youth Steady, a charity which deals with the mental health of young people, I manage and contribute to the production of most of the content that goes on our site and social media platforms ...'

As I talked, uninterrupted, I felt my nerves seep away. This is *fine*. I'm alright in interviews, past the part where I have to have a back-and-forth interaction with other human beings, because although I'm incredibly awkward socially, I'm also a huge show-off. Also, I've done so much preparation and filled my head with so many facts, opinions and answers to practice questions that actually doing the interview feels like I've opened a tap in my brain and it's all pouring out of me. I feel light, I feel free. *I'm weirdly enjoying this.* I sat up a little straighter, threw my shoulders back, cracked a few jokes that actually landed and elicited a chuckle. By the time the interview was over, I was practically glowing with the mix of endorphins and adrenaline.

Hire me, bitches! I'm great!

'Okay, so I think that's just about everything,' Rama said as I finished telling him all about how I think Instagram Stories would be an excellent way of connecting with and informing millennials and Generation X about Foreign Office policies. 'Just one question, actually – why are you leaving your current role?'

'Oh!' I said, taken aback. What do I say? That I'm bored as hell, my boss is a sociopath, and if I have to watch as one more peer gets a book deal or buys a house or has a baby while I'm stuck in the same life I've had for almost three years I might throw myself off a building just to insert some excitement? No, that probably won't go down well.

'I love Youth Steady,' I stammered, stalling for time. 'It's a great place to work, and I really passionately believe in the cause. But, well ...' *Oh, shit. Think, Amy, think.* 'The thing is ...' Shit. Shit. *Shitballsfuckingtwatbags.* Wait! No, I have it. 'The thing is, when I saw this role, I just thought it was too good *not* to apply for.'

Rama barked with laughter. Leanne and Jean smiled indulgently and I glowed so brightly, I lit up the room.

Nailed it.

'Good answer,' Rama said, neatening his papers and standing up to shake my hand. I shook it back firmly, grinning. 'Thanks for coming in, Amy. We'll be in touch.'

'Thank you! I hope you have a lovely day,' I burbled as Jean gestured me out of the room and led me back to reception.

'That went well, I thought,' she said cheerfully as she swiped her card and held the door open for me to go through.

'Do you think so?'

'Definitely.' She walked me back to the security gates and turned to face me directly, smiling much more openly than she had when I'd met her an hour ago. 'Thanks so much for coming in – I'm sure I'll be speaking to you soon.'

'Right!' I burbled, my pleasure so intense that it made me clumsy. 'Absolutely, yes! Thank you so much. See you soon!'

I went back out through security and burst back out into the sunshine. The air choking me just 90 minutes ago felt fresh and sweet in my lungs, now. I jumped on the first bus I saw and let it take me back into central London, not caring where I was going or how I was getting there because I'd booked a day's holiday and wanted to ride this wave of joy for as long as I could. I took a seat on the top deck, right at the front, and texted everyone to tell them how brilliantly it had gone. Throwing my phone in my bag euphorically, I rested my head on the window and beamed at the world outside with gold-tinted glasses. I felt bubbly, like champagne. I felt so wonderful it was like one single body wasn't enough to contain it.

That had been brilliant. *Brilliant.* There was no way they weren't going to offer me the job. There was *No. Way.* And now I knew how to make it work, I could do the same for the next one! I shivered, imagining how fantastic I'd feel next week when I had *two* jobs to choose from. It was just as I thought: underneath all the depression telling me that I was useless, I'm brilliant and fantastic, and people recognise it, and there's a world out there beyond Steady. A place out there for me, no matter how it usually feels.

I sighed happily, watching the world pass me by, for once utterly connected rather than standing on the outskirts, looking in. This was my time to succeed. This was *my turn*. And it felt so bloody great to, just for once, feel like I was first in line.

Wednesday, 14 March

The email from Jean came through the next day while I was researching a new article on disordered eating. I saw the notification flash up and my heart leapt in my mouth. *This is it! This is the email that's going to change my life!* I flung myself at my phone and started reading like I was drowning and the email was the bubble of fresh, clean air that would save me.

'*Dear Mrs Jones,*' it began. '*We are sorry to tell you …*'

Wait! What?

'*… that you have been unsuccessful in your application for the position of online content officer. We'd like to thank you for your interest, and wish you the best of luck in the future.*'

I stared at the email in shock, my throat closing up, a sharp prickling behind my eyes. Abruptly, I pushed my chair back, grabbed my coat and walked out, trying to move normally enough so that no one would think anything was wrong, but quickly enough so that I could get out before I exploded. I walked down the stairs, out the front door and down the street, turning corners and going down alleyways until I found myself alone in a small square of dirt pretending to be a park. I sat down on a bench, put my head in my hands and sobbed.

There's no escape, is there? This is my life, forever. The problem isn't that I'm undiscovered or I'm not trying hard enough, or I'm in the wrong place. It's just that I'm not good enough. *I'm just not good enough.*

My phone buzzed. I glanced at the screen: it was a text.

CLAIRE: You okay, babe? Where've you gone?

I sniffed, wiping my nose on the back of my hand. I'd spent a hurried tea break that morning whispering to Claire about how well it had gone. She'd been so happy for me. I couldn't bear to tell her I'd fucked it up, again. Not just because I didn't want to disappoint her, but because my pride really wouldn't let me admit just how wrong and stupid I'd been.

AMY: I'm fine! Needed coffee. Want anything?
CLAIRE: Ooh! I'd love a hot chocolate

Balls! Fine. I stood up, sniffing heavily, winding my way back towards the office via a cafe. I got the drinks, and bought a bar of tiffin while I was there. The drinks made it back to the office, but the tiffin was stinging my throat and sitting uncomfortably in my belly by the time I was halfway back.

I delivered Claire's hot chocolate to her with a smile. She smiled back cautiously.

'Thanks, pet. Everything okay?'

'Everything is *great*,' I said meaningfully, winking with the eye furthest away from Adam. She smirked imperceptibly, nodded, and went back to her work. I settled back in my chair, sighing deeply. My amazing skills of deception come in handy once again.

For the rest of the day, while my face was pointed towards NHS pages on disordered eating, my brain was entirely elsewhere. One more interview, tomorrow. One more chance.

Please, God, don't let me fuck it up.

Thursday, 15 March

This final interview had to be a bit cloak-and-dagger. What with the doctor's appointments and the random Tuesday booked in as annual leave, I had a feeling that Adam was getting suspicious. Part of me didn't give a toss – he could think I was off giving sexual favours to Russian diplomats for all I cared – but a bigger part is still a total Goody Two-Shoes who wants to play by the rules and have everyone like me and be my friend. So, rather than lying and say I had another medical appointment, I booked this interview for 7.45am so that I could rush back to the office afterwards and complain bitterly about how terrible the train service from my flat is.

For the other interviews, the jobs in the charity sector and the Civil Service, I'd known how to dress. They were staid, formal organisations so I'd needed a staid, formal outfit. But this was for a *magazine*, and I was being interviewed by a *journalist*. Not just a journalist, a *magazine editor*. People in the media were all super cool and fashionable, judging by Instagram, all the events Penny dragged me to, and *The Devil Wears Prada*. My dowdy christening dress and Doc Martens really weren't going to cut it.

So, I'd dressed up. Today's interview outfit was a pair of fancy new ankle boots under paperbag trousers (Penny assured me they were very fashionable right now) and a silk white blouse covered in swans, with liquid eyeliner, fuchsia lipstick and more eyebrow pencil than I usually went for. When I looked in the mirror, I felt like a little girl playing dress-up. I struck a pose, took a photo, and sent it to my best girls.

AMY: What do you think?
PENNY: You look GORGEOUS. Go get 'em xxx
FRANKIE: I'd do you. Good luck, babes!
JANAE: Sorry, can't talk, am blinded by your hotness
JANAE: But seriously, GOOD LUCK. You're gonna be
    amazing xxx

Fuck it, let's do this. I left the house, breathing deeply to keep myself calm, and walked briskly towards the station. I managed to get on a train three trains before the one originally planned, so by the time I got to where I needed to catch the bus from, there was plenty of time to spare. Again. I bimbled over to the bus stop, wondering if there was a handy bookshop near my destination that I could hide in before the interview and spotted a little coffee kiosk tucked away in the station.

Coffee! That'd be nice. Rather than rush around when I got there I'd get myself a nice coffee now, sip it slowly on the bus, and arrive in a state of gentle serenity, fuelled by caffeine and sugar. I queued up behind several very angry bankers (*Why are bankers always so angry? Doesn't all the money and the endless supply of cocaine make them happy?*), ordered a mocha and clutched it happily as I weaved my way through the crowd to the bus stop. The heat from the mug seeped through my palms, keeping them warm despite the bitterly cold morning. My chest lightened. *It's fine*, I thought. *This is all going to be fine*.

That's when I fell over. I caught the heel of the new boots on a wonky paving slab and, unused to wearing anything other than trainers and Doc Martens, I couldn't get my balance in time. One hand reached out to protect my face from the pavement rapidly coming up to meet it, the other tried to keep hold of the coffee, instinctively squeezing it tightly. About the same time that my shoulders hit the floor, the coffee lid burst off and the contents rushed out with it. Before I was really aware of what was going on, I was lying on the floor, my top covered in sticky, chocolatey coffee, palm bleeding. I coughed, winded, gasping in pain as the hot liquid met my chest.

'Oh God, are you okay?' asked a kind-faced woman with a pram, rushing over.

'Are you burnt? Do you need an ambulance?' a studenty-looking bloke said, already unlocking his phone.

'No, no, I'm fine,' I stammered, sitting up and plucking the hot material of my poor, ruined blouse from my chest. 'Fuck! Ow! Sorry.'

'Don't be sorry, take a moment. You really stacked it,' the woman said, kneeling down beside me while the man put his phone away, clearly disappointed. She handed me a packet of wet wipes and helped me clean myself up, throwing the empty coffee cup away and fussing over me while her wide-eyed toddler watched with the air of a king unamused by his jester. I managed to hold it together for long enough to reassure them that I was fine, get myself back on my feet and catch my bus. It was only when I got myself a seat, on the top deck and right at the back where I could at least pretend I had some privacy, that I let myself bawl.

Is God actively trying to fuck with me these days? I'm in no way religious, but this week surely has to be the proof we all need to accept that (a) there is a God, and (b) they are a total fuckwit. Snot dribbled down my face and I wiped it away with an old napkin found in the bottom of my bag. A smear of pink came away with it, and I laughed bleakly. There goes my carefully applied pink lipstick. The only thing that had even a chance of distracting from the giant brown stain across my beautiful silk blouse. Looks like I wasn't going to get this job either, then – no one was going to hire this train wreck.

By the time I got to the Pret where we were having our interview, I was all cried out. I was all *everything-ed* out. All the highs and lows of the past few weeks had been purged in the form of tears, snot, and little hiccupy sobs that I think the person in front of me was filming and putting on Twitter. I'm not nervous. I'm not excited. I'm not even sad.

I'm just so tired, and I have no energy left to feel anything.

I nipped into the loo and tried to do something about my appearance. My make-up was cried off entirely, my hair all over the place from clutching it while I sobbed, my outfit totally fucked. *Ah, well … Even if I can't polish the turd that is my appearance right now, I can at least clean it up a bit.* I found a clean corner of the coffee-stained wet wipes and wiped away the remaining crumbs of pink clinging to the corners of my mouth and the black streaks under my eyes. I wet my hands and ran them through my hair to flatten it. Although there was nothing I could do to salvage my top, I decided to undo the top few buttons so that it was at least a bit more comfortable. Looking at myself in the mirror, I laughed miserably. I was so far away from the woman in the photo sent to my friends that morning, I could have been a different species.

Might as well get this over with, then. I went back into the cafe and got myself a juice (didn't fancy a coffee, somehow). As soon as I'd settled myself in the corner and taken my coat off, my interviewer arrived: Grace Chambers, a woman who at 36 already had a CV that made Penny moan with envy. I waved at her awkwardly and she waved back.

'Do you want anything?' she mouthed, pointing towards the counter and miming swigging a drink. I shook my head and raised my juice, mouthing back my thanks. She nodded, her brow creasing ever so slightly in confusion as she clocked my stained top, and went to the counter. I waited to feel sick with nerves and shame, but it didn't come – I was all feelings-ed out.

'Hi,' said Grace awkwardly as she approached my table, clutching a flat white and a banana. I stood up to shake her hand. She had a firm handshake, but I was slightly taken aback to see that she had bitten nails. In fact, I thought as I sat back down and she took her coat off, she didn't look anything like I thought she would. She didn't seem to be wearing *any* make-up – not in that 'I look natural but actually, I've got 32 different types of product on' way, but in a genuine 'I just don't wear make-up' way. Her hair was not the sleek, highlighted waterfall I'd seen in her headshot; it was just hair, normal hair that might have seen a hairdryer but certainly hadn't seen a straightener. And her *outfit*. A parka. A white t-shirt. Jeans. Expensive jeans, not the ones I usually get when I go to a big ASDA, but still. My gaze kept travelling down and I almost yelped out loud when

I noticed she was wearing Doc Martens. Fuck, if I'd know *that* I could have saved myself a lot of embarrassment and a mildly serious chest burn!

Speaking of the chest burn, I figured it was probably less embarrassing to tell her than to pretend I hadn't noticed. As she sat, I shrugged self-consciously.

'I tripped over this morning while carrying a coffee,' I said awkwardly. 'Not my finest moment!'

'Oh my God, are you okay?' she asked, her face all concern.

'Yes, thank you, I'm fine,' I replied cautiously. *Is she genuinely concerned? She's not disgusted or laughing at me?* 'My pride was more hurt than anything else.'

'I know that feeling,' she sighed, taking the lid off her coffee and pouring in a sugar sachet. 'Our office is still small and we don't have a lot of space, so I keep tripping over things, trying to get to my desk. Utterly humiliating.' She paused, then looked up at me in alarm. 'Not that anyone makes me feel bad about it, though. It's, um, it's not that kind of office. We're nice, I promise.'

'No, of course,' I said slowly, trying to figure out what the fuck was going on. Was this editor, this publishing legend, really this awkward around some tit with coffee all down her top? *Was this a trap?* 'But it's always the stuff you say to yourself that's more awkward than the stuff other people say to you, isn't it?'

'Indeed,' Grace laughed wryly. She sat back in her chair and took a sip of coffee. Not knowing what to say, I watched her silently. She fidgeted in her chair and examined her nails. Christ! If aliens were watching us now, I swear they'd vaporise the whole planet instead of trying to make contact because they'd rightly decide we're just too fucking awkward to deal with.

'So,' she said eventually, smiling at me. The smile didn't quite meet her eyes. 'Tell me about what you do at … Youth Steady, isn't it?'

So I told her. Then she asked about how we know what topics to cover, and I told her that, too. Aware that I'd fucked the entire thing already by turning up covered in coffee and looking such a mess, I didn't feel any pressure to get it 'right'.

I just talked for a bit, and then she talked for a bit, and then I talked back. It wasn't an interview in any sense of the word, it was just a chat. But really, with my lack of experience and having made such a total mess of the morning, what else did I expect?

'So, you've told me all about what you do and what Youth Steady does and what you're good at, but tell me, what do you actually *want* to do?' she asked after about half an hour. 'What would make you happy?' *Christ, there's a question.* Well, actually it's two very different questions, but I didn't think 'A lifetime supply of Toffee Crisps and having Mindy Kaling as my best friend' was a helpful or productive answer here.

I opened my mouth to say, 'I want to be a journalist and eventually write novels,' and then closed it again. Did I want to do that, really, or was that just what I thought I *should* be doing? Is it not just the path that my life had been going on up until recently, what my best friend and partner-in-crime was doing? Would that life, Penny's life, the life that she thrived on but always made me feel strangely anxious even just watching it, really make me happy? Is that really, *really*, what I wanted to do?

'I ... I want to make good things,' I said carefully. 'I like making things. I like the satisfaction I get when I finish a script, or write the copy for a leaflet, or publish a new blog post. I like it even more when those things are good – good because they're, y'know, *good*. They're high-quality and well-made and all that stuff, but also good because they're putting good into the world. I like helping teenagers, and I like it when we get a message that says some of the work I've done has made a difference to someone's life. That's all I want to do, really. Work hard, and make good things.' I paused, and looked back at Grace; she was watching me carefully. 'If that doesn't sound too much like something from a Home Bargains motivational poster, I mean.'

She laughed, and nodded thoughtfully. 'I get that. But, you're doing that where you are. Why are you looking for other roles?'

I blew out my breath again, my fringe fluttering. I was tempted to bring out the 'This role seemed too good to pass up' line again, but I was still so exhausted, I didn't think I had the energy to pull it off. *Honesty? Yeah, sod it.*

'I'm bored,' I said, looking her straight in the eye. 'I love my job, and my team are amazing, but it's been almost three years of doing the same thing. I'm happiest when I'm learning and developing, trying new things and growing as a worker and as a writer. I know Steady would love to do more, but charities aren't the most flexible of places and it's just not possible. I want to do more and, to be honest, I know I can do more. So, as much as I love the place, it's time for me to move on. For my own, er, sanity.'

She nodded thoughtfully throughout my little speech, staring at the table in front of her. When I finished, she looked up at me and smiled. It touched her eyes this time – weirdly, she seemed reassured. But what would she need reassuring about?

'Thanks for meeting me, Amy,' she said, standing up. Surprised at this sudden change in direction, I half-stood up too. She clocked my confusion. 'You need to leave to go to work now, right?'

I glanced at my watch: 8.45. I was going to be *very* late. I leapt out of my chair and threw my coat on, shoving my basically untouched juice in my bag. We left together, then turned to face each other and say goodbye.

'It was lovely to meet you,' I said.

'Yes, you too,' she replied, wrapping a scarf round her neck. 'I'll be in touch.'

'Yes, thank you,' I said, cringing. 'I'm really sorry, but I'm going to have to dash off.'

'Oh yes, no problem, you go ...'

'Thanks, bye!'

'Bye!'

And that was how I left Grace Chambers standing on the street outside Pret, looking slightly baffled as I jogged away from her towards the Tube. If my rambling, stained blouse and mad hair hadn't put her off, the sight of my arse wobbling everywhere in those paperbag trousers certainly would. Although to be honest, it could have been worse: I could have fallen over again.

Friday, 16 March

I was in the kitchen, making myself a 3pm instant hot chocolate, when Adam came in behind me. I stepped to one side, letting him get to the mugs and the kettle to make himself one of the disgusting herbal teas he liked. When he'd finished, I expected him to stalk back to his desk like he usually did. Instead, he turned to lean against the counter, watching me stir a few splashes of hot water into the powder in order to get a lump-free paste to add the milk to.

I glanced at him uneasily, but he wasn't looking at me: he was staring into his mug like he'd find the secrets of the universe there. The microwave pinged and I poured the milk into my mug. I was about to leave when he said casually, 'How are the interviews going?'

There was almost a repeat of the previous morning. I jumped so hard that the chocolate slopped over the side of the mug. Putting it back on the counter, I reached for kitchen towel, studiously avoiding his eye. Even not looking directly at him, I could see his smirk from across the room.

'What do you mean?' I said coolly, wiping the floor.

'I'm not stupid, Amy,' he replied gently – or at least, as gently as I'd ever heard him speak. 'Doctor's appointments, coming in late in fancy clothes, random days off, jumping every time you get a text ... You're going for job interviews.'

I stood to face him, my face frozen in fear.

He laughed sharply. 'Don't worry, you're not in trouble for it. I'm glad you're going for other jobs, it's a good thing.'

The floor dropped out of the room. He's *glad* I'm going for other jobs? He thinks it's *good* that I'm leaving? I was right: he hates me. He thinks I'm useless. He wants me gone. I know I've always suspected that, but somehow having it confirmed is *so much worse* than I thought it would be. What's worse is everyone agrees with him: none of the other jobs want me. So, now I'm stuck here, forever, with him – a boss who I know now openly dislikes me and wants me gone. *Just great*. This week really is *just fucking fantastic*, isn't it?

I didn't say all this, though. He definitely thinks I'm useless, he doesn't need to know I'm insane too. Instead, I repeated 'A good thing' through numb lips, picked up my mug and turned to leave – stopping in my tracks when Adam swore as energetically as I usually did.

'No, not like that ...' he said as I turned back to face him. He was scowling again, but for some reason I got the feeling that it wasn't directed at me. 'We'll be sad to lose you, but you need to leave. We can't give you what you deserve here.' Pause. 'You've gotten everything you can out of this role, now. Someone as talented as you, you should be reaching for more.'

'Talented?' I said, trying to ignore the rush of blood in my ears. 'But I thought you didn't rate me. I thought you thought I was crap.'

'Why?' he said, genuine surprise in his voice. A spark of anger flickered inside me. Adam's unexpected compliment had given me the gas it needed to catch. It burst into flame, and suddenly I was talking without being fully aware of what I was saying.

'You never say anything I do is good. You never really even talk to me. You never praise me or thank me, or show *any* indication that I'm anything other than a fly buzzing in your ear. Why on earth *would* I think that I wasn't crap?'

He shrugged and took a swig of tea, utterly unmoved. 'I'm not that kind of man, Amy. I assumed you knew what you were doing was good because the quality of your work was so good. Did *you* think it was good?'

'Yes, but ...'

'Then you need to trust that.' He stood up straight and walked past me to leave. 'You shouldn't need the validation of other people to make yourself feel good about what you do. Know you're great anyway. But, just so you know ...' He paused in the doorway, not looking at me. 'Yes, I *am* proud of you and your work. I'll be sad to see you go, but you're going on to better things. Okay?'

I looked up at him, and nodded shortly. 'Okay.' He nodded and left. I immediately took up his place, leaning against the counter and trying to absorb what had happened.

Shit. I'm not shit? All these years I've been working with Adam, trying desperately to impress him, and it turns out he was impressed the whole time. In some ways, it was a huge relief, but in other ways I wanted to go back in time and throttle him for not at any point saying, 'Hey, just so you know, I'm not the kind of guy to give you praise when you do anything good. We cool?' It would have saved so much heartache.

But it was the last part of what Adam had said that was really niggling: 'You shouldn't need the validation of other people to make yourself feel good about what you do.' *Shouldn't I?* Don't we all do that? Isn't that just the easiest way to know you're on the right path? I tried to brush off what he was saying, rationalise it away, but deep in my gut, I knew he was right: I'd known within six months that Adam was never going to be my best pal, so why had I spent another two years trying to impress him? Why had I spent all that time chasing his approval – approval I knew was never going to come – when instead I could have been focusing on making something that I felt proud of? Something that *I* thought was good. When I wasn't in a self-hate spiral, I had a pretty decent opinion of the work I did. Why wasn't I listening to *those* voices, to those feelings of pride and satisfaction, rather than the ones that whispered to me that unless everyone in the entire world loved what I did and I was the most impressive person ever to have graced this earth, I was essentially useless?

I walked back to my desk slowly, my mind racing. Okay, so I hadn't gotten any of those jobs, but that's okay! That doesn't mean I'm never going to get any job, and it's not a reflection on me as a person or as a worker. I *am* good. I know I'm good – I just need to find the right role, the right place that appreciates it. Meanwhile, I just need to chill the hell out here. I'm ready to leave, but not because I can't make this job work any more but because I've made it work for over two years, and now it's time to make something else work instead. And I can keep doing good work here, too, until I find something else. Because I'm good! I'm *good! I'm fucking good!* And Adam, it turns out, isn't too bad himself. I had just read him wrong.

I was so wrapped up in my own thoughts – *delicious, happy, self-validating thoughts* – that it took me a while to notice a new email notification on my phone. I took a sip of hot chocolate and opened it up: Grace. All the joy I had whooshing through me dropped out of my stomach in less than a second. *Ah, shit.* Even if I know it's not necessarily my fault, it's never nice to read a rejection, is it?

> '*Hi, Amy. Really lovely to meet you yesterday,*' the email read. '*I don't think there's any point in hanging round with this – I'd like to offer you a job. I'm not sure what as yet, maybe a video producer, maybe a writer, maybe a bit of both, but could we meet for coffee next week to discuss? We can both wear brown tops, just in case. Fyi: I've already tripped over Robyn's shoes twice so far today, so I think you'll fit in just fine. Grace x*'

'Amy, are you okay?' Fee asked in alarm. Everyone looked at me – probably because tears were streaming down my face. Fee rushed round the table to put their arm around me, Claire dived into her bag for some tissues, and Nish ran off to the kitchen to get me some water. But I only glanced across at Adam and smiled, tears dribbling into the corners of my mouth, and held up my phone. He nodded curtly and looked back at his computer screen, a strange mix of pride and sadness on his face. As much as I wanted to stare at him and absorb the truth about how he rates me, I looked away, back at the email, back at my friends. This wasn't about him, it was about me. *It should always have been about me.* And Christ, am I glad to finally believe it.

MONDAY, 12 MARCH
TO-DO

☑ *Job interview: Tuesday @ 10am, (Foreign Office)*

☑ *Job interview: Pret @ 8am, (UPSTART)*

☑ *Prep for interview #1*

☑ *Prep for interview #2*

☑ *Hear back from (Safeguard) interview*

☑ *Draft letter of resignation* ✎

☑ *Disordered eating piece (suppose I should do my actual job even as I'm trying to leave it...)*

TO-DONE

- Swam twice

- Two good interviews

- EXCELLENT flicked eyeliner, twice 👁

- Still went to a job interview even though I was covered in coffee

- FINISHED MY BOOK

- Managed not to cry openly in front of people at work when sad

- Cried openly in front of people when happy, which I'm taking as a win

- ☆ Total life revelation ☆

- Got a job. <u>GOT A FUCKING JOB!</u>

SESSION FIVE

'Because what the fuck do I have to be depressed about, really?' I burst out. We were 30 minutes into our penultimate session, and it was going super well. 'I'm so lucky. I'm so, *so* lucky. I have everything going for me. I'm healthy. I have enough money and I have a flat and I have food and ... and it's fine. Everything is *fine*.'

Bjorg didn't react. I looked at her calm face and hot, angry word-vomit exploded from me before I could stop it.

'I don't deserve to feel like this!' I shouted. 'I don't deserve help and medication and therapy, because there are other people who actually have reason to feel like this and cope with it, and ... and they could use the help and I'm just wasting it, because I'm pathetic. I'm *pathetic*!'

I sat back in my chair and crossed my arms across my chest, angry tears wriggling down my face. Bjorg still looked so fucking calm. What would I have to do? Start throwing things? Fashion a noose in front of her? *God, I hate her*. I mean, I love her, but I hate her and her fucking logic and understanding too.

'Mental health doesn't work like that, Amy,' she said placidly. 'It's not like you have to "earn" being depressed. Anyone can be depressed, for any reason.'

'I hate it.' I glowered. 'I hate it. I just want to get on with things, like everyone else does, rather than fussing for no fucking reason. I want an easy life, like everyone else, not to constantly have to fight with my own fucking brain.'

'How do you know everyone else has an easy life and doesn't have to fight their brain?' Bjorg said, raising an eyebrow.

'It's entirely normal to have difficult feelings, and to struggle sometimes. Just because you don't see people struggling, it doesn't mean they're not.'

'I know, I know,' I said, miserably. 'I just … It feels like everyone else is so in control of what they're doing, where they're going, how they're feeling. I want to feel like I'm in control, but no matter what I do, my brain always gets in the way.'

'Huh,' said Bjorg, nodding thoughtfully. 'And what do you do to make yourself feel in control?'

'I write lists.'

'Lists?'

'Yeah.' I pulled my phone out of my pocket and opened my Notes app, turning the screen to show her the number of lists I had saved within. 'Lists of things I want to do and achieve, films I want to watch, books I want to read, and daily To-Do Lists. They're, like, little plans for life. I wanted a way to keep myself on track, and stop myself worrying about forgetting things or becoming stressed. And then I make those To-Done Lists I talked about in, uh, week two? Week three? To try and remind myself that I can achieve *something*.'

'So, you started making lists in order to make yourself feel better, encourage yourself to keep going, and make you feel like you're in control of your life?' Bjorg said slowly.

'Yes! Exactly that.'

'Huh. And how is that working for you?' she asked innocently.

I gaped.

'I mean, I … uh …'

'You don't have to answer now, we're at the end of the session. But maybe think about it for next week. Are your lists making you feel the way you want to? Do you think you can do that? Is that okay?'

No, it's not okay, you wonderful Scandinavian monster! It's not okay at all. If you take my lists away from me, what do I have left to show that I'm useful?

'Absolutely,' I said brightly. 'Yup, I can do that.'
'Okay. And, before you go …'
'I have no intention of harming myself in any way, no.'
'Good! See you next week.'
'Have a good one.'

TO-DO

- ☐ Find perfect first day outfit

- ☐ Find nice shoes I can walk in that aren't trainers

- ☐ But then, also, trainers — but not the trainers I'd usually get. Fashionable trainers?

- ☐ Buy a small, entirely impractical, but very pretty shoulder bag

- ☐ Buy cropped linen dungarees

- ☐ Buy high-necked midi dress

☐ *Buy jumpsuit. Aim to get one which is in itself ugly, but makes you look good, because that's fashion*

☐ *Leopard print?!*

☐ *Get something healthy for tea.*

FIFTEEN

I know it's a cliche for a woman to say she hates shopping – like, it makes her some kind of magical unicorn woman who just isn't *like* those other girls, y'know? – but fuck me, I *hate* shopping. I used to quite like it when I was younger, when Mum and I would spend our Saturdays wandering round the shops together and I'd come home with a bagful of clothes and what felt like an entirely new personality to go with them, but now it's just three hours of finding new and innovative ways to hate myself. However, I was starting my new job in a fortnight and I didn't think I could turn up to an office full of *journalists* wearing the same crap I'd been wearing to Steady for the past few years. I'd attended enough of Penny's parties to know that journalists all look really *cool*, and they all shop in the places my eyes usually slide right over, and they wear stuff that looks horrific on its own but somehow works when it's on them and 'teamed' with other 'pieces'. In contrast, I tended to wear jeans and whatever stripy jersey-top bought in the sales was clean that day. So, if I was going to fit in at *Upstart* – and God, I really wanted to fit in – then I needed to update my wardrobe.

I had set aside one of my remaining holiday days specifically to go shopping midweek, because the only thing worse than shopping was shopping on a Saturday with the rest of the world. Penny had offered to come with me, but again, I was trying to make this as painless as possible and the last time we'd gone shopping, I'd asked if we could go into H&M so I could buy a pair of trousers I loved, only to find their biggest size didn't fit.

Instead, I'd encouraged Penny to try on more and more things, my voice getting higher and higher as she stepped out of the changing room, looking more and more beautiful with each passing outfit, and gone home with nothing while she had to get an Uber because she couldn't get the Tube with all her bags. So, no, not today. I needed to spend all my energy finding some clothes that didn't make me want to throw up on myself.

I stepped through the doors into the big shopping centre, darted to the side so I could lean against the wall, and opened Pinterest on my phone to remind myself of what I needed to get today. I'd stalked the Instagram account and most recent articles of *Upstart*'s fashion editor, Angelina, to get a good sense of what I *should* be wearing, and it was far removed from what I usually wore. Midi dresses with trainers seemed to be a good shout – not the battered Converse I wore, mind, but box-fresh Nikes in gleaming white or pastel pink, or completely impractical materials like suede – as did wide-legged cropped trousers, especially dungarees, and leopard print. And last week, she'd written how jumpsuits were the most important thing you could have in your wardrobe right now, so I should probably get at least one of those, too.

Okay, deep breath. I looked up and scanned the floor for a shop that *wasn't* a WHSmith or a Boots. *Zara ... Fine, let's try there.* Ignoring the fact that I really would rather be buying stationery or a new eyeshadow palette, I marched towards Zara and threw myself into the intimidatingly shiny interiors, determined to find the outfit of my dreams.

Almost immediately, I saw a swishy mid-length leopard-print skirt that looked like something Ivy would wear. *Success!* I plucked the largest size they had from the rail and draped it over my arm, trying to look like the kind of person who did this all the time. Then I wandered round the rest of the store, trying to find other things on my list. *Look, here was a jumpsuit!* It was long and baggy and shapeless, but with an elasticated waistband. To be honest, it looked like the kind of thing Taggie used to wear in her upcycling-old-furniture phase, but I think that meant it was *exactly* the kind of thing I should be wearing right now. I added it to my arm, and scoured the rest of the shop for more prizes.

A high-necked midi dress in two different patterns that looked like the kind of thing a rag doll would wear. *On the arm.* Another dress, this time with a strange asymmetric hem so that it finished both mid-thigh and mid-calf. *Sure, why not? On the arm.* Cropped trousers in poo-brown made from ... was that velvet *and* corduroy? *Wow! Okay, yes, on the arm, and I should get a top to try with it.* How about this plain black one ... for £34? *Shit! Okay, fine, and let's try this high-neck, blush-pink blouse, too, and this yellow and plum paisley patterned one.* My arm was starting to ache, but the only way to tell what's going to make you look like a fashionable, grown-up lady and what's like a child running amok in Oxfam's reject pile is to try *everything* on, so if something didn't actively make me want to die, it was worth a go, right?

Arms full, I headed to the changing room. Because it was midweek and incredibly quiet, there was no one guarding the doors. Grateful, I slipped into a cubicle as far away from the entrance as possible. I hung up my spoils and tried to avoid eye contact with the enormous, full-length mirror as I took off my normal, boring, unfashionable clothes. Hoiking my knickers up over my roll of belly fat to better keep it sucked in, I stood, hands on hips, and surveyed the clothes hanging on the wall, like a chubby, naked Peter Pan deciding which Lost Boy he was going to torment first.

My eyes landed on the poo-brown trousers and paisley shirt. I slid the shirt off the hanger, marvelling at how soft and lovely it felt in my hands, undid the top few buttons and started to wiggle it over my head. *Oh ...* I'd picked the biggest size they had and it looked baggy, but still wasn't big enough. I managed to wrestle it on and it fitted fairly well on the waist, but the top buttons wouldn't do up, my boobs burst out of the front and it was so tight on my arms they looked like over-stuffed sausages.

Cool. Okay, fine. Well, even if I don't get this top, I can tell what the colours and everything would look like with the trousers. I unclipped them from the hanger, again marvelling at how nice they *felt*, even if they did look utterly bizarre, and stepped into them. *Ah* ... Again, I'd picked the biggest size, but I had to fight to get them over my hips and there was no way in hell I would be able to do them up unless I sliced my belly off, like carving a roast ham.

I was starting to feel very hot. Forcing the trousers off my hips, I kicked them off my legs, undid the buttons on the blouse, ripped it off and threw them both into a corner. *It's fine. Just because they didn't fit doesn't mean that the other clothes won't.* I blindly grabbed another hanger – one of the dresses – and tried that on. Nope, couldn't even get it over my shoulders. I managed to get the other dress on, but then I couldn't zip it up. The leopard-print skirt looked great, but the last inch of zip wouldn't do up. I could get the jumpsuit on and done up, but it was so tight on the hips that I was worried it'd burst open at the seams if I tried to sit down and it perfectly cupped my lower belly flab – my *gunt* – and made it look like I was smuggling a large pouch of milk in my knickers.

The only thing that I could possibly have worn was the plain black top. Even then it strained obscenely across my breasts. I stared at myself in the mirror for a while, marvelling how my chest looked like two puppies fighting in a bin bag and wondering what would make me feel worse: leaving the shop with nothing at all, or with a £34 top that I knew I would never, ever wear? I wrenched it over my head and threw it in the corner with the other rejects. *Although it's not the clothes' fault, really, is it? It's me – I should be me in the reject corner, not them.*

I hung everything back up, got dressed, and left as quickly as possible, shoving the clothes on the changing-room rail as I went and trying not to make eye contact with anyone until

I was safely out of the store. Back in the bright, anonymous safety of the shopping centre, I power-walked as far away from the shop as possible and took deep, steadying breaths to calm myself down, willing the tears stinging my eyes to disappear. *It's fine*, I murmured as I dodged between giggling groups of girls bunking off school and small armies of mothers with prams. *You're fine. Just because you had that one experience in that one shop doesn't mean you're never going to be able to buy clothes. Just try again somewhere else.*

So, I tried the next lot of shops on my list – Mint Velvet, Boden, Warehouse, Mango, Jigsaw, Whistles – and had exactly the same experience. Trousers got stuck on my thighs. The zips wouldn't do up, or I'd force them to the top and hear an ominous rip when I turned to look in the mirror. A dress got stuck on my upper arms as I tried to take it off, so I ended up lurching wildly round the changing room, arms above my head, as I attempted to ease the fabric away. At one point someone opened the curtain on me, looking for their friend Val, and was treated to the sight of me with no trousers on and my hands down my top as I tried to rearrange my boobs to make them look less comically enormous in a polo neck.

The only stuff that I could get on properly were oversized tents, the kind of clothes that only work if it's obvious there's a teeny-weeny slip of a woman hiding underneath. On me, they looked lumpen and ungainly, and sort of like I was going to act as a wedding marquee for a family of leprechauns later that evening. I stared in the mirror, wearing a long, pale-yellow dress which reached below my knees and somehow managed to highlight all my lumpy bits on the way down while simultaneously standing a good foot away from my skin. I imagined walking into my first day at *Upstart* looking like this, and had to dig my nails into the heels of my hands to stop myself from bursting into tears.

Suddenly exhausted, I flopped down on the little leatherette stool and dug in my bag for my phone.

AMY: How do you buy clothes?

AMY: Everything looks awful on me

AMY: I'm going to have to turn up to my new job wrapped in a bedsheet

PENNY: I think you could pull it off with the right accessories

AMY: Do you think I can tell Grace that I can't accept the job because I'm too chronically ugly to take it?

PENNY: I will literally never speak to you again if you do that

PENNY: You don't need to buy new clothes to fit in, just treat yourself to something that makes you happy. You're gorgeous and you always look fantastic x

'You have to think that, you're my best friend,' I muttered darkly as I shoved my stupid t-shirt back on my stupid body. I gathered up the clothes I'd been trying on – the beautiful, wonderful clothes that would look chic on anyone else but crappy on me – and handed them back to the shop assistant, being as nice and kind as possible to ensure she didn't look down on me for being the kind of ugly elephant that couldn't even fit into their biggest sizes, the kind of moose that didn't *deserve* to be in their shop. I left the shop, walking briskly and resisting the urge to walk straight home and hide under the duvet.

No, I thought miserably. I can't go home. I haven't bought anything yet, and I just *can't* start my new job wearing the same shitty stuff I've had for years. This job is supposed to be, if not a new start, at least a new chapter. This is me moving on, progressing, breaking out of the rut I've been stuck in for so long. It's supposed to be me starting to believe in myself. If I walk into *Upstart* wearing worn-out jeans with holes on the inner thighs and a top that's been through the wash a few too many times, I'm still going to be the worn-out girl who's been stuck doing and thinking the same old shit a few too many times. I'm not just looking for an outfit that's going to make me fit in with my colleagues, but one that will make me feel like I'm the kind of person who *could*.

Right, I'd take a break and then get back to it. What should I do? Well, the only thing to do in shopping centres apart from shop is eat, really. I glanced at my phone: lunchtime.

Fine, I'll go to the food court, get some lunch, calm the hell down and get back to it.

The food court was slap-bang in the middle of the shopping centre. I wandered round, trying to get close enough to read the menus, but not so close I'd have to do that awkward 'Oh, just looking, thanks!' thing with the people behind the counter. There was a KFC, a Burger King, an ITSU, a Spudulike, a Pizza Hut Express, a salad bar and a noodle bar.

Oh, shit. Here's a new problem: what should I eat?

Burger King was out, obviously, because who even eats Burger King nowadays unless it's the only place open in a motorway service station? KFC? I love KFC, but it's not exactly healthy eating, is it? I thought back to the sleeves of that dress stuck on the plump, pale flesh of my arms, and felt a hot, uncomfortable blush on my back of my neck. No, probably best not to have a KFC, or a Pizza Hut.

Is itsu healthy? The only stuff I like is the stuff with sticky rice and teriyaki sauce poured over it, but that's not going to help me fit into pretty dresses, is it? Okay, how about a jacket potato? That always used to be my staple meal when I was eating on Slim Success, but what about all those studies I see on the news every day about how carbs are basically the devil? So, no jacket potato. And no noodles either. The salad bar, then? I approached it carefully, standing on tiptoes to peer at what was on offer. Limp lettuce, pale strips of red onion and deflated-looking chicken, apparently. Soggy chickpeas for £1.50 extra.

I sighed heavily, and joined the queue. Although miserable at the thought of having to eat this terrible salad, a part of me was a little bit proud, too. It felt like I was taking control of myself. Forcing myself to eat a salad that was probably going to leave me ravenous in two hours' time was another achievement, another thing to tick off my list. A step towards getting the healthy body that I wanted – and by that, I mean the *slim* body that I wanted. Because let's face it, whenever the majority of influencers and chefs and whatever talk about a 'healthy body', that's really what they mean. A slim body, not a body that looks like mine.

The queue shuffled forward, and I shuffled with it. *Does everyone eat like this?* I genuinely couldn't remember the last time I didn't feel proud of what I was eating because it was 'healthy', e.g. eating in a way that'll help me lose weight, or guilty because I was eating something unhealthy – or, conversely, like I was patting myself on the back for eating something 'unhealthy' because I was actively *not* dieting. The rules for how I should and could eat were ever-changing, and they rattled round my head constantly.

The food hall was buzzing with people. I looked at them enviously, studying their bodies and their plates and trying to match the two together, to find the pattern, the secret, the key to how to eat to look the way I want. And I couldn't do it: there was no pattern. There were thin people eating KFC as well as fat people. Old people who looked like they'd be blown away by a particularly strong gust of wind eating jacket potatoes alongside solid-looking blokes in hi-vis vests. My eye fell on a group of teenagers who looked so similar they were like a glitch in the matrix: they were eating everything from sushi to salads to pizza to burgers, all mixed together, all happy, all chatting away and enjoying themselves. The ones eating salads didn't look smug, the ones eating 'junk food' didn't look guilty – they were just eating.

Why don't I get to just eat?

Stepping out of the salad queue, I fumbled for my phone. I was halfway through texting my best girls before I re-read what I'd written and closed the phone. *Why am I doing this?* I talk to them endlessly about weight and dieting, and they are endlessly patient with what must be, by now, a hideously boring part of our friendship. But I need to talk to them about it, because I need to *know*. I compare myself, my body, to them and theirs constantly. I look at what they eat and how they move, and cry about the fact that they can eat chocolate croissants and chorizo at brunch and stay slim, whereas I am resolutely blubbery even after going for the fruit plate, or eggs, or even just coffee. But why do I *care*? And why am I spending so much of my time with my friends thinking about how we look and eat? *What does it matter*?

By now, I was pacing the food hall, scowling at the food around me, the people around me. I was suddenly furious, my brain scorched black with rage at the amount of time spent hating myself for how I look and assuming others felt the same when I had absolutely *no evidence* that's the case. In fact, I know it's the opposite, because that's how I feel. I don't care how other people look. I've read articles about how society demonises fat people and sees them as lazy and bad, and how that's bollocks, and I agree. I've read the scientific studies about how being fat doesn't necessarily mean bad health. *For Christ's sake, I'm an example!* Apart from my BMI, I'm well within the healthy range for all the tests at the doctor. I follow all the body positive accounts with beautiful photos of fat people of all genders, ages, colours and sizes, and sigh over photos of beautiful fat women on Instagram with big bottoms or wobbly arms or overhangs of stomach fat posing in bikinis and short dresses and crop tops, and I think they look amazing! I would never, ever think that someone who was fat was lesser, so why on earth don't I apply that knowledge to myself?

A family at a table in front of me stood up, and I threw myself in their empty seats, shooting daggers at the couple who had tried to sneak around me to get to them first. I opened my phone and made a list of all the things I do with my body. I thought about dancing at Janae's wedding, playing Nintendo games with my siblings, snuggling under a duvet with Garry, going swimming, prancing round my room in a dress that I love, writing, attending fancy book launches, hugging my friends, going for job interviews, putting photos and videos of myself online, decorating cakes, walking my parents' dogs. Being fat doesn't stop me from living, it doesn't stop me from enjoying life. Being thinner wouldn't make me smarter, more popular, more successful. All it would do is, maybe, stop me *obsessing* over how I look and what I eat.

But really, would it even do that? The only time I've successfully dieted, back when I was 21 and got down to a size 10/12, I had to monitor every single thing I ate to see if it was on plan. The only reason it worked was because I was at university and had a lot of spare time to devote to it – I fell off the dieting wagon the second I had exams or moving out to think about. No, even being thin won't stop me obsessing over my body and food. So, why don't I try to just stop obsessing?

I slumped back in my chair, exhausted. I don't think I'm ever going to *like* my body like it is. I've spent too many years being bullied for my weight, trying and failing to diet, watching TV shows and films where fat people are always the butt of the joke to ever get to the point of true love for how I look. But maybe I can start to accept that it doesn't really matter if I don't like my body, the same way I accepted it doesn't really matter that I can't sing like Charlotte Church (shut up, *Tissues and Issues* is a great album). Not having a body that looks the way I want it to won't hold me back, and it doesn't have to take over my life. There's so, so much more to me than the meat sack I exist in, everyone else can see that.

Maybe it's time I do, too.

I stood up abruptly and walked round the food court again. If I want a burger or a pizza or a KFC, I should fucking well have one. Who cares? *Who. Cares?* But actually, I don't really want one right now. What do I *really want* to eat? I stopped in front of Spudulike and breathed in the smell: charred potato skin, oozing cheese, crisp side salad. My stomach grumbled.

I ordered a jacket potato with cheese and beans and a lemonade. I took it to the quietest corner of the food court I could find (still so rammed, it was like trying to get to the fancy biscuit shelf in ASDA on Christmas Eve), sat by myself with my phone in my pocket and ate it very slowly, stopping when full, and making a new plan of attack.

There is no way a midi dress with a weird hem will suddenly make me look like Angelina and Grace and all the other cool, stylish women in the *Upstart* office. That's okay – I don't need to dress or look like them to be good enough for them. *For fuck's sake, Grace hired me when I'd poured coffee all over myself!* Penny was my best friend through all my worst fashion periods, including when everything I wore was from Tammy Girl (highlight: a scarlet halter top with glow-in-the-dark stars and moons all over it) and when I exclusively wore dusky pink cords with floral shirts. So, I don't need to dress up who I am to be acceptable. I *am* acceptable – no, I'm *great* – just as I am. So, fuck it! This afternoon, I'm not going to look for fashionable clothes or cool clothes or clothes you'd see on the style pages of magazines. I'll look for the clothes that make me feel as great as my friends, loved ones and new colleagues think I am.

First stop was Schuh. My list called for sporty-looking trainers, so I deleted it and instead bought a pair of navy sneakers with big yellow daisies printed all over them and a pair of Doc Marten Chelsea boots with red roses embroidered up the sides. The sneakers were ridiculous and the Doc Martens would probably look more at home in Camden than a fancy Bloomsbury office, but they made me so happy that when I walked out of the shop, I felt like I was floating several feet off the floor.

Next, I went into TK Maxx. I'd been looking at getting a chic, teeny-tiny handbag to store my phone and keys in, and then carrying all my stuff in a canvas shopping bag. It looked very delicate on Angelina, but to be honest, the idea made me sweat with how impractical it was. So instead, I went to the men's section and found a pale blue Herschel backpack with a laptop slot in it, £75 down to £20, and then found some cheery pin badges in Primark to add to the front. By the time I went into Dorothy Perkins (traditionally, where I bought my clothes), I was feeling very pleased with myself indeed.

Which is when I saw her. *Her.* My nemesis from swimming, wandering round the jeans section with someone I assumed was her sister. It took me a moment or two to recognise her because she looked very different fully clothed. Even though it was June, she was in a long-sleeved, baggy top and an awkward skirt which hung off her and billowed round her legs. She looked awkward, or like she was trying to hide – a far cry from the confident water goddess I saw in the pool each morning.

Ducking around her, I went to the other side of the shop, my hands running over rails. I filled my arms with clothes I loved, relief filling my heart because I could get things in my actual size rather than getting the biggest size and hoping for the best. A navy dress with a scoop neck, patterned in pink and white flowers. A white blouse with multi-coloured pastel spots and yellow cigarette pants. A fitted white dress with sky-blue swirls and a full skirt. Another navy dress, this time covered in cherries. A green tea dress with white spots. Bottle-green skinny jeans. A denim dungaree dress. A black wrap dress with a vibrant yellow ribbon twirling over it. I filled my arms with colour and headed to the changing room, hoping at least one thing would fit.

Reader, it all fitted! Not all of it looked good, mind – the blouse made me look like I had some kind of tropical disease, the skinny jeans gave me a pancake bum and the dungaree dress fell too far right on the 'Cute/An Extra In Schoolgirl Porn' scale – but I didn't get stuck in anything, and after the morning, that felt like a *huge* win. And actually, a lot of it looked lovely! I smiled into the mirror and a pretty, happy woman smiled back. It's amazing the difference dressing to be kind to yourself, rather than the person you wish you were, can make.

Just as I was admiring the way the wrap dress swooshed around my knees (and how good my boobs looked in it), I became aware of two women having a loud conversation, a few cubicles down.

'No, it's no good,' one of them said in a sharp, clipped voice. 'It looks terrible!'

'Let me see,' said the other voice. The sound of a curtain being pulled back. 'Oh, no, it looks lovely on you!'

'No, it doesn't,' the first woman interjected. 'I told you it wouldn't – it shows off how gross and huge my shoulders are.'

'Your shoulders aren't huge,' the other woman sighed, with the air of someone who has said that exact same sentence a thousand times before.

'Yes, they are,' the first woman said. I recognised all too clearly the breathy, tight voice of someone trying her hardest not to cry. 'They have been since I was 12. And they make my tits look even smaller than they already are.'

'Your tits are fine. Although yeah, maybe they look a little small in that dress ...'

'I told you, it looks terrible.'

'No, it doesn't!' the second woman said, frustrated. 'It's gorgeous. I'm going to see if they've got any chicken fillets. Stay there, don't take it off! It looks great on you, honestly.'

'It doesn't look any more terrible than anything else would, I suppose,' the first woman sighed.

Can you hear someone rolling their eyes? Because I swear I could tell the second woman rolled her eyes before leaving in search of some fake boobs.

I got dressed quietly, gathered up my spoils and pulled back the curtain. Already I knew who I would see when I walked into the corridor, but it was still a bit of a surprise to see my nemesis, sportswoman supreme, whose lithe body and swimming prowess I had envied for months, staring miserably into the big mirror in a beautiful, electric blue lacy dress.

It didn't make her shoulders look big. Of course it didn't! I mean, her tits looked tiny, but that's because they *were* tiny.

But tiny boobs are great! She had a body I would commit some fairly serious crimes for. At the sound of the curtain being pulled back, she looked up and met my eyes in the mirror. I waited for a flicker of recognition, but nothing. She had no idea who I was. She did look slightly embarrassed, though, and her face was hot and teary, like mine that morning. I smiled warmly at her.

'That dress looks *amazing* on you,' I said sincerely. She started, taken aback. 'The colour really makes your eyes pop, and you're got such *great* arms!'

'Really?' she said, turning to the mirror, her eyes moving away from her shoulders. Yes, *really*, you're *obviously* gorgeous, read the goddamn room! I took a breath, and increased the wattage of my smile.

'Yes, really,' I said, brushing past her. 'You look great.'

'Oh. Uh, thank you!' she said, smiling slightly.

'No problem. Have a lovely day!' I replied as I left, and I truly meant it. It's sad to think this woman I'd been so envious of for such a long time because I wished my body could look and work like hers didn't feel *her* body was enough, either. I've seen that haunted, humiliated look in the mirror and heard that crack in my own voice too many times not to feel immensely sad for anyone who feels the same way. If I can give her a compliment and make her feel a bit better, well, why not? I fully expect to hate her guts again the second we get back in the pool, but for now? This. This is nice.

I paid for my clothes and left the shop, a jaunty spring in my step, swinging my bags off my wrist. *Where next? Another shop? A cafe for a hot chocolate? Another shopping centre? Home?* My heart felt light even while my body felt heavy, and for a second it felt like anything was possible as long as I wanted it to be. I peered in my bag at the bright, gently rustling fabrics within and beamed involuntarily. It felt good to be nice to myself, to do something *with* my body instead of against it. I'm never going to be the biggest fan of how I look, but that's fine. As long as I remember my body is on my team – and more crucially, act like I'm on its team in return – then I might just be okay.

WEDNESDAY, 20 JUNE

TO-DO

☑ Find perfect first day outfit

☑ Find nice shoes I can walk in that aren't trainers

☐ ~~But then, also, trainers — but not the trainers I'd usually get. Fashionable trainers?~~

☐ ~~Buy a small, entirely impractical, but very pretty shoulder bag~~

☐ ~~Buy cropped linen dungarees~~

☐ ~~Buy high-necked midi dress~~ High-necked things still make me look like I've got water balloons hiding up my top

- ☐ ~~Buy jumpsuit. Aim to get one which is in itself ugly, but makes you look good, because that's fashion~~

....

- ☐ ~~Leopard print?!~~

....

- ☐ Get something healthy for tea — I got the ingredients for a ragu, with peppery rocket and balsamic dressing. Is that healthy?
  Who cares? It's delicious!

....

TO-DONE

- Went shopping 🛍

- Did excellent research into clothes, even though I then ignored it all

- Tried lots of new shops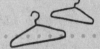

- Tried lots of new looks

- Rightfully decided I didn't want to wear anything from said shops or those looks

- Resisted going home and hiding when I was sad

- Had a slight mental revelation in the middle of a food court

- Enjoyed a delicious lunch

- *Bought excellent new trainers*
- *Bought excellent new DMs* 🛍
- *Bought v nice practical work bag*
- *Bought five lovely new dresses*
- *Bought fabulous yellow cigarette pants*
- *Made someone feel a little bit better* ✓
- *Made a toddler in a cafe smile* 😄
- *Went food shopping*
- *Cooked excellent tea*
- *Did fashion show for Garry and had excellent sex afterwards. New clothes are a hit!* ✧ ✧

SESSION SIX

This session feels strange. Weighted. I only get six sessions with Bjorg – seriously, we need better mental health funding in this country – so this is it, the last time I'm going to see her. As much as I've mentally cursed her, her mum and the horse she rode in on these past six weeks, life has been so much easier knowing I have her to talk to about things. The sessions themselves have been horrible, but life outside has felt easier. Kinder. Less like prolonged periods of mental torture. It's like I've remembered how to breathe, or at least taken off a very uncomfortable bra at the end of a long working day.

I know that if I could just talk to Bjorg for an hour a fortnight for the rest of my life, I'd probably never need antidepressants again. But that's not an option, so now I've only got 45 minutes left with her and every word feels like it's the most important one I'll ever say or hear. And so, after the pleasantries and the basics, I brought up the one thing I really didn't want to talk about, the thing I'd spent years relying on, which I knew she was going to dismantle with a raised eyebrow and a kind word. As soon as there was a gap in the conversation I took a deep breath, steeled myself, and brought up my lists.

'I don't think my lists are actually that helpful,' I announced quietly.

'Why's that?'

'Because I always put so much on them, then I never manage to get everything done.' Silence. I know this trick. An old trick, beloved by journalists and therapists alike, but knowledge of its power doesn't diminish it in the slightest, and so I plough on. 'I set the bar too high for myself and then feel terrible when I don't manage to achieve it all. But realistically, I could never achieve all the things that I want to on my lists. I'm setting myself up to fail.'

'That's interesting,' Bjorg said. I do genuinely think she means it when she says this, you know. 'Do you think you often put too much pressure on yourself?'

'I know what you're getting at,' I said, smiling sardonically. 'You think I put too much pressure on myself.' She shrugged lightly. 'And yes, I agree – I do. I do so much, but just because I'm not doing everything that every other person in the whole entire world does, I think I'm basically doing nothing. It's irrational. And crazy. And I wouldn't expect this much of any of my peers, or of my 11-year-old self. I need to …' I took a deep breath. 'I need to give myself a break.'

Bjorg smiled widely, like she was pleased with – or proud of – me. My tummy glowed with pride that I'd done something right, something she liked.

Ugh, Jones, you're pathetic! Once a teacher's pet …

'So, how are you going to do that?'

'Well …' I started cautiously, not wanting to disappoint. 'I don't want to give up my To-Do Lists entirely, because I do find it useful to keep track of everything I have to do and get it out of my head. But I don't want to put everything on them any more. I don't want to view my life as a series of tasks or things to tick off any more. So, keep the lists to actual tasks. Use the To-Done Lists on bad days to remind myself that I actually do a hell of a lot. And to remind myself that I don't need to achieve things to be … ack. To be enough.'

'I like that idea,' she said. 'Use them when you need them to remind yourself that you're pretty …' she paused, then seemed to internally shrug, '… that you're pretty fucking great already, yeah? Yes, that's a good idea.'

'Yeah,' I said, laughing. 'Yeah. Something like that.'

'Good.'

We sat in silence for a moment or so, beaming at each other. It felt nice to beam at someone. It felt good that this person – this clever, kind, irritatingly fucking perceptive person who'd made me see things differently – thought I was pretty fucking great, and was coming up with good ideas of how to remind myself of that. And it felt wonderful that for the first time in forever, I had hope that life could be bearable even if I had to live it as me.

'So,' she said, glancing down at my questionnaire, 'I think we have to leave it here. But looking at your scores, you're scoring so much lower than you were when you started.' She grinned. 'That's really good. And I think that if you use the tools we've talked about here, you'll keep feeling better. Just keep putting the work in, and you'll be—'

'Thank you,' I interrupted. 'Seriously, thank you. You've been great and I wouldn't feel this well without you.'

She smiled and blinked slowly, sleepily – she really was like a cat.

'Thank you. It's been really lovely working with you. Oh, but, one more thing before we finish …'

'I promise, I'm not going to fucking kill myself,' I deadpanned.

She laughed, and nodded firmly.

'Fair enough. Good luck. Not that you need it, you're going to do great!'

TO-DONE

- Six sessions of therapy. And I wasn't late for a single one

- Been honest in therapy, even when it was hard 😢

- Managed to keep going to work through therapy and emotional upheaval

- Found good ways to deal with negative thought patterns and anxiety

- Showered _at least_ twice a week through all this

- Kept up my newsletter

- Kept up my relationship with my parents, husband and friends despite brain falling out of arse

- Asked for help when I needed it, even when it was horrible

- Not killed self, even when I really wanted to

TO-DONE:

I mean — when you put it like that, that's not bad, really.

TO-DO

- ☐ Put a load of washing on
- ☐ Put all washing away
- ☐ Energy bills
- ☐ Clean kitchen
- ☐ Go food shopping
- ☐ Read up on teen culture to prepare for new job
- ☐ Mental health newsletter
- ☐ Exercise
- ☐ Read that book that Grace was tweeting about
- ☐ Make dinner
- ☐ Find new podcast and listen to a few episodes

SIXTEEN

I woke up slowly, the sun sneaking through a gap in the curtains and creeping across my face, nudging at my eyes until I couldn't ignore it any more. I rolled over and checked the time on my phone: 9.17am. Sighing, I flipped onto my back and stared at the ceiling, luxuriating in the soft nest of duvet I'd wrapped myself in since Garry left for work four hours earlier, and in the feeling of being totally, completely still.

And, to be honest, congratulating myself on having avoided a hangover. Yesterday was both my last day at Steady and my leaving party, and Adam made up for three years of pastoral stinginess by being *very* generous with the drinks. The bar served cocktails by the pint, and although not a big boozer, I cannot resist a brightly coloured drink with a cocktail umbrella and mint leaves or fruit floating in it. They slip down as easily as eating sweeties, and I think I had three pints within the first 90 minutes.

Thankfully – and possibly because I didn't spend years abusing it as a teenager – my liver is in cracking shape, so while seriously drunk, I still remained in total control. Well … *ish*. I do remember stumbling out of the toilet and being very surprised about bumping into men coming in, realising I'd actually used the men's loo and being too drunk and giggly to be embarrassed about it. That's not *particularly* in control, is it?

And … oh God, I remember asking Rowena and Claire about childbirth and if contractions felt like big orgasms in reverse. And cornering Rosie Lucas and telling her that I wanted to 'solve the mystery that is *you*' before asking her really inane life questions for an hour. And that Nish had had to walk me to the bus stop because no one was convinced I'd be able to make it there on my own. And then Garry had come to meet me and walk me home, even though it was midnight and he was on an early shift, but I was flicking through emotions so quickly that I kept stopping and sitting down on the pavement to laugh or cry hysterically, or rant about how mental health services in this country were being cut and telling us to 'just talk about it' was never going to be enough. The journey ended up with me sat on our doorstep, head in my hands, sobbing uncontrollably, while Garry tried to convince the people across the road that he wasn't the reason I was crying and that he was trying to help me get into bed to sleep off £40-worth of spirits, after which I'd probably feel much better, while I wailed, 'It's just not *fair*, why is everything so *sad*?'

But apart from that, *total* control.

I grinned. It had been a good night. A nice goodbye to a job that, for all I'd outgrown it, had been incredibly important to me. A job that helped me become the person I am, really. A job that was maybe not as cool as Janae's or prolific as Penny's, or as exciting as Frankie's, but that did good for the world, that made me a better writer, and that was important to me. I'm glad I had it – and, simultaneously, I'm glad it's time to say goodbye.

Speaking of Penny, Frankie and Janae … I picked up my phone again and opened Instagram. I may not have a hangover, but I could really go for a big breakfast and a fancy coffee right now. But no, they all had plans: Penny and Ollie were spending the day decorating their new house, Janae and Emily were having a creative weekend with some of their friends in a big caravan in Wales, while Frankie was doing a Marvel movie marathon at her local cinema. *Alright, then: no friends today. That's okay!* I put my phone down and looked around for Flick. She was curled up on the chair in the corner of the room, having made a little nest out of the clean washing. I pursed my lips and made a little kissy noise, but she ignored me.

'Flick,' I crooned. 'Flick!' She raised her head and looked at me, eyes half-closed. I feigned a look of delight. 'There she is! Good girl! Come on, Flick, come on …' I patted the duvet next to me, still making the kissy noises. She looked at where I was patting, then back at me, nonplussed. I changed tactic, scratching the bed instead, making my fingers scuttle back and forth like a bug in the hope she'd chase after them. She watched for a while, totally unmoved, then yawned widely and settled back down to sleep. I let my hand flop back onto the duvet. *Oh, alright then. No cuddles for Amy, I guess – and no bloody Dreamies for ungrateful Flick, either.*

I opened up my To-Do List and scanned through the items on it. *Urgh.* None of them looked particularly appealing, to be honest. I might not be hungover, but I was still riding the hedonistic wave from last night and wasn't quite ready to crash back onto the shore. Closing the app, I stretched luxuriously, letting out a little involuntary squeak and wriggling back into a comfy position afterwards. *Mmm … bed! Bed is nice. Maybe I'll just stay here a little while longer.*

'A little while' ended up being an hour and a half. For a while I lay still and dozed, enjoying the warmth of the sun on my face and listening to the people outside as they went about their day. Then I opened my phone and scrolled through Tumblr until my eyes went funny. I tried to do the same on Twitter, but closed it almost immediately. There were too many stories about politicians fighting and Donald Trump saying Awful Things on there, and while I usually tried to read as much of it as possible because I know I should stay updated, today wasn't the day for that.

Today wasn't the day for that *at all.*

Eventually, I got up. I could probably have held off my grumbling stomach for a little while longer, but combined with the incessant wailing of a baby in the next flat over, it became too much to bear. I swung out of bed and looked down in surprise when I realised I was only wearing a pair of knickers and the vest top I'd had on under my skirt and cardigan last night. Vague memories of Garry swearing under his breath as he tried to undo my bra for me, and me refusing to get into my PJs because I wanted to 'be one with the night'. I laughed, then grimaced as the cool bedroom air prickled my skin, making my leg hairs stand up uncomfortably.

'No wonder you cry so hard, baby,' I murmured, picking my PJ bottoms up from the floor and putting them on. 'I want to cry just getting out of bed. I can't imagine what it must be like being pulled from a nice, warm uterus. I think I'd cry all the time, too.'

Slippers on, I shuffled into the kitchen. My cupboards were, as usual, fairly empty – I cursed myself for not having been productive enough earlier in the week to do a meal plan and online shop. If I'd had buttermilk and blueberries, I could have made pancakes or something. I could have done some lovely baked eggs and tomatoes with coriander and a good, crusty sourdough. If I'd just put a *little bit of thought* into it, I could have treated myself to a fancy breakfast today rather than making do with the eggs in the cupboard and the bread in the freezer. *Loser, loser, loser*, I thought, crossly.

While the bread defrosted in the toaster, I put a frying pan over a medium-low heat. I snapped on the grill and added an ample knob of creamy, salted butter, spreading it with a spatula and watching it heat and bubble until foamy and thick. The toast went under the grill and I whisked the eggs together in a *Monsters, Inc.* mug, with lots of salt and black pepper from the grinders I bought from Sainsbury's when I moved in with Garry. I tipped them into the pan with more butter and a splash of milk, and stirred slowly until they became creamy and light. When the toast was golden brown on both sides and just starting to blacken at the edges, I buttered it and tipped the eggs on top, followed by a *very* generous squirt of brown sauce. I brought the plate into the living room, along with a cup of tea so strong you could stand a spoon in it, and sat at the table.

Fuck, these are good eggs, I thought as I ate, watching a fox explore downstairs' garden out of the window. *Like, really good eggs.* Soft and fluffy, and the bread was caramelised and crisp even though it came from the freezer, and although the abundance of butter may have teetered on obscene, it was bloody worth it. By the time my plate was clear – and I mean *clear*, because I saved some bread till the end and mopped up all the good, rich juices left on the plate with it – my heart was as full as my stomach. Okay, it wasn't a fancy stack of pancakes or a warm, bubbling bowl of huevos rancheros, but it felt good. I sighed happily as the fox curled up in a patch of sun and started to snooze. It felt really, *really* good.

I checked the time: almost noon. Time to start being productive! I got dressed (in my scratty jeans and the Hufflepuff jumper Garry got me for my birthday a few years ago – I know I had my lovely new clothes ready, but today was a day for comfort, not style), gave the cat a scratch (she totally ignored me. Didn't even open her eyes) and sat down in the living room to check my list. *Ugh!* So much of it seemed like so much *effort*. Sorting out the washing, cleaning the kitchen, doing anything which required leaving the house … *No, thank you!* A finger of guilt trailed up my spine, but I dashed it away and tried to look for another way in.

What about the fun things on the list? Reading, listening to podcasts? But it wasn't just reading, was it? It was reading that book that Grace was tweeting about, the novel that had just won the Baileys Prize, the one I'd been carrying around for months and never quite gotten round to. And it wasn't just listening to a podcast, it was finding a *new* podcast I could talk about in the office to my new colleagues, one that would make me seem cultured and cool because I didn't think my Hamilton fan podcast, *My Dad Wrote A Porno*, or the podcasts by the comedians I fancied really said good things about me.

It was all so exhausting. When did reading, something I used to do as easily as breathing as a kid, become so exhausting? *Probably*, I thought guiltily, *when I stopped seeing entertainment as entertainment and started seeing it as another achievement to tick off*. I feel oddly embarrassed by the fact that I haven't seen all the films everyone raves about or the Netflix shows they all seem to be able to binge in a weekend, or the important, worthy books that really hold up a mirror to society that everyone talks about. And not embarrassed because I might be missing out on some really incredible entertainment or art, but because I feel it's a failure within me that I haven't consumed it and had it impact on my life. Fucking weird, isn't it? I don't think my mum ever felt like this about *Coronation Street*, so why do I still feel guilty that I haven't watched *Daredevil* Season 2 yet?

And it's not just entertainment, it's everything. *Everything!* I open my list app and scroll back through months, years of lists. Say happy anniversary to Garry. Make sure Mum has a good time at the Christmas party. Janae's wedding. Go to a club. Play a game. Enjoy time with friends. Have a romantic weekend with my husband. Attend a party. Go swimming. Meet friends for brunch. These aren't achievements, they're not tasks, not things to tick off a list – they're my *life*!

When did I start turning things that should be enjoyable into an endless list of tasks, a series of obligations? When did my life become one long quest to achieve, rather than just be? *I can't even cook myself breakfast without stressing I'm not doing it well enough, for Christ's sake*. My To-Do Lists should be for tasks, actual tasks I need to complete. My life is not a task, not something to tick off. My life is *brilliant*, and I should enjoy it.

Swiping back through the app, I rested on today's list: 'Read the book Grace was tweeting about'. *Delete*. You know what? I've been trying to read that fucking book for months. I don't like it, I don't care about it, I don't want to read it. I stood up suddenly and marched to my bookshelf, yanking it off the shelf. *No, thank you!* I take a carrier bag and put the book in it, along with a few others on my shelf that I bought because they were impressive rather than because I actually wanted to read them: *I don't need you in my life*.

What I *do* need is a few hours with a book, though. I ran my fingers across the spines of my books and settled on one decorated in glorious purple and gold: *Chocolat*, a book I've read so many times before I can probably quote it to you. It's not new, it's not going to impress anyone, but fuck it, I love it, and it's what I want to read. I took it, and my tea, back to bed, nestled on top of the duvet, tried and failed to encourage the cat over to me, and spend a few hours having glorious, unproductive fun until I was broken out of my reading reverie by my phone beeping. I set the book down on the bed, careful not to crack the spine more than it already was, and checked the notification.

GARRY: Hey you. Going to the pub with Raf and Ben,
      be home late
AMY: Okay. Don't get too drunk x
GARRY: Ha! You can talk. See you later x

I stretched – my neck and arms were sore. It was 3.20pm. I opened the list again. I'd had a lovely day so far, but there were still quite a lot of chores that needed doing. I could very easily put some washing in, or maybe clean the kitchen. I dog-eared my book and wandered back through the flat, surveying the kitchen through beady eyes. It wasn't *too* bad, really. I needed to give the hob a wipe and there was some washing-up, but nothing urgent that needed doing.

And, in fact ... I opened the cupboard where I kept all my store things. I had chocolate chips, and I had condensed milk and flour, and I knew I had butter in the fridge. So, cookies? Sure! I wondered for a second about doing mindful baking, then remembered I had an episode of *Crazy Ex-Girlfriend* to watch on Netflix. Feeling a little guilty about neglecting my mental health, I propped the iPad up on the bread bin and gathered my ingredients. But after an hour or so, when I'd finished taking rounds and rounds of gooey, delicious cookies out of the oven and singing tunelessly along with Broadway-trained singers, I felt more peaceful and cheery than I ever had while staring into the ingredients as I stirred them and trying to really *feel* my feelings. Baking was fun and made me feel good. Trying to do it specifically *to* feel good ... Just a bit awkward and stressful, really.

Cookie in hand – and when I say 'cookie', I really mean two or three – I flopped back onto the sofa and checked the time: 4.35pm. Okay, really, it was time to do something, now. I opened the list and checked what I had left to do. I sucked in my breath as I looked at the third item: energy bills.

Energy bills.

No! You know what? I can do this, I can bloody well do this. I made cookies! I drank several pints of mojito last night and don't have a hangover! I managed to get a job while covered in coffee! I pay all my other bills on time, every month, no problem! I'm a responsible human and I can pay my goddamn energy bills. Adrenaline rushing through me, I grabbed my laptop and logged onto the EasyPower website. I found my account details and the contact number for bills enquiries. I typed the number in my phone and pressed call. I listened as it dialled, connected, and then ...

'We're sorry, but our bills enquiries department is now closed. Please call back between 8am and 8pm, Monday to Friday, or from 9am to 3pm Saturday.' Click.

Slowly, I moved the phone away from my ear and gaped at the screen: call disconnected. I stared at it, dumbstruck, and suddenly felt a wave of relief wash over me. *Oh, thank God! I don't have to do it today, I can do it another day.* The mix of adrenaline and relief made me giddy, and I laughed out loud. *Oh, Christ!* I might be a responsible human and I might be a million miles less mad than I was a year ago, but the idea of having to sort out this energy bills clusterfuck is still *utterly* terrifying.

So, what now? I closed my laptop and checked my list again. Washing. Cleaning. Exercise. Eh? The clock says it's almost 5pm, and I haven't done a single thing today, and you know what? I don't care, I just don't care! I've done nothing all day, for the first time in a long, long time, and it feels wonderful. Wonderful in a way that I haven't felt in months? Years? Since I left university? It feels like a gap has been filled, an empty space in my life has suddenly revealed itself to me.

I've done nothing, and I feel brilliant about it.

I know, rationally, focusing on achieving is stupid, but to feel it, to really *feel* it in my blood and my guts and my bones, is amazing. There is more to life than ticking things off! There is *more* to life than being productive – no, scrap that, not even *being* productive, but *feeling* productive. For years, I've put so much on my To-Do Lists that no normal human being could ever hope to do it all without having a mental breakdown, and when I looked at it at the end of the day and saw the things that I hadn't done – at the bins not being taken out, the washing not being put in, the kitchen not being cleaned – I felt *guilt*, actual guilt, that I hadn't done it. *Why?* I'm not a worse person for not having ticked things off my list, my worth is not measured by productivity – and you know, I think I might be actively ruining my life by trying to make it so.

Because if you think that doing more is the same as *being* more, then it's never enough. There's always more to do, more to achieve, more items you can add to a list just to tick them off. I could always take on another hobby, consume more 'worthwhile' culture, do more exercise, travel more, write more, cook more. When I was exhausted, I would hate myself for not working harder – and then feel guilty for the time I spent hating myself when I should have been doing something to actively make myself feel better. If I wasn't working, I was worthless.

Look, To-Do Lists are incredibly useful things. My brain is too full to keep everything it needs in place, and when I started these lists, it was really helpful so that I didn't worry about forgetting them. But my lists quickly became more than that: an emotional crutch, a way of proving to myself that I was acceptable, that I was working hard enough, doing enough to be a worthwhile human being. Those little ticks were a sign that I was doing something, being something, making something, and I took any gaps as a sign that I was a failure.

But I'm *not* a failure. I have a family I love, amazing friends, a strong relationship with a great husband, a career, a flat, hobbies. On the spectrum of human achievement, I'm pretty far over to the good side. I'm so lucky to have the life I have, and constantly comparing it to the lives of others, pushing myself to do more, won't make it better: my life is enough, *I* am enough.

I love working hard and getting things done, but I also love lounging around and talking nonsense with people I love, and watching crap TV and splashing around in a swimming pool because I like being in the water. I've spent so long wanting to be successful that I sacrificed the things I really love in order to do more, but it didn't work – it just didn't. I don't want to focus on apparent success any more. Right now, I'd rather be happy.

And right now, I thought as I looked around my living room, I *am* happy. I probably won't always feel this happy – I've gone through depression and misery far too many times to think that revelations about my psyche are enough to fix me forever, it's hard to keep on feeling good about yourself and your life when the world is geared towards making you feel crap, and there will always be something else ready to trip me up – but I feel positive that whatever happens, I'll be able to get through it. I'm strong enough to get through it, good enough to get through it. Besides, it's unrealistic to go through life being happy all the time. God, can you imagine what an annoying twat you'd be?

I opened Instagram on my phone and flicked through what my friends had done with their days. Janae and Emily had made good progress on their comic book about a mermaid who falls in love with a princess and lures her away to the sea. Penny and Ollie had painted their living room in one of Farrow & Ball's newest shades, and were now eating fish and chips on the floor and beaming. Frankie was several films deep, currently watching *Iron Man 2*. Claire and Edie had gone to the seaside. Ivy had spent the day writing her next book. Carla and Val had gone engagement ring shopping. Bloody hell, even Freddy had posted something: a photo of him and Laura having a family dinner with the caption 'The gang's back together again'.

On and on my feed went: people who'd gone on weekend breaks, people at weddings, doing talks and panels, upcycling furniture and having big boozy brunches and showing off their latest reads. I grinned. All these days, all these *lives*, looked AMAZING. I bet everyone had a really brilliant day. But *I* had a brilliant day too. Sure, I didn't get an Instagram post out of it, but maybe that doesn't matter. I used to worry if something happened and I didn't show off about it online, did it really matter at all? But now, I'm not going to show off to anyone but myself – I'm the only person I have to please, really. And you know, I thought Berkeley was a pretentious prick when I studied him at university, so I'm hardly going to take his theories on perception into the rest of my life with me.

I closed my phone and put it down decisively on the sofa next to me. *I don't want to do any of those things on my To-Do List today*, I thought. *Instead, I'm going to have a bath. A nice, warm bubble bath.* I turned the hot tap on, emptied a good half of a bottle of Radox into the stream of water and retrieved my book from the bedroom, setting it up next to the bath along with a small pile of my cookies, a hair mask and a scented vanilla candle. Nothing worth showing off about. Nothing that I've really achieved by doing it. But all perfect little moments of joy, all lovely, nice things, and reasons to be happy.

And there are so many reasons to be happy in my life. The way Janae rocks me from side to side when she hugs me hello. The little trill Flick does when I come home from work. Garry's hair when he first wakes up, when it's all fluffy and he looks like Professor Weeto; a perfectly roasted potato, singing in the car with the windows down, sunlight shining on my face and slowly bringing me into a new, beautiful day. I don't need to rely on feeling like I'm good in order to be happy. The world is full of small happinesses and taking the time to truly enjoy them is a surer, safer route to feeling truly content.

But even if I do need to feel good about myself sometimes, there are so many reasons I have to do that without relying on constant achievement. There are the emails from people who tell me that the newsletter I wrote really helped them. The way Penny casually tells me she loves me, thinks I'm brilliant, like it's such a normal part of the world that she doesn't even need to make a big deal out of it. My parents, who adore me unconditionally. My husband, who hates basically everyone but still somehow likes me. All the millions of things I do each day without even thinking about it – getting up, getting dressed in an outfit that looks good, being kind to people, cracking jokes, going to work, all the billions of tiny things I do to survive and exist and *live* ... They make me enough. As I am, *I* am enough: I am worthwhile and I am good, and I am enough.

It's hard to remember that sometimes, though, I thought as I stepped into the bubbly bathwater. My skin flushed pink and I wriggled with equal amounts of delight and pain from the hot water. *There really are a lot of reasons to feel good about the world and myself, but when I'm down and depressed, they're all hidden away behind a fog of despair. I really need to try and figure out how to remember them better. Maybe I should make a list to keep track?*

Or maybe, I thought as I sank beneath the bubbles in bliss, *for once, I should just live.*

SATURDAY, 30 JUNE
TO-DO

- ☐ Put a load of washing on
- ☐ Put all washing away
- → Energy bills Move to next week, maybe see if Garry can hold your hand while you call £
- ☐ Clean kitchen
- ☐ Go food shopping
- ☐ Read up on <u>teen culture</u> to prepare for new job
- ☐ Mental health newsletter
- ☐ Exercise
- ☐ ~~Read that book that Grace was tweeting about~~
- ☐ Make dinner
- ☐ ~~Find new podcast and listen to a few episodes~~

TO-DONE

Had a bloody
lovely day!
And really,
that's <u>the</u> <u>only</u>
<u>thing</u> <u>that</u>
<u>matters</u>

USEFUL LINKS

In this book – as in in my life – I didn't get help until I was at crisis point. This is a remarkably stupid thing to do. Although making comparisons between mental and physical health is often fallacious, not getting help with your mental health until you're so desperate you want to walk into a lake (or in front of a bus or train, as is my most common impulse) is like not getting help with an infected toenail until your whole foot is about to drop off. The earlier you can get at the poison, the easier it will be to remove.

Mind is the best resource there is for all things mental health – if you are unsure and need information, advice or urgent help with mental health, you can find them at https://www.mind. org.uk/.

If you aren't ready for that yet but you still feel like you could use someone to talk to, then the Samaritans are there for you. You can read about them on their website – https://www. samaritans.org/ – or call them on 116 123.

If you're under 19 and you need help, Childline is specifically designed for you. I worked there for almost three years (my boss was a lot nicer than Adam, don't worry) as a Digital Producer and Facebook host, and I was consistently amazed by the level of care and respect they provide for young people. You can email or instant message them https://www.childline.org.uk/, call on 0800 1111, or use the website/the For Me! app to read information, post on the message boards and get advice.

If you're a man and you're concerned about your mental health but don't feel like any of the above are for you, that's okay! I love the work of https://www.thecalmzone.net/, who are specifically trying to help men who feel like they could use help with their mental health. Mental health is the biggest killer of men under 45 in the UK. The patriarchy tells men that talking about their feelings makes them less of a man, but frankly, this is bollocks. If you need help, then please, please get it.

Everyone has a level of mental health, whether that's something that needs medical treatment or not. To look after yours, there are a number of apps which will help you do some meditation or mindfulness. I like https://www.calm.com/ and https://www.headspace.com/, because they don't feel as wanky as some others do.

I am lucky in that my friends understand mental health, and I can talk to them openly about how I'm feeling without awkwardness. Not everyone is that lucky. To combat this, Bryony Gordon set up the brilliant Mental Health Mates – outdoor meet-ups all over the country which let you meet other people who might be feeling the same way. Find your nearest walk at www.mentalhealthmates.co.uk

If you've got a friend or loved one who you think is feeling down and you want to help, firstly, I love you and you are exactly the kind of good people we need in the world. Secondly, if you're not sure where to start, here are some resources that might help: Heads Together has an excellent list of things to say to someone who is depressed that are actually helpful rather than platitudes https://www.headstogether.org.uk/10-things-to-say-to-someone-with-depression/ and Blurt has developed a Buddy Box which is a box

of nice things to remind your friend that they are loved https://
www.blurtitout.org/buddybox/. Both of these websites are also
full of information and support, so worth looking into.

Eating disorders are complicated things. In this book, I talk
about the struggles I had and have with my body, and my
relationship to food. If you've been affected by this, BEAT is
the best resource I know of. Find them online at https://www.
beateatingdisorders.org.uk/ – if you'd rather talk on the phone,
the number is 0808 801 0677.

But most of all, if you recognised yourself in this book, please
get help from your doctor. No matter what your brain tells you
when you're at your lowest, you deserve help, professional help
from people who know what they're doing. I couldn't have
gotten through my depression without the help of my friends,
but also, my friends couldn't do for me what antidepressants
and therapy did – and it would have been unfair for me to expect
them to. If you're nervous about what therapy might entail,
the BACP is a great source of information – https://www.bacp.
co.uk/about-therapy/what-happens-in-therapy/

The best place to start with accessing mental health services is via
your GP. If your GP isn't understanding, you are allowed – and
again, you deserve – to ask to see another GP. Mental health funding
in the UK is being slashed, but I've still had utterly exceptional
mental-health care from the NHS whenever I've needed it. In
some areas, you can self-refer for psychological therapies (IAPT)
help. To find out how to access mental health help in your area,
look on https://www.nhs.uk/using-the-nhs/nhs-services/
mental-health-services/how-to-access-mental-health-services/.

Finally, if you are ever in danger, please call 999 immediately.
You're not wasting time, they'd rather you did call than you
didn't – and, for what it's worth, so would I.

ACKNOWLEDGEMENTS

Thank you to everyone who has read this book and thought 'Hang on, didn't we have that conversation ...?' Of course we didn't. This memoir is entirely made up and any resemblance to any persons living or dead is entirely coincidental, which means you can't sue me. Ha.

Thank you to Robyn Drury, for being there right from the very very beginning and believing in me before anyone else really knew or cared who I was. This 100 per cent would not have happened without you. Thank you for making my dreams come true, and for holding my hand on the way. And to everyone at Ebury who has been in turn excited, kind, encouraging and, when I'm talking bollocks on Twitter about what a terrible writer I am and how this is all going to be an enormous failure, gently chiding. I couldn't have asked for a better team to help me get through the brilliantly terrifying whirlwind that has been my first book.

To Diana Beaumont, agent-extraordinaire, who studied me at Rooftop Book Club years ago and said 'Hey, you look interesting, here's my card' and who leapt into action and got to grips with a project I'd been working on for a year within a couple of *days* when I needed her to. I look forward to cooing over red lipsticks and Dominic West with you for years to come.

To the Wilder-Heritages. To Stu for encouraging me even way back when I was writing about my tea and liveblogging *GBBO* as a hobby. To Robyn, who read the entire book in sections as it was being written and kept nagging me for more; I don't think I would have written anything past the third chapter if it wasn't for you demanding it. To Herbie and Ned for the cuddles, the Disco Elephants, and the repeated renditions of 'Old MacDonald Had A Farm'.

Huge thanks to everyone who was at The Pool. I've never met a group of people who are more focused, dedicated, hard-working and talented than you were. Thank you for taking a rando who had never worked in media before and treating her like she was worthwhile and had something to say. You encouraged me, inspired me, made me better and showed me what it meant to be truly brilliant. We all deserved better. I hope that you all get it, and soon.

Thanks to Becky, for being my creative partner and the closest thing to a wife I could have while being married to someone else. Thanks to Janina and Jamie, who somehow make me feel better about myself even though our relationship consists primarily of screaming "FUCK YOU" at each other on secret Twitter accounts. To Holly, who has been my mentor and my manager and my life coach and, all the way through, my darling, wonderful friend. To Alice, my high-love, low-key friend and writing partner who is the perfect balance of tough love and endless, exuberant support. To Ashley and Lauren, my best girls, for being there right from the start, back when I was just a weirdo from Nuneaton who stalked them on Twitter, and for being there through my brain breaking into pieces (twice) and holding my hand across WhatsApp while I tried to put it back together again. To all of the above for being the Penny, Frankie and Janae of my real lives. I love you all so much, and I wouldn't have made it through my real-life chapter six without you. Thank you for my survival. Thank you even more for my life.

Thanks to my parents for, y'know, having me. Thanks to Dad for my brain, and for never treating me as anything other than an equal, even if that meant having to debate you about every single opinion and thought I had when I was only seven years old. Thanks to Mum for my heart, and for teaching me to never give up – it came in useful when it came to the aforementioned debates. Thank you for being proud of me even when you didn't understand me, for being the best cheerleaders I could hope for, and for letting me write about our ridiculous family so honestly.

Thank you to Garry. I only gave myself two chapters to write about you because I knew that could write solidly for two decades and it wouldn't be enough. You're the most ridiculous, frustrating, brilliant human being I have ever met. Throughout this book-making process I've had a mental health collapse, a miscarriage, been made redundant, had an identity breakdown and suffered from hideous, debilitating pregnancy nausea – and you've been there through it all, making me laugh and making sure I still wash my face occasionally. Thank you for loving me. Thank you for making me better. Thank you for not sulking at how completely I mocked you in this book. I love you. And it's your turn to take the bins out.

And finally, thank you to everyone I've ever spoken to, online or in real life, about mental health or vulnerability or anything else where the words have been difficult to find. I spent so much of my life feeling entirely alone and like I didn't fit, and those thousands of tiny conversations have been like a life raft in a storm. Thank you for your understanding. Thank you for your honesty. And thank you so much for your kindness. No matter how it feels, we aren't alone. We never are. Thank you for helping me believe it.